3⁵⁵

The End

The End

Closing Words for a Millennium

by

Mark Morton
and
Gail Noble

Bain & Cox, Publishers
Winnipeg • Buffalo

First published 1999 by Bain & Cox, Publishers
an imprint of Blizzard Publishing Inc.
73 Furby Street, Winnipeg, Canada R3C 2A2.

Distributed in the United States by General Distribution Services,
85 River Rock Dr., Unit 202, Buffalo, NY 14207-2170.

Cover design by Otium.
Printed for Bain & Cox in Canada by Printcrafters.

5   4   3   2   1

The End: Closing Words for a Millennium

Bain & Cox, Publishers gratefully acknowledge the support of the
Manitoba Arts Council and the Canada Council for its publishing
program.

Cataloguing in Publication Data

Morton, Mark
  The End, closing words for a millennium
    ISBN 0-921368-83-6
1. Millennium celebrations (Year 2000).
2. Anniversaries.   I. Noble, Gail.   II. Title.
D857.M67 1999   394.2   C99-920049-6

For Janet Hamilton and David Morton,
who will not see the end

Rise, and greet the author of time

Keep cool: it will be all one a hundred years hence.
—Ralph Waldo Emerson

Contents

An accounting conundrum — zero and Little Denis — what was that again? (a chronological crisis) — the editor insists — the Kaiser demands — Schiller and Goethe waffle — betting on perplexity — singing the century — unerring principles for finding Saturday — where are we now? — 100 of this, 99 of that — in 1800 they'd had enough — in 1900 they had more — the saga of Sir Courtney — and the parodies ensuing — doomed to repetition?

The untimely demise of the Rat Pack — then the trumpet's blast — scintillations and the fires of joy — din evoked — the electric age of celebration — throng control — not everyone's cup of champagne — bloomers, fishers, golfers, actors — waking the president — he carried her over the century threshold — get out of jail free! — was having a wonderful time — the quieter way — the rise and fall of Frank D. Higbee — his run-in with Mark Twain — a sorry tale of schemes gone awry — final achievements

Trying out the digits — the world at hand — the weather above — the climate within — final dates — the glossy and the gruesome — waltzing the century out — dangers! — and so to bed — better girls — a great whacking lunch

The retro gaze — taking stock — finance to football — a gate, a door, a mountaintop — the enthralling Mrs. Thrale — the uses of dust —

greatest books of the century — the master dogma — lists and coun-
ter-lists — women's lot transformed — flimsy picture books — bigger
and littler

List of reproductions and illustrations

Thanks and Acknowledgments

Ian Ainsworth, Ben Ainsworth, Georgia Ainsworth, Harry Ainsworth, Charmagne Reimer, Esmé Keith, David Roberts, Gregg Shilliday, Neil Besner, David Milligan, Lynda Noble, George Mills, Jacob Engel, Clarise Foster, Peter Atwood, Tanya Ho, Heidi Harms, Patty Hawkins, Rhoda Glasberg, Howard Engel, Ashley Peoples, Andrew Burashko, Beverley Slopen, Mary-Anne Fraser, Rick Montgomery (*Kansas City Star*), Nellie Perret, Joan Ste-Marie, Faith MacDonald, Todd Sprecken, Hillel Schwartz, Howard Tyner (*Chicago Tribune*), Frederick Bauman (Library of Congress), Paul Hudson (International Time Capsule Society), Jim Zwick, Judy Baker, Richard S. Levy, Will Jarvis (International Time Capsule Society), Carissa Almeida, Greg Gingras, Rachel Jeal, Tanis MacDonald, Kristine Nutting, Christina Penner, Laurie Watson, Jennifer Selby, the Manitoba Arts Council, the City of Winnipeg Arts Advisory Council, the University of Winnipeg Library, Robarts Library, the Library of Congress, Farley, Eccles, and Rex. And Toto too.

FRIEND, I'D LIKE to share with you a truth that will make your hair stand on end. On Friday, December 31, 1999, at exactly midnight, as a hundred million clocks chime the final stroke of twelve, the following terrible event will occur.

Absolutely nothing.

It's true—setting aside some minor concerns about a computer bug— nothing apocalyptic is going to happen. The Messiah is not going to descend. No asteroid will plunge into the heart of Los Angeles. Your achy leg will still ache and your house will still need a fresh coat of paint. Your brother-in-law will still be a lazy son of a gun. None of that will change. Why would it? Sure, it's the end of one century and the start of another, but a century is that wispiest of things: an idea. You can't touch a century. You can't weigh one. You can't even give one away. Centuries don't really exist. If humans were to vanish from the earth tomorrow, all the centuries would vanish with them.

But that's the paradox: centuries don't exist, and yet we (and our computers) act as if they do. We treat them like they dropped down from heaven along with cherry pie and dogs. But they're actually just a product of our imaginations, an arbitrary construct.

After all, it's really just an accident that humans use a base-ten numbering system. If we used a base-eight system, or a base-two system like computers do, who knows what century we'd be in?

And after all, most people know that the starting point for our centuries—the birth of Jesus—isn't quite accurate: he was likely born about seven years before the year that divides B.C. from A.D.

And after all, billions of people use other calendar systems. For them, the end of the century is still decades away.

In short, nothing could be more arbitrary, more accidental, more meaningless than December 31, 1999. It's just a number, like 6 or π or 783-8914.

So why are we all going to treat December 31, 1999 as if it were a pivotal moment in history?

On that day, a party of global proportions will erupt. A million people will jam Times Square in New York. Thousands of others will circle the earth on special millennium charters, zipping from time zone to time zone to experience the turn of the millennium again and again. Hundreds of couples will begin reciting their wedding vows as the clock strikes twelve. Cranky men will mail off letters-to-the-editor, pointing out that the century doesn't really end until December 31, 2000. Newspapers will be filled with editorials brooding upon the meaning of time, change, and history. Radio stations will begin playing the top hundred songs of the twentieth century. Science columnists will speculate on what discoveries will be made in the twenty-first century, what diseases will be conquered, what planets we will colonize. Apocalypse-mongers will huddle together, waiting for the hand of God to swing down and smite us. Some poor souls will go one step farther: they'll beat God to the punch by stepping off a building or in front of a subway train.

To figure out why we're going to make such a fuss at such an arbitrary moment, we've got to travel back in time to A.D. 525. See that monk scribbling Roman numerals by candlelight? You can almost hear him muttering: "LX divided by V equals XII, carry the VIII … drat, I wish we'd hurry up and invent the number zero." That's Dionysius Exiguus, hired by the Pope to figure out a more effective way of calculating the date of Easter. Now, imagine that above the desk of Dionysius is a calendar (a promotional item from Acme Parchment Services): this chimerical wall item doesn't read A.D. 525. It reads 1278, because Dionysius and his monkish colleagues dated all historical events from the founding of ancient Rome. Or rather, Dionysius used the Roman calendar up until the moment that he sat down at his desk and invented a new one. He decided to re-date and Christianize all of history, making the starting point the birth of Jesus. The manger, the star, the wise men, the shepherds—all that, proposed the devout Dionysius, took place in the year A.D. 1.

Dionysius's bold new calendar system caught on with all the fury of a wet newspaper. Imagine the feedback the poor monk must have gotten from his local bishop: "So, Dionysius, you want us to memorize new dates for every historical event that's ever occurred?" If you happened to be in Canada in 1972, think "metric system" and you'll have a sense of the inertia that Dionysius was up against.

Still, by the ninth century, Dionysius's time-scheme was widely employed throughout the vast Holy Roman Empire and so one might expect that people living at the end of that century, or at the end of subsequent ones, would start to perceive those "turns" as somehow significant. But until we arrive at the end of the seventeenth century, very few people living at the end of earlier centuries seem to have thought the change in date—from '99 to '00 (or from '00 to '01)—worth remarking upon. Needless to say, this also means that the fabled "millennium panic" that supposedly paralysed medieval Christians on December 31, 999 was just that—a fable. People did not gather in churches on the last night of the tenth century to wait for God to whisk them to heaven or blast them to hell. End-of-the-world anxieties flared up recurrently in the Middle Ages, but there is very little evidence to suggest that the very end of the tenth century was marked by any special apocalyptic fervour.

In fact, until the last half of the eighteenth century when the industrial revolution started packing labourers into factories from 7:00 a.m. to 6:00 p.m., Monday to Saturday, the rhythm of most people's lives was determined by the sun and seasons, not by clocks and calendars. Thus, something as artificial and arbitrary as a change in date meant little to most people, even if it was the end of one century and the beginning of the next.

Even when people did "mark time" in a more systematic manner—as in a letter or a will—they often used a more meaningful benchmark like a great battle or the reign of a sovereign: "St. Crispin's Day of this eighth year of King Henry VIII." To take a literary example, consider how the grave digger responds to Hamlet's question about how long he has dug holes for a living: "Of all the days i' the year, I came to it that day / that our last king Hamlet overcame Fortinbras." A grave digger in Shakespeare's England, or Hamlet's Denmark, would likely have *known* that the actual year was, say, 1585, but he and his friends would not have *thought* of it in those terms. (To get a sense of how much things have changed, try dating your next cheque "Arbour Day, this seventh year of Clinton's reign.")

Even among learned individuals, other calendar systems continued to compete with the "Christian" one invented by Dionysius. One of the six thousand end-of-the-century newspapers, books, and journals we thumbed through in our research for this book was an old English almanac. At the top of its title page it said, "For the Year 1699," but at the bottom it added "From the World's Creation the year 5701." Start from one benchmark and you're at the end of the seventeenth century; start from another, and it's already long over.

It wasn't just the number of the year that was in flux three centuries ago. People also couldn't agree on when the year ended and began. In England many started the new year on the supposed birthday of Christ, December 25. Others insisted on a date close to the vernal equinox, March 25. And still others held to the date established by Julius Caesar, January 1. That explains why *Poor Robin's Almanac* for 1700 glossed January 1 as "New-yeares day" but the *London Post* didn't change the year on its masthead from 1700 to 1701 until its March 25 issue. Every year, for a three-month stretch, you and your neighbour might be living in different years.

Eventually, European nations and their trading partners started to exorcise the confusion by officially adopting the Gregorian calendar (a refinement of the one invented by Dionysius). France, Italy, Portugal, and

A brief Chronology of memorable Things

Since	
the Creation of the World	5702
the General Deluge of *Noah's* Flood	4047
Julius Cæsar conquer'd *Britain*	1750
the Destruction of *Jerusalem* by *Titus Vespasian*	1629
Lucius the first Christian King of *Britain*	1519
Duke *William* conquer'd *England*	633
the Invention of Guns	321
the Art of Printing first found out	259
Tilbury-Camp on St. *James's* Day	111
the Gun-powder Treason, *November* 5.	91
the long Parliament began	59
the Loyal Earl of *Strafford* beheaded	59
the Pious Bishop *Laud* murthered	55
King *Charles* the First barbarously murthered	51
the Loyal Lord *Capel* murthered	51
the Fatal Fight at *Worcester*	49
Cromwel made himself Protector	45
the Reverend Dr. *Hewyt* murthered	39
King *Charles* the Second happily restored	39
the great Plague in *London*, whereof died 100000	34
London almost consumed with Fire	33
600 Houses burnt in *Southwark*	23
the Prince of *Orange* married to the Lady *Mary*	22
the great Frost which lasted 13 Weeks	15
the Bloody Assizes in the *West*	14
King *James* the Second abdicated	11
King *William* and Queen *Mary* crowned	10
the terrible Earthquake in *Jamaca*	7
the Earthquake in *England*	7

from *Poor Robin, An Almanac*, 1699 (and opposite page)

Spain endorsed it in 1582, Britain followed in 1752, Japan waited till 1873, and Greece held off till 1923.

You can imagine what started to happen. As one nation after another banished all calendar systems but one, people started to think about the calendar, about centuries, and about time, differently. It wasn't, say, *either* 1760 *or* 5763 depending on which benchmark you chose. It wasn't *either* 1760 *or* 1761 depending on which New Year's Day you observed. If it was 1760, then it was 1760 and that's final. The acceptance of a sole standard meant that calendar time came to be objectified, turned into an absolute, as seemingly real and unyielding as a chunk of iron. It was no longer a system that we casually devise and shape, but an inflexible force that encompasses us.

Language, too, over the last three or four hundred years, helped to change how we think about time and the experience of living through the

A Brief Chronology of other Things.

SInce the Ballad of *Chevy-Chafe* was firft Invented,   202
   Since *Hobfon* the Carrier flourifhed,   58
Since the Rat (oh woful cafe to think upon) eat up the Cat, 3
   Reader, this Story's true which thou doft read,
   A Rat eat up a Cat of Ginger-bread.
Since Geefe went bare-foot,   5609
Since the firft beginning of *Sellinger's Round,*   186
Since Tobacco was firft brought over to *England* in a Coach, 108
   Reader, we do not flam you with a Fable,
   But write fuch things are very memorable.
Since the firft putting of Plumbs into Bag-Puddings,   1002
Since Men firft wore Perriwigs,   325
Since the Pox was firft Invented,   4 12
   Which Pox is now a Genteel fafhion grown,
   Though very few to have it will be known.
Since the Invention of Eating and Drinking,   5702
Since *Hobfon* the Carrier flourifhed,   75
Since the Countryman fhit at *Will. Lilly's* Door,   42
   And made the Aftrologer too for h s Credit,
   To erect a Scheme to know who 'twas that did it.
Since Alderman *Hoyle* went to Heaven in a String,   50
Since the beginning of the laft Year,   1
Since *Scoggin* found out his Flea-Powder,   83
   An excellent Med'cine being us'd aright
   To put thofe Negro Back-biters to flight.
Since Men firft wore Night-Caps,   420
Since the 6rft ufing *Italian* Padlocks.   371
Since Married Men lay on Pillows made of Horn-fhavings,   97
   For many a Man fo with a Wife is fped,
   On fuch a Pillow he doth lay his Head.
Since *Tho. Abbey,* at the *Red Bull* in *New——* brought up a Pint
   of Vinegar in ftead of a Pint of Canary.

end of a century. According to the *Oxford English Dictionary*, it wasn't until 1626 that the word "century" was first used to mean "a hundred years." The word had existed in English since 1533 but denoted only a military unit in the ancient Roman army (a century of centurions) or a hundred items of anything—a collection of a hundred sermons, for instance, might be referred to as "a century of homilies." Significantly, other "time" words appeared in English at the same time that "century" acquired its "hundred years" sense: "decade" in 1605, "epoch" in 1614, and "era" in 1646. With such words now at their disposal, speakers of English were more apt to conceive of time and history in terms of discrete units: epochs, eras, decades, and centuries, all of which have beginnings and ends, but especially the latter two, whose precise boundaries are determined by an inflexible base-ten counting system. The same sort of semantic developments also occurred in other cultures and languages. To take a single example, in the seventeenth century the French *siècle* changed from meaning "an age" (an undefined division of time) to meaning "century" (that is, a one-hundred year unit).

Later historical developments also contributed to the reification of calendar time. As watches became more common throughout the seventeenth and eighteenth century, our sense of time shifted out of our minds and into our pockets or onto our wrists. Even more important was the spread of railways in the late nineteenth century. If you're going to have different trains hurtling down the same stretch of track, you've got to be awfully conscious of time. That's why Sanford Fleming, a Canadian railway engineer, proposed the idea of "standard time" in the late 1870s. A few decades later, in 1907, an Englishman named William Willet came up with the idea of "daylight savings" time.

As the proponents of daylight savings blathered on about how it would make workers more productive, labour groups began to press for a shorter workday, for vacation days, and for the right to take Saturday off as well as Sunday. Soon, a new concept developed: the weekend. Unlike the cyclic understanding of time—the moon waxed and waned recurrently, the seasons revolved endlessly—the weekend polarized time. You had work time and you had play time, and the frenetic transition from one to the other occurred at exactly 5:00 p.m. on Friday afternoon.

Throughout the twentieth century, changes in technology and social conditions continued to make us ever more conscious of time. You have thirty-year bonds, you retire at sixty-five, you watch the news at 10:00 p.m., you have a timepiece strapped to your wrist, hanging on your walls, blinking on your VCR, on your microwave, on your computer screen (and threatening to go haywire at exactly one second past midnight on December 31, 1999). Never before has the world been so in control of time and time so in control of the world. We try to manipulate it by carving it into zones, pushing it forward in the spring and pulling it back in the fall; but it manipulates us, dividing our lives into weekdays and weekends, into work time and holiday time, career and retirement. It's all a far cry from the days when no one was sure whether it was 1700, 1701, or 5702.

No wonder that on December 31, 1999, when 1999 turns to 2000, we will all feel the shock of time—like driving through your hometown and seeing that your childhood house is now a vacant lot. "Oh no!" you cry. Or maybe "Thank God!" But either way, the change makes you pause, think, and feel.

When North Americans travel to the great cities of Europe—the "old country"—what often startles them is the sudden realization that they're standing in a place where millions have stood before. Travel to Notre Dame in Paris, climb to the top, and close your eyes: you can feel the convergence of earlier presences. Napoleon, Molière, Queen Victoria, Churchill, Bud Harris from Sioux Falls, Idaho—they've all panted up the

*   *   *   *   *

OBITUARY.

CENTURY.—At midnight on Monday, at Greenwich Observatory, after a long illness, the Nineteenth Century, aged one hundred years, much respected.

"Let it die" (for goodness' sake, and don't write "reviews" of it. Other papers please copy).   RASPER.

---

from *Vanity Fair*, January 3, 1901

same steep staircase, stroked the same fearsome gargoyles, gazed down upon the same rippling Seine. It's just a tower of stone, but like any historied place it connects us to those who have come before. Recurrent moments in history do the same thing. When we celebrate Christmas or Passover—or the end of a century—we're connecting ourselves not just with people across the table, or across Times Square, who are celebrating the same holiday. We're also connecting with everyone who has ever celebrated that holiday before us and with everyone who will ever celebrate it after us. The moment reaches through space and time, and unites us.

Of course, our *fin-de-siècle* predecessors were not exclusively fixated on the end of their century. On the last day of the nineteenth century, for instance, the *Boston Herald* ran a back-page item about a German doctor's recent success in hypnotizing dogs, chickens, and lobsters. Closer to the front of the paper were the "hard news" stories: more skirmishes in the Boer War, debate about American Imperialism in the Philippines, the inauguration of the Australian Commonwealth, the saloon smashings of Carrie A. Nation and her prohibitionist allies.

But still, overshadowing all these stories was the one on everyone's mind—the turn of the century. Just think: *a new century!* Why, nobody could remember the turn of the last century. I've got to scribble my thoughts about the century's end into my diary! I've got to write a poem, an ode, to the new century! I've got to hurry and get to City Hall and cheer and wait for the bells to chime midnight! Those were the sorts of things that ordinary people did, by the hundreds of thousands, as one century gave way to the next. Journalists and academics wrote buoyant or cynical or solemn essays about the "accomplishments" of the dying century or the anticipated marvels of the century to come. Ministers wrote century sermons, musicians wrote century songs, ad-men promoted countless "End-Of-The-Century Sales!!!" and novelists wrote fantastic tales about people living at the end of the far off and unfathomable year 2000.

All this, and more, happened at the end of the nineteenth century. And as we'll see in the upcoming chapters, it had happened before, though more quietly, at the end of the eighteenth century. And some of it happened even before that, at the end of the seventeenth century.

That's where this book comes in. As we hurtle towards the biggest, loudest, and most frenzied *fin-de-siècle* celebrations the planet has yet seen, we hope to put it all in perspective by providing snapshots from journals, diaries, newspapers, books, and other sources, of what our predecessors—our counterparts—wrote and reported to mark the end of previous centuries.

Snapshots—hundreds of them. Some ridiculous, some sublime. There's John Mackay, arguing that the eighteenth century doesn't end when everyone thinks it ends. There's a trapper on the frozen Canadian prairies, scribbling "January 1" on the top corner of his diary but too cold to care that he's just entered the nineteenth century. There's Sigmund Freud, a hundred years later, complaining that the new century contains the date of his death. There's a contributor for the *Chicago Tribune*, reporting that the humans of the next century will lack teeth and little toes. There's con man Frank Higbee, almost ruining the American Red Cross by getting it to endorse his huge *fin-de-siècle* parties. This book is chock full of such snapshots, which makes it a kind of literary photo-album, one in which you'll turn the pages and recognize your own end-of-the-millennium self.

Mark Morton and Gail Noble

May 1999 (from the world's creation, 6001)

Chapter One

The Century Squabble

> I am aware that the Astronomer Royal says that the next century will begin on January 1, 1901—the last year of the century being 1900, and that the present era begins with the year A.D. 1, and the year before is B.C. 1, there being no year 0. This pedantic view is not new to me. It is of course absurd.
>
> —*Punch*, January 1900

ONE DAY, THREE WOMEN attending the same convention decided to cut expenses by sharing a hotel room. At the front desk, the bellhop—covering for the manager who was grabbing some lunch—told them the room was thirty dollars. Each woman handed over ten dollars, and they proceeded up to their room. When the stalwart manager returned, he discovered the bellhop had overcharged the women: the room was only twenty-five dollars. He handed the bellhop five dollars, and told him to return it to the women. On the way, the sneaky bellhop decided to keep a little something for his trouble, so he pocketed two dollars. He then knocked on the door, explained the mistake, and handed each of the three women a single dollar. This meant that each woman originally paid ten dollars, but then received one back, so that each woman actually paid nine dollars. Since there were three women, they collectively paid twenty-seven dollars. The bellhop had two dollars in his pocket. Twenty-seven plus two totals twenty-nine. Where did the other dollar go?

Anyone who has ever taken a course in accounting, or who has ever been treasurer of their local tennis club, will not be taken in by the preceding "ledger"-demain. But to others, the mystery of the supposedly missing dollar can be maddening. Until solved, the puzzle threatens to explode a fundamental assumption about the universe: that numbers make sense, that 30 is always 30, and that 30 is never 29.

An analogous puzzle arose at the end of the seventeenth century and has resurfaced at the end of every century since. The debate in its essence is this: is the last day of a century December 31 of the year that ends in '99, or is it December 31 of the year that ends in '00? The crux of the matter is

THE PROBLEM OF THE DAY---HOW OLD ARE WE?

When Does the 19th Century End?

Old 1899—"I am the most important year that ever lived. I mark the close of the most remarkable century in the world's history."

Young 1900—"Hold on, old fellow! I am coming and the nineteenth century will not be over until I have lived 365 days."

from *Nassau County Review*, 1899

whether that sixth-century deviser of our calendar, Dionysius Exiguus, designated the first year after the birth of Jesus to be A.D. 0 or A.D. 1. If A.D. 0 (which historians say is unlikely), then all centuries must end on the last day of '99; if A.D. 1 (which the evidence points to), then all centuries must end on the last day of '00, for example, December 31, 2000. When previous centuries rose on the horizon, there was much throwing about of brains on this subject. But for us, perhaps the question is not such a burning one. Who, for the sake of calendrical rigor, is going to ignore the thrill of hailing all those zeroes and that alien "2"?

The century debate unleashed a flood of intellectual activity—analogies, puzzles, stories, parodies, pseudomathematica. None of these forms of cerebral play interest us much these days. The nineteenth-century clergyman who indulged his dream of order by engaging in a little recreational mathematics has a few successors among us, but not enough to fill thirty column-feet in the *London Times* over a two-week period. We might *The opinion generally adopted I now forget* be tempted to see our predecessors' century squabbles as quaint, a manifestation of a culture that allowed a few privileged fellows (and they were all fellows) the leisure and learning to puzzle over arcane questions. Today we might even pathologize such thinkers as obsessive-compulsives or autistic savants, which is too bad, for there is something to be said for their energetic pursuit of the "truth." While we accumulate information, they made order. While we pile sticks, they built nests—though sometimes, as we will see, uninhabitable ones.

Many writers of memoirs record the heated debates that took place in every household as 1800 and 1900 loomed nearer, but it is ironic how the passage of a few decades blurs the "correct" view. In the end, it seems, the right answer doesn't matter very much. Writing in 1862, the poet Ann Taylor, sister of Jane Taylor who penned "Twinkle, Twinkle, Little Star," recalled that

> The year 1800 commenced, as did I believe the year 1700, and will, I daresay, the year 1900, with a warm, general, still unsettled dispute as to the period at which the old century should be understood to close, and the new one begin ... There was just a year's difference in the calculations of the disputants, though to each the question appeared to admit not a shadow of a doubt. Did the eighteenth century close on the 31st of December 1799, or of 1800? The opinion generally adopted I now forget. Close, however, it did, and here we are more than half through another!

The war poet Siegfried Sassoon, looking back in 1939, recalled the squabble but mis-remembered the positions taken by his English stepfather, Mr. Hamilton, and his German grandmother. The trouble was exacerbated by the German emperor Kaiser Wilhelm II who, according to Sassoon, "announced that the twentieth century wouldn't really begin until the first of January 1901." (In fact the Kaiser had taken the opposite position—he decreed January 1, 1900 as the first day of the *grotesquely, obviously, almost indecently, absurd* twentieth century.) Grandma, known as "Fraulein" in Sassoon's memoirs, naturally accepted her Kaiser's decree and supported him with "bigoted pertinacity." In contrast,

> Mr. Hamilton, who shared the national indignation against the Kaiser for telegraphing hearty congratulations to President Kruger because the British were doing so badly against the Boers, was fully in favour of starting the new century a year earlier. Just as they looked like losing their tempers at luncheon the controversy would close down, only to begin all over again next day. The final result was

a stalemate, but arguing continued up to the actual chronological crisis. On New Year's Day [of 1900] Mr. Hamilton, who had spent Christmas with us and was just off for his holiday, beamingly inquired of Fraulein what the Kaiser was proposing to do about babies born in Germany during the year 1900, as they couldn't begin to be alive before next January. Fraulein gave no sign of having heard him. She had made up her mind that she was still knitting in the old century, and Mr. Hamilton made no further attempt to convince her that she wasn't.

The battle of the century's end was waged not only round the hearth, but in hundreds of newspapers across Europe and North America. The editor of the *New York Times* lambasted those contributors who maintained that the century ended on December 31, 1899. That belief, the editor insisted, was "grotesquely, obviously, almost indecently, absurd." What was especially shocking, he added, was that this view was held

> not only by people densely illiterate and therefore in a measure pardonable, but also by hundreds of persons who in youth were familiar with reading books and arithmetics, and who had managed to reach adult age without any particular familiarity with the interior of insane asylums.

These "unfortunate and deluded individuals," continued the editor, "argued the wrong side of the case at dreadful length"; they "wrote innumerable letters to the newspapers"; they "wearied their relatives and alienated their friends"—all in a "desperate effort to prove that even if there never was a Year Zero, there should have been one."

The editor spared no one who championed the "wrong" side of the century dispute. When Pope Leo XIII in the last month of 1899 issued a decree implying that 1900 was the beginning of the *the destinies of colleges for women* century, the editor ridiculed the pontiff's "infallible authority" in the matter. (Pope Leo later clarified his position, saying that what he meant was that January 1, 1900 was actually the beginning of the last year of the century.) When fourteen college presidents were invited by the *Boston Herald* to weigh in on the issue, the editor of the *New York Times* poo-pooed the argument put forth by Caroline Hazard of Wellesley University. "According to my way of thinking," Hazard had written,

> the twentieth century begins one second past midnight of December 31, 1899—January 1, 1900. Midnight marks the conclusion of the 1900th year of the Christian era. The 1900th year, understand, is different from the year 1900, because when we write 1900 we are not at the completion of the 1900 and first year, which we write 1901. But anything beyond midnight on the 1st of January of the coming year is time that must be reckoned in the 1901st year.

True, not the clearest explanation, but the *New York Times* editor took it all very personally. He slammed Hazard as well as Clark Seelye of Smith

College for their singular belief in "an imaginary, non-existent and impossible Year Zero," a year which had led them to the "false conclusion that the twentieth century begins on the first of January, 1900." With such deficient minds, the editor suggested, it was hardly surprising that "these two very obviously mistaken persons are guiding the destinies of colleges for women."

But despite the drubbing he gave the Pope and the college presidents, it was the German emperor, Kaiser Wilhelm II, whom the *New York Times* editor really blasted. While most western nations—including Canada, Britain, the United States, and France— *was ever such freak in dating?* had declared that December 31, 1900 was the "official" end of the century, Kaiser Wilhelm stubbornly ordered his subjects to celebrate December 31, 1899: at the stroke of midnight on that date, the Kaiser's military leaders, courtiers, and other well-wishers were to file past his majesty and welcome him into the new century. When word of these plans reached the editor of the *New York Times* on December 20, 1899, he sneered that "the German emperor must stand in solitary grandeur as the only man of any prominence who cannot count up to one hundred." Not letting the matter drop, the editor returned to it a few weeks later on January 8, 1900, laughing that "The emperor has declared that at some period unrevealed there was a century with only ninety-nine years in it." Months later, on November 9, 1900, the editor was still at it. The century debate had been settled, he claimed, because "the dictum of logic and common sense has been accepted by everybody—except the German emperor" and his "delightfully docile subjects."

The *Worcester Telegraph* echoed these sentiments, stating that "There is no appeal from Willie's decision, according to Willie's thinking." Likewise *Punch*, in its issue of December 20, 1899, asserted that Germans "must ditto" the Kaiser's view, and went on to compare their leader to Sigismund, the Holy Roman Emperor who once claimed he had the power to alter Latin grammar:

> Twas the Holy Roman Kaiser, over a thousand years ago,
> In a speech made "schema" feminine—which caused a monk
>   to stammer,
> "My liege, it is a neuter word!"—said his liege, "I'd have you know
> I'm Emperor, and aught I say is *ipso facto* grammar!"

> Even so a modern autocrat will arithmetic defy,
> And chronologic laws override with a mere "*Sic volo!*", stating
> That the Twentieth Century has begun (and his folk must
>   ditto cry)
> Ere nineteen hundred years are past—was there ever such freak
>   in dating?

To give them credit, though, perhaps the German people were not so much docile as canny: much like us, they may have asked—"why limit

HOW THE TWENTIETH CENTURY
Breaks upon the British Empire.

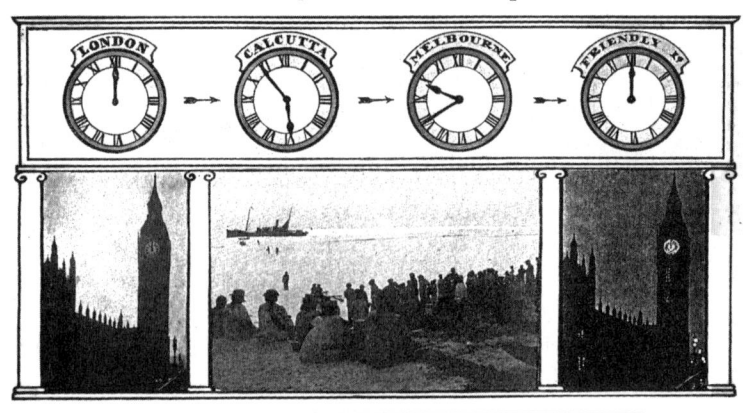

from *The Sphere*, December 29, 1900 (and opposite page)

ourselves to just one end-of-the-century bash when we can have another one a year later?" When December 31, 1900 rolled around, the streets of Berlin and other German cities were again jammed with "new-century" revellers.

Why the Kaiser declared 1900 to be the first year of the twentieth century is open to speculation. Known more for his bombast than his brain, perhaps he simply could not fathom the mathematical explanation of why 1901 was the "correct" beginning of the century. More likely, though, is that the Kaiser's century decree was politically motivated. Along with his councillors, the German emperor was convinced that his nation was on the verge of regaining its ancient splendour. Given this vision of Germany's imminent glory, small wonder that Kaiser Wilhelm II was eager to abandon the nineteenth century, which had seen the shrivelling of German prestige, and commence a brand-spanking-new one. For better or worse, the Kaiser's mandate to begin the century a year early had the political advantage of herding all German citizens into the twentieth century before any other nation.

One hundred years earlier, in 1800, no one in Germany was quite certain what century they were living in. Writing on January 1, 1800, the poet **Mon Dieu, En Quel Siècle Vivons Nous?** Friedrich von Schiller sent Johann Wolfgang von Goethe "kind greetings for the new year and the new century"—yet twelve months later Goethe invited Schiller to a new century party, one at which Goethe's *Iphigenie* and Haydn's *Creation* were performed. On January 3, 1800, Goethe wished a happy new century to Prince August of Gotha, a German blue blood—yet one year later another blue blood, the duchess of Wurtemberg, sent new-century felicitations from her home in Bavaria to George III, king of Eng-

THE COMING OF THE NEW CENTURY
Its Spasmodic Career across the Map.

The first people to enter the new century may, perhaps, be on a vessel crossing the date line at midnight on December 31, 1900. The vessel shown here is one of the Canadian Pacific fleet which regularly crosses the 180 deg. line on her journeys from Vancouver to Hong Kong. Should she pass at the auspicious moment it will be possible for the bow watch who has entered the twentieth century to hail the man at the stern who, but a few yards away, is still a century behind

land. To the south, in France, the same confusion reigned: in 1800, a theatre in Paris produced a play entitled *Mon Dieu, en quel siècle vivons nous?*—that is, *My God, What Century Are We Living In?*

Across the English Channel, King George III likely considered the new-century felicitations from the duchess of Wurtemberg to be quite timely: there the first day of 1801 established the union of Great Britain and Ireland, a "great event," as the *London Times* then proclaimed, "dating its commencement from the awful epoch of a new century." The special day was celebrated with the ringing of bells, hoisting of flags, and firing of cannons.

For some the century debate was a good opportunity for a bet or at least a free lunch. Richard Brinsley Sheridan, statesman and playwright, bet his friend Joseph Richardson that 1799 was the last year of the century. A mutual friend listened to the two disputants and ruled against *the more uncertain and confused the better* Sheridan, who was already deeply in debt. Sydney Smith, the founder of the *Edinburgh Review*, recalled a professor at Oxford who won "a very large wager" by proving that 1800 was the last year of the century. Nor was he the only academic to profit—Thomas Holcroft, writing in his diary, recalled meeting a mathematics professor from Cambridge—known as "F"—who literally fed off the confusion about when the century ended. Whenever he learned that two gentleman had made a wager regarding the century's end, "F" would volunteer to adjudicate their debate—but only over a "sumptuous dinner." "F"—wrote Holcroft—"revelled in the idea of disputes which produced wagers of eating and drinking, and said they were very proper, and the more uncertain and confused the better." Confused is certainly how Holcroft felt after discussing the century question with Professor "F" and his friend Geddes:

> Geddes was still more incomprehensible—for if I understood him, the century begins with the year 99. I asked him to explain. He said he could only do it by a diagram, but added that after Christ was born, the year 1 was not completed till he was one year old; to which

I answered, this I believed nobody would dispute. As I found they either did not understand themselves, or at least were unintelligible to me, I dropped the question.

The debate also raged on the other side of the planet. The *Connecticut Courrant* published these anonymous verses on January 1, 1801:

Precisely at twelve o'clock last night
The eighteenth century took its flight.
Full many a calculating head
Has racked its brains, its ink has shed,
To prove by metaphysics fine,
A hundred means but ninety-nine,
While at their wisdom others wondered,
But took one more to make a hundred.

Strange at the eighteenth century's close
While light in beams effulgent glows,
When bright illuminated ray
Has chased the darkness far away,
Heads filled with mathematic lore,
Dispute if two and two make four.

Go on, ye scientific sages,
Collect your light a few more ages,
Perhaps as swells the vast amount,
A century hence you'll learn to count.

Nor were anglophones the only ones embroiled in the end-of-the-century controversy. Pamphlets sprang up everywhere, from Paris ("Quand a Fini le XVIII siècle? Quand a Commencé le XIX?") to Rotterdam ("Voorstelling dat het Jaar 1800, en niet het Jaar 1801, het Begin der Negentiende eeuw is of moet Zijn") to Berlin ("Ein Gespräch über die Frage: ob das Neue Jahrhundert mid dem Jahre 1800 oder mid 1801 Anfängt?"). For the most part, these pamphlets employed the same sort of arguments as their English-language counterparts. One treatise from Leipzig, however, stands out—its author incorporated a musical canon into the argument. The year 1800, he wrote, is like the last note of a canon: the second voice begins when the first has ended its last note, not when it begins it. Likewise, all of the eighteenth century must be "sung" before the nineteenth century begins its part.

Ach! Ach!
Ach! Ach!

Although the Leipzigian's argument may have been sound, the canon itself was no great shakes. The lyrics consisted of nothing more than the question "When does the nineteenth century begin?" interspersed occasionally with a guttural "Ach! Ach! Ach! Ach!"

Toe-tapper or not, the "musical" argument from Leipzig at least had the virtue of being short (an especially difficult task in German, where the author was stuck with words like *Jubilaumssinfonienkomponisten*). That virtue was lacking in many English treatises where the century-question spawned works of eye-blearing length and brain-numbing complexity.

from *Musikalische Zeitung*, September, 1799

For example, John Mackay's *The Commencement of the Nineteenth Century Determined upon Unerring Principles* ran forty-seven pages, with another fourteen pages of appendices.

Mackay begins his argument by presenting himself as a paragon of good sense. Acknowledging that "much keenness of temper has been shown by some of the contending parties," he promises to approach the century issue calmly and logically. He deplores those disputants whose arguments *tending only to perplex the matter* "display ignorance in its highest pitch" and who "have endeavoured to get the better of their adversary by asking questions not connected with the subject and tending only to perplex the matter." In no time at all, Mackay promises, the reader will at last understand why the eighteenth century ends on December 31, 1799.

Mackay argues by citing dozens of authorities including historians, specialists in ecclesiastical calendars, parliamentary records, encyclopaedias, poets, and the ever-popular Todd's *Perpetuum Kalendarium Astronomicum*—all of which make passing reference to 1799 as the last year of the eighteenth century. But the real heart of Mackay's argument is a set of astronomical tables that, Mackay says, reveal precisely where the heavenly bodies were located during the year zero:

> The mean longitude of the sun, at the instant of mean noon of the first day of the year zero, under the meridian of Greenwich, according to Mayer's Tables, page vi, is 9S 7°49′20″.9; and that of the moon at the same instant, page xxvi, is 11S 21°46′24″.9.

Mackay's point is this: if the location of the sun and moon can be calculated backwards to the year zero, then there must have been a year

THE

COMMENCEMENT

OF THE

NINETEENTH CENTURY,

DETERMINED

UPON UNERRING PRINCIPLES.

BY

ANDREW MACKAY, LL.D. F.R.S. EDIN. &c.

ABERDEEN:

PRINTED FOR THE AUTHOR,

BY W. RETTIE;

AND SOLD BY J. WHITE, FLEET STREET; W. HEATHER, LEADENHALL
STREET; D. STEEL, UNION ROW, MINORIES, LONDON;
A. CONSTABLE, EDINBURGH; BRASH
& REID, GLASGOW, &c.

1800.

title page from Andrew MacKay's essay

zero. Whether or not his year zero is actually the year 1 B.C. he does not
say. Be that as it may, Mackay is satisfied that he has "thus established in
the most solid manner, and upon unexceptionable principles, that the
first year of the vulgar era of Christ was denominated Zero." From here—
ground zero, so to speak—he begins to build upwards to his conclusion:

> It hence follows, that as soon as the first year was completed, and
> the second commenced, then that year would be marked or dated
> "1," signifying, therefore, that one year was elapsed and the second
> flowing on. In like manner, the interval of time between the begin-
> ning of the second and third was dated "2"; and, therefore, the third
> year was completed with the expiry of the year marked "2." The
> fourth year of the era was completed at the termination of the year
> marked "3."

At this point, things look bad for Mackay's reader—in an entire paragraph,
Mackay has only progressed from year zero to year three. Mercifully,
though, Mackay finds a way to accelerate his argument:

And hence, by carrying forward the reckoning in the same manner, the first century will be found to be completed at the termination of the year denominated 99. Therefore the eighteenth century terminated with the last day of the year marked 1799.

But Mackay isn't done just yet. He cunningly anticipates how his adversaries might object to his argument: if there really was a year zero, then what historical incidents occurred during it? To answer the objection, or rather to sidestep it, Mackay once again unfurls his astronomical tables and discovers that "in the year zero a very remarkable total eclipse of the moon happened on January 9. That the year zero began upon Thursday … That the year zero was a leap year."

But as he continues to pore over his astronomical tables looking for more evidence of "historical incidents," Mackay loses sight of his argument. As if suddenly ravished by the cosmic secrets contained in his wondrous tables, he turns seer and makes several peculiar predictions:

> The year 10,000 will begin upon Saturday … the planet Venus will appear like a black round spot, upon the sun's disk, upwards of 7h.52′, in the afternoon of Monday, June 14th, 2984.

Mackay, of course, could not have anticipated what any fan of "Star Trek" now knows: that in the year 2162 the planet earth, along with other members of the intergalactic Federation, will cease to use the seven-day week and switch to a "stardate" calendar system.

Mackay's chief adversary in the century dispute was John Rose, author of *The Grand Chronological Dispute, or The Question in What Century is the Present Year 1800?* Rose contended that December 31, 1800 was the true turn of the century and in the introduction to his treatise he promises to "remove the film from the eyes" of people like Mackay "who maintain that the eighteenth century expired with the year 1799." His undertaking, Rose realizes, is a dangerous one, since "this momentous question has been agitated with a zeal sufficient to kindle the flames of war amid rival nations."

the year 10,000 will begin upon Saturday

For Rose, the century dispute cannot be settled by consulting dusty authorities or arcane astronomical tables. Instead he turns his imagination to the creation of "helpful" analogies. He begins, for instance, by drawing a parallel between the passing of a hundred years and a man walking a hundred miles.

> Suppose he were to take the proposed journey, and to compute his walk at a mile a year. When he came to the date of his 100th year he had many weary steps to make before he could have come to the 100th mile-mark. The fact is, he would be in the date of his mile 100 from the beginning of it.

Kindergarten Teacher—Now children, let me hear you count.

The reply rational.	*The reply otherwise.*
Children—One, two, three, four, five, six, seven, eight, etc.	Children—Nothing, one, two, three, four, five, six, seven, etc.

School Teacher—Tommy, what is a century?

Tommy—One hundred years.	Tommy—One hundred years.

Teacher—Give an example.

Tommy—From the first day of the first year to the last day of the one hundredth year.	Tommy—From the first day of the year before the first to the last day of the year before the one hundredth.

Merchant—Mr. Jones, please arrange these cancelled checks in bundles of one hundred and file them away.

Mr. Jones does so, marking the bundles thus:	Mr. Jones seems puzzled at not finding check numbe zero, so with many misgivings adds check number 100 to his first bundle and is amazed that his second one begins with number 101.
Nos. 1-100.	
Nos. 101-200.	
Nos. 201-300, etc.	

Bank Customer—Will you be kind enough to let me have ones for this $100 bill.

Cashier—With pleasure. (Counts out): One dollar, two dollars, three dollars, four dollars, five, six, seven, . . . ninety-nine and a hundred. Here you are, sir. (Customer goes away satisfied.)	Cashier—With pleasure. (Lays first bill aside, murmuring: No dollar). Then: One dollar, two dollars, three dollars, four dollars, five, six, seven. . . . and ninety-nine. Here you are, sir. (Customer does *not* go away.)

from *The Literary Digest*, December 30, 1899

Despite the implausibility of the man travelling for one hundred years at the molasses-like pace of seven inches per hour, the analogy is clear

let there be a cuckoo

enough. In fact, the analogy of the hundred-mile journey was proposed by countless century squabblers, which is perhaps why Rose felt the need to elaborate on it, to put his own scholarly stamp upon it. He does so by going on to demand that his aged traveller turn around and retrace his steps:

> Let him walk back again, a mile a year: he would then at the end of his first year's travel arrive at the 99th mile-mark; at the end of the 99th year, at the 1st mile mark; at which point he would have to commence his 100th mile journey and his 100th year's date together; and he would then find, travelling at his old rate, that he must once more close the centenary year before his trial could be ended.

Reversing the hundred-mile walk has already left his readers scratching their heads, but Rose does not stop there—he now proposes a more ingenious analogy, this time comparing the passing of a century to a clock whose face is inscribed not with twelve, but a hundred hours:

> Let us place before us a clock describing 100 hours. Let each hour be the representative of a year and let the revolution of each hour be described by a small hand traversing its time in 365 distinct divisions ... When the small hand has made 99 revolutions, and the

other hand has, in due course, arrived at the point marked 99, it will be fully as plain that 99 years are passed; and that the instant the hands set off again they will be describing the 100th year—that is, they will represent the first day (alias January 1) of the year 100, which cannot be complete till the small hand has described all the parts thereof, when both hands will be again, for the first time since their departure, where they originally set out.

Rose goes on to insist that an imaginary cuckoo be hooked up to the clock's imaginary mechanism, so that each of the hundred "hours" will be chirped. For readers who remain unconvinced by his baroque analogy, Rose invites them to sit and watch the hands of such a *pigmies in science* clock for eighteen hours, an activity which, he claims, will assuredly demonstrate that the eighteenth century ends on December 31, 1800.

Unlike Mackay and Rose, some end-of-the-eighteenth-century squabblers argued their position in just a few cranky lines. In the *Gentleman's Magazine*, we read:

> Mr. URBAN,   Dec. 31, 1799
>
> For the satisfaction of such of your ingenious correspondents as are capable of conviction, I beg your insertion of the following short dialogue between my master and me; which may serve, perhaps, to deliver them out of those cruel and unaccountable embarrassments under which they have so long been labouring.
>
> Q. What is a century?
>
> A. A series of a hundred years.
>
> Q. What is the last number in a series of one hundred?
>
> A. The number 100.
>
> Q. What is the last number in a century?
>
> A. Why, Sir, if an hundred years and a century be the same thing, then, whatever is the last number of one must be the last number of the other. I answer again, therefore, the number 100.
>
> Q. And what do you infer from this?
>
> A. Why, Sir, that if 100 be the last number of a series of one hundred, and also of a century, then 1800 must be the last number of an eighteenth series, and also of the eighteenth century.
>
> Master. Right, my lad. Now go and tell Mr. Urban's correspondents, and the scribbling chronologists in the newspapers, what pigmies in science they are compared with.
>
> —A SCHOOL-BOY

Other participants in the century squabble were even more terse, engaging in little more than *ad hominem* attacks on their adversaries. On January 11, 1801, the editor of London's *Bell's Weekly Messenger* complained bitterly about "the idle controversy *no more brains than an oyster* which has of late convulsed so many brains" and put forth a three-sentence argument intended to "disappoint the snares of public delusion." The editor of Philadelphia's *Porcupine's Gazette*, writing in the first issue of 1800, did not even bother with an argument, merely snapping that "We are now in the last year of the century, and whoever denies this has no more brains than an oyster." Another clipped response came from the editor of the *London Times*, William Walter, who was rendered nigh apoplectic by the very existence of the century debate. In his editorial of December 26, 1799, Walter announced that

> We have uniformly rejected all letters, and declined all discussion upon the question of when the present century ends as it is one of the most absurd that can engage the public attention, and we are astonished to find it has been the subject of so much dispute, since it appears to be perfectly plain. The present century will not terminate till Jan. 1, 1801, unless it can be made out that 99 are 100 ... It is a silly, childish discussion, and only exposes the want of brains of those who maintain the contrary opinion to that we have stated.

To Walter we might say—you ain't seen nothing yet. A hundred years later his successor at the *London Times*, editor George Buckle, did not think to impose an embargo on letters disputing the end of the nineteenth century. The result was a deluge. The story begins on December 29, 1899. Sir Courtenay Boyle, a low-level government official, contributed a polite letter of the by-Jove-isn't-that-interesting sort:

> Sir,—
> Will you allow me to say a few words with regard to a question which has attracted some attention here and elsewhere—namely, what day should be considered the first day of the 20th century?
> The question what day is the commencement of the 20th century of the common era is not, I think, soluble for the following reasons.
> The common era was, there is no reason to doubt, first devised by Dionysius, an abbot of the sixth century, and first brought into use by the Carlovingian Kings ... The founders of the era, as indeed the founders of any other, had two courses open to them. They
>
> *Your obedient* might either have described the events of the first 12
> *servant* months after the Nativity as having happened Anno Domini Nati (or for short Anno Domini) and the events of the second 12 months as having happened Anno Domini 1, or the first as having happened Anno Domini 1 and the second as having happened Anno Domini 2. Either course would have been as correct as the other ... To my mind it is slightly more probable that the sequence was Anno Domini, Anno Domini 1, than that it was Anno Domini 1, Anno Domini 2. If parents fix events by the birth of a child, they say so and so happened "the year Alfred was born," and so and so happened "the year Alfred was 1," thus making the sequence 0 1 2, not 1 2 3. Of this probability other thinkers may take a different view. But again I submit that no conclusive evidence exists either way ...
> Inasmuch as those persons who desire to reach the 20th century are probably more numerous than those who care nothing for any such record, it seems to me that they should be gratified at the earliest moment. There is no reason why essayists, preachers, and

TO THE EDITOR OF THE TIMES.

" In France, as in England, there have been disputes about the commencement of the 19th century. The astronomer Lalande thus determines the question, which, he says, was equally agitated at the end of the last century, he having in his library a pamphlet published on the subject. 'Many persons imagine that, because after having counted 17 they commence 18, the century must, be changed ; but this is a mistake', for when 100 years are to be counted we must pass from 99 and we arrive at 100 : we have changed the 10 before we have finished the 100. Whatever calculation is to be made we commence by 1 and finish by 100 ; nobody has ever thought of commencing at 0 and finishing by 99.' Thus he concludes the year 1800 incontestably belongs to the 18th or old century."

from the *London Times*, January 2, 1900

paragraphists should have to postpone their eloquence on the subject till 1901, and I therefore venture to think that we may in this country follow the example of Germany and treat Monday next as the first day of the 20th century. May it be a fortunate one for our Sovereign and her people!

> Your obedient Servant,
> Courtenay Boyle

Boyle's tone was deferential: he politely granted that "other thinkers may take a different view" and his final appeal was to sentiment, endorsing the earlier date because it would please the multitudes who yearned to greet the new century as soon as possible. Considering his conciliatory tone, his jaw must have dropped when he opened the next day's *London Times*—December 30, 1899—and found himself under attack from someone calling himself "Scaliger" after the sixteenth-century chronologist who authored *The Improvement of Time*.

Sir,—

If Sir Courtenay Boyle really wishes the century to end with the end of the year 1899 I am afraid he must still wait for another year before his wish can be gratified. It doesn't matter a pin whether Dionysius the Little made his era begin with the year 1 or the year 0, nor does it matter whether we choose to think that he might just as well have made it begin with the year zero as with the numeral one. Chronologers and astronomers both make it begin with the numeral one in all their reckonings. If we are now to assume that this is a mistake, the consequences will be rather startling. Every date given in terms of the Christian era is based on the assumption that that era began with A.D. 1. If we are now to reject that assumption, we must alter all dates accordingly, thus:—An event assigned to the year 1 really happened in the year 0. An event assigned to the year 2 really happened in the year 1. An event assigned to the year n really happened in they year n-1. Of two things, one, then: either all

---

TO THE EDITOR OF THE TIMES.

Sir.—A great deal of confusion seems to have been caused by the mistaken comparison between the numeration of the years of our era and those of a man's age. We say a man is 50, which means he has completed 50 years ; but we say this is the year 1900, which means that the era is in its 1900th year and has only completed its 1899th year. Just as a man in his 51st year has only completed his 50th year.

We cannot begin the 20th century until the era has completed its 1900th year and is in its 1901st year, or "the year 1901."   Yours faithfully,

HAROLD B. BARKWORTH.

Royal Societies' Club, St. James's-street, S.W.

---

from the *London Times*, January 2, 1900

our dates are wrong from the year 1 to the present time, or the 20th century cannot begin for another year.

I am, Sir, your obedient servant,

Scaliger

In the same day's paper, another contributor was even more infuriated by Boyle's take on the century problem. Sir Herbert Stephen, a cousin of Virginia Woolf, wrote:

December 29, 1899

Sir,—

It is not credible that the inventors of the Christian Era can have given the number 1 to the second year it contained.

Has Sir Courtenay Boyle ever seen a book in which the second page of the text was numbered 1, and the hundredth 99?

Has he ever known of a company the first hundred shares of which were numbered 0 to 99?

Has he ever himself numbered sheets of manuscripts and numbered the second 1, the third 2, and so on? ...

The first year of the first century of the Christian Era was the year 1, and the first year of the 20th century will be the year 1901.

I am, sir, your obedient servant,

Herbert Stephen

Boyle countered this parry from Stephen with a thrust of his own, published the day after New Year's, 1900:

Sir,—

Sir Herbert Stephen asks whether I have ever seen a book in which the second page of the text was numbered 1 and the hundredth 99. May I ask Sir Herbert Stephen how he connotes the hours of the day? Does he consider 1:15 a.m. a moment in the first hour of the day or of the second? ... Does he record temperature from the starting point of zero or of one? In simple numeration is not 0.25 a part of the first unit and 1.45 a part of the second?

Your obedient servant,
Courtenay Boyle

Not to be outdone, Stephen spotted an apparent chink in Boyle's analogies and moved in for the kill with his reply of January 3:

Sir,—

Sir Courtenay Boyle seems to me to have changed his ground. When he began his first letter he thought the question of the century "not soluble." He appears now to have solved it in the wrong way ...

"1:15 a.m." indicates a moment in the second hour of the day. It does not follow that "1, January 20," or "January 20, 1," would mean the 20th of January in the second year. Numbers are not used as the specific names of entire hours. Each number, in relation to hours, means a moment in each hour—namely, the latter end of it. With years it is otherwise. It is now 1900, and will continue to be 1900 for 11 months and some days longer. If the whole hour from 1 a.m. to 2 a.m. were known as 2, I daresay we should describe a quarter past 1 as "2:15." As we do not, Sir Courtenay's analogy is delusive.

I am, Sir, your obedient servant,
Herbert Stephen

For two days, Boyle was silent. The readers of the *Times*, dozens of whom carried on the squabble with irate letters of their own, no doubt wondered if Boyle had been dumbstruck by Stephen's mighty reasoning. Perhaps, some readers thought to themselves, he had even been converted to Stephen's view of the matter. Then, on January 6, it became clear what Boyle had been up to: he had been rooting through decades of back issues of the *London Times*, seeking some scrap of information that would turn the tables on Stephen and his ilk. He found it, he thought, in this thunderbolt—a *London Times* editorial from mid-century implying that the last day of 1849, not the last day of 1850, was the mid-point of the century:

Sir,—

May I be permitted to recall to your memory that on December 31, 1849 the first leading article in the *Times* thus began:—"The close of a year marked by a rapid succession of extraordinary events—the close of the first half of the 19th century which now bequeaths to posterity its unclouded tale—invites us to survey the course of the last 12 months."

May it be said of thunderbolts as it was said of Cleopatra:—"Age cannot wither them, nor custom stale their infinite variety"?

Your obedient servant,
Courtenay Boyle
Travellers' Club, Pall-mall, S.W.

But Boyle's imagined victory over Stephen was overshadowed by another letter on the same page of the newspaper. This one, contributed by a fresh contender, Henry Wilson, was not so much an argument against Boyle's case as a damning *ad hominem* attack on Boyle's professional competence and personal sanity:

> Sir,—
> This controversy is chiefly interesting from the light it throws on the workings of the human mind. Can we wonder at the Titus Oates craze, or pilgrimages to Lourdes, or the Flagellants, or Mormonism, when persons now, of education and position, gravely treat it as an arguable question whether 99 are equal to 100 or not?
> ... Sir Courtenay mixed up the question of whether 1,900 full years have passed since the date Dionysius fixed on as the one to reckon from, with the totally irrelevant question of whether Christ was actually born on that day or five years earlier.
> Sir Courtenay Boyle says that from 0.1 to 0.99 is a complete hundred. Now if I were a doctor and were called in to decide on the state of a person's mind, I would hand him the change for a £5 note in silver and tell him to count it back to me. If when he put down the 99th shilling he said that he had paid me in full, it would only be a question whether his destination should be a prison or an asylum.
>
> Farnborough, Kent
> Henry Wilson

From a public drubbing such as this, there was no recovery. Boyle fell silent, withdrawing from the century dispute, apparently for good.

However, one year later, on December 31, 1900, an anonymous notice appeared in the classified ads of the *London Times*, so small it was probably overlooked by most readers:

> To the English Public and the Public Abroad,   Dec. 25, 1900
> A widespread haziness about the beginning of the Century should be dispersed. A century is a series of one hundred consecutive years and must therefore begin with a year and end with a year. The 20th century could not begin on the 1st of January, 1901, because the tenth decade ended with the 31st of December, 1899, and so terminated the 19th century. The 1st of January, 1900, inaugurated the 20th century and its first birthday will be on the first of next month.

To the sentimental, this small advertisement conjures a melancholy scenario: Sir Courtenay Boyle, his bowler soiled and his trousers tattered, shambling down to the offices of the *London Times* on Christmas day, 1900, spending his last few pounds on a classified ad, bent on getting the last word in the now-stale century debate, a debate that cost him his reputation, his sanity, and—ultimately—his position as a low-level government official.

In the two weeks following Boyle's initial contribution, an astonishing seventy-seven letters appeared in the *London Times*, written by sixty-five different authors, and totalling about thirty feet of column space. Of these authors, only about ten—including Boyle—endorsed the end of 1899 as the turn of the century, while a whopping fifty argued for the end of 1900—a ratio of one to five. The remaining fifteen or so contributors include those whose letters were so muddled that it is not evident which side they were supporting, and those who muddied *MDCCCCLXXXVIII* the already turbid waters by inquiring after matters not relevant to the actual debate. Typical of the muddled thinkers was W. Day:

> Sir,—
> December 29
>
> I was 76 last birthday and shall be 77 next birthday, when I shall have completed my 77th year. We leave the year behind as we go on. The same with our hundredth year. We have lived it to the full and it is behind us, and if we lived 20 centuries it would be the same. Another year is not required to be thrown in to complete the time; to require this would be to assume that the first two years count as one only, or that otherwise we were done out of a year somehow or other.
>
> Yours faithfully
> W. Day

More lucid, but less germane, were the left-field queries submitted by two individuals who concealed their identities in an alphabet soup of initials:

> Sir,—
>
> Will one of your numerous correspondents who discourse so learnedly of Consuls, before and after Plancus, tell the proper manner of expressing 1900 in Roman numerals?
> Should it be MDCCCC or MDCD or simply MCM?
> The last seems preferable for brevity's sake, for if the first be adopted the year 1988 will require 18 letters—viz. MDCCCCLXXXVIII.
> The question has some interest for editors and printers.
>
> Yours faithfully,
> S.P.Q.R.

> Sir,—
> December 30
>
> Can any one inform us at what point on the earth's surface the 20th century will first begin? It will begin in Bombay before it does in London, and in London before it does in New York.
>
> Yours obediently,
> L.Y.L.

While S.P.Q.R.'s query about the Roman numerals went unheeded, L.Y.L. received a curt response from a Mr. Hastings C. Dent that "the 20th century begins at 180 degrees east latitude."

The *London Times* century debate came to an end on January 11, 1900. This armistice signalled not resolution but exhaustion. By January 9, contributors had already begun to preface their arguments with apologies for "wearying" and "tiring" the public with "this somewhat profitless contro-

---

TO THE EDITOR OF THE TIMES.

Sir,—Does not the idea of a year 0 at the beginning of our era destroy itself, for no one ever heard of it ? Even if it were the year 0, it would still remain the first year, and we should have the first year known as year 0, the second year as year 1, and the third year as year 2. This would be ridiculous. In all computations the first is one, the second two, and the end of the 100th completes a century. I begin to wonder if the Roman centurion counted his men 0 to 99. Does any one count 100 that way ? Practically the whole question is, How do we count 100, from 0 to 99 or from 1 to 100 ? Does any one, or did any one, ever count the former way ? Mr. Buchanan's " arithmetically sound " thesis is quite unsound. Apply it to his child, and he does not begin the year 1 of his existence until he enters upon his second year, which is absurd.

Yours truly, C. P. N.

---

from the *London Times*, January 2, 1900

versy." On the same day, a Parisian contributor to the *London Times* warned that "This controversy is very amusing, and there is no reason why it should not continue until the end of all the centuries, except that one may have too much of a good thing."

What really quashed the squabble, however, was the intervention of *Punch,* a satirical magazine whose reputation for exposing folly struck fear into the hearts of all pedants. One such pedant was J. Y. Buchanan, whose labyrinthine argument had been published in the *Times* on December 30, 1899:

1900 years 1 month 5 days 12 hours 20 minutes 15 seconds

Sir,—

The determination of the moment when the 19th century ends and the 20th begins appears still to vex the minds of many people. The German Emperor has declared it to be the midnight which separates December 31, 1899 from January 1, 1900. The following considerations will show that his Majesty's decision is arithmetically sound.

The conventional date of the birth of Christ is the zero of reckoning of our era, and it is written 0 years 0 days 0 seconds. One second later the date would be written 0 years 0 days 1 second A.D. The first year of the era ends at the instant which may be written either 0 years 365 days 0 seconds A.D. or 1 year 0 days 0 seconds A.D. Similarly the tenth year of the era ends at the date 9 years 365 days 0 seconds A.D. or 10 years 0 days 0 seconds A.D. This is the date of the end of the first century of our era. The date of the end of the 19th century is given by adding 1800 years to either of these dates. In the one case we get 1,899 years 365 days 0 seconds A.D., and in the other 1,900 years 0 days 0 seconds A.D. Each of these dates expresses the moment which occurs midway between 11 p.m. on December 31, 1899 and 1 a.m. on January 1, 1900.

J. Y. Buchanan

A few days later, a parody appeared in *Punch* from "J. Y. Babbage," the pseudonym poking fun at both J. Y. Buchanan and Charles Babbage, a professor of mathematics who had designed a mechanical computer in the early nineteenth century:

Sir,—

The Christian era started at 0 years 0 months 0 days 0 hours 0 minutes 0 seconds. When it was one second old, it was dated 0 years 0 months 0 days 0 hours 0 minutes 1 second A.D. I think nobody will deny this. Consequently, when it was two seconds old, it follows quite clearly that the date was 0 years 0 months 0 days 0 hours 2 seconds. Proceeding thus carefully second by second (every second is of equal importance), we shall not, I imagine, find a single opponent left to confute the contention that we are now in the 20th century.

What could be more previous?

J. Y. Babbage, President of the Statistical Babblers' Asylum

Dated: 1900 years 1 month 5 days 12 hours 20 minutes 15 seconds

Although the parody was only slightly more absurd than the original letter from Buchanan, it was successful enough that *Punch* followed it the next week with a reporter's account of a visit to "Professor Babbage" at his institution:

I found the savant engaged in argument with an attendant. He broke off, however, at my approach, and without waiting to receive my credentials, said to me somewhat peremptorily, "Think of a number!"

"Nineteen Hundred," I replied, thinking aloud.

Professor Babbage at this pricked up his ears, and appeared to take a deeper interest in my case.

"Oh, you too have got it!" he cried.

"Yes, Master, I want to get an authoritative opinion—"

"Yes, I know. I am aware that the Astronomer Royal says that the next century will begin on January 1, 1901—the last year of the century being 1900, and that the present era begins with the year A.D. 1, and the year before is B.C. 1, there being no year 0. This pedantic view is not new to me. It is of course absurd."

"The more correct view, then, is—"

"That of Nature's philosopher, the man in the street, preferably the back street. He knows, as well as you or I do, that there never was a year one. Eighteen hundred and ninety-nine years ago the Sun went round the Earth, so the year wasn't counted. If it had a date, I should prefer to call it Naughty-naught. Then, later on, when our reckoning was adopted, the wise minds of the dark age started arbitrarily in such a way as to allow the second century to begin on an even number."

"Why was that?"

"Well, I have no positive proof, but you can take my word it was so. You see, it is so much nicer and more sensible to suppose that the year one hundred is in the second century. (The first century, by the way, can well afford to do without a year or two.) Thus, 1 = 2, and we gain a year all round—you take my point?"

"I see, and so 19 = 20, and—"

"Quite right! Before we have finished nineteen hundred years, we are already in the twentieth hundred. What could be more previous? That's what we want, my boy—push! We're pushing for the new century, and people like ourselves, with our wits about us, will get there first! As for the others," he continued, his voice rising to a scream, "those who will have it that 1900 is the last year of the nineteenth century—well, they ought to be in a lunatic asylum!"

At this point the attendant made a hurried communication to the professor, and the interview was terminated with the pronouncement which I am glad to make known to the world that is still at large.

Other parodies followed in the *Punch* of January 10, 1900, each one sharp enough to make the disputants in the *Times* century squabble wince with shame:

Sir,—

I am a firm believer in the German Emperor, and a martyr to the cause of my belief. Having been further convinced by Sir Courtenay Boyle, and by the actual experiment in counting 0, 1, 2, 3, ... up to 99, that £99 is change for a hundred-pound note, I am now starting the new century under remand. It is, I am afraid, quite clear from the bigoted turn of mind of the presiding Magistrate, that this year will be a year 0, as far as I personally am concerned. It could not, therefore, be the last year of the nineteenth century.

our 1900th bottle of
Automatic Hairwash

Yours regretfully,
An Ex-Cashier

Sir,—

On December 31, 1899, as the clock was striking midnight, we packed up our 1900th bottle of Automatic Hairwash (which has created such a furore in fashionable circles, price 3s. 6d. only), and started upon the next hundred. The Twentieth century has therefore begun.

Yours obediently,
De Capille, Ltd.

Dere Sir,—

I had a berthday this morning and mammy says i interred my tenth yere. Daddy says you inter a thing wen it is finished and dun with, i have therefor dun with ten and must be eleven by now tho i was borne in 1891 i think the rithmytic must be rong sumware daddy could not be becos he rites to the Times and says it is now the new sentry in fack the middel of nex weak alreddy. Thinking yow wood like to no i am yore loving,

Tommy Wrottar

By January 15, 1900, the editor of the *Temperance Caterer*, a prohibitionist newsletter, was lamenting the energy that had been wasted by the squabblers, noting that "none of them have demonstrated the utility of the problem" and adding "What, in the name of common sense, does it matter?" A few weeks later, a contributor to the *Contemporary Review* calling himself Hobhouse published "The Battle of the Centuries," a painstaking analysis of the letters published by the *London Times*. "I expected," he remarked, "that when the mistake was once

What, in the name of common sense, does it matter?

exposed the dispute would end, but finding that fresh combatants were ever entering the field I thought the phenomenon so marvellous as to deserve study." After fourteen pages of study, Hobhouse arrived at this noisome bit of Darwinism: the "Twenties" (the disputants who put 1900 in the twentieth century) were less evolved than the "Nineteens" (the disputants who put 1900 in the nineteenth century). "I do not insinuate," he insinuated,

> that the Twenties as a whole are more backward than the Nineteens as a whole. But it is consistent with the observation, that in all of us there lingers something of ancestral and primitive character, showing itself in different ways among different individuals, and requiring correction from the majority who in that particular matter have been better trained. The inability to deal correctly with large numbers may be one of these survivals from our ancestors.

If Hobhouse's explanation for the existence and ferocity of the century-squabble seems off-target, perhaps we can find its real *raison d'être* in the double nature of time. First, there is the time that we experience, the dimension we live in and through, like a boat carried down a river. Then there is the time that we measure, the time we parcel up, arbitrarily, into seconds, days, weekends, fortnights, and centuries. We spend most of our lives acting as if these two faces of time are one and the same. On those infrequent occasions when our experience of time collides with our measurement of time—like when we appear to gain a day on February 29, or appear to lose a day by crossing the international date line—we feel a bit discombobulated.

When it comes to the turn of a century, our experience of time again clashes with our measuring of time. Our everyday experience with counting things—like eggs or dollars—tells us that the moment we reach the year 1800, or 1900, or 2000 we have embarked upon a new era. However, our precise rules for measuring time tell us that, barring a year zero, we have to wait for 1801, 1901, or 2001 before a new century truly begins. Some people privilege the subjectivity of experience and lean toward the "00" date; others privilege the objectivity of measurement and back the "01" date. While the former group is likely in the majority, the latter group

PORTRAIT OF A CALCULATING GENTLEMAN (NOT AT ALL A BAD LOOKING CHAP)
WHO HAS SOLVED THE PROBLEM AS TO WHETHER WE ARE IN THE
NINETEENTH OR TWENTIETH CENTURY.

from *Punch*, January 10, 1900

is louder: they are predisposed by temperament to write ornery letters to the editor explaining why everyone else is wrong.

Strange, though, that the accepted wisdom at the end of the eighteenth and nineteenth century was the opposite of that which now prevails. Whereas the newspapers and elected officials of the late eighteenth and nineteenth centuries sanctioned the "objectively" correct date—the first day of 1801 or 1901—their late-twentieth-century counterparts are now endorsing the "subjective" date, the one that "feels" right: the first day of 2000. That, at least, is when our leaders will be making forward-looking speeches, when newspapers will be filled with "new-millennium" editorials, and when almost everyone will be nursing hangovers of the century.

The reason the consensus is different this time around has much to do with the prospect of computer systems failing as 1999 becomes 2000. The odometer effect, the visual impact of all four digits changing as we go from 1999 to 2000, is also a forceful impetus, as is the power of the marketplace. Whether they know it or not, corporate executives are already echoing the words of Professor Babbage: "That's what we want, my boy— push! We're pushing for the new century, and people like ourselves, with our wits about us, will get there first!" Why wait for 2001 to sell New Century Cola when we can sell it a year earlier?

Could it be, then, that the twenty-first century will be rung in on December 31, 1999 with no disputes about the date, moment, or location of its entry? That was the prediction made a hundred years ago by the squabble-worn editor of the *Chicago Tribune*: "It is absurd to imagine that what has already happened once can happen again." Absurd? That never stopped us before.

Chapter Two

Century Celebrations
Civil, Uncivil, and Thwarted

> This society will not celebrate the advent of the twentieth century. We really have no excuse to celebrate at this time of year—it is not bug weather. —The American Entomological Society, 1900

LET'S FACE IT—New Year's Eve is cheesy. True, we could celebrate, in folksy fashion, with a cup o' hot cider, banging tin pots on the porch with grandma. But when we imagine the classic New Year's Eve, it's a boozy night on the town with Frank and the rest of the Rat Pack. Fireworks, sparkling lights, balloons, confetti, noise-makers, cocktails, champagne, too much of everything. We're expected to abandon good taste and decorum, for one night excused from sobriety, and practice a kind of parody adulthood—costumed in grown-ups' dress-up clothes, sipping on a flute of Dom Perignon, but wearing a little paper dunce cap and blowing on an extendable paper horn.

The problem is that these goofy, glitzy New Year's Eve traditions crystallized in the 1950s and '60s, when people were ingenuous enough to pull it off. Put a paper dunce cap on Liza and she still looked like she was having a ball. Put one on Alanis Morissette and she looks like a grieving clown. Nowadays, we're too self-concious to play along, to strut our stuff for the fun of it. Even at forty, we're more likely to have sneakers and overalls in our closets than a tux or little black number.

So how will we celebrate the millennium without being totally retro and ironic? Perhaps as they did one and two hundred years ago—with wholesome public festivities, bright and noisy, that leave us nothing to live down the next day. Still, a new century, a new millennium, like a new year, must make itself known by excess and as with extremity of all kinds, there's a story in it.

On January 1, 1801 a few cannons loaded with forty-two-pounders were enough to thrill the multitude. By January 1, 1901, it took forty lyddite bombs to elicit "oohs" and "ahs" from a merry-making throng. How much explosive power will it take to herald the thrilling turn of the millennium?

In 1996, Sydney, Australia, set off sixteen thousand fireworks in a practice event for the year 2000. New York's Times Square, too tight a fit for fireworks, already advertises that three thousand pounds of confetti will fall at the stroke of midnight. That celebration will also include the famous lowering of the ball (the emperor's new clothes of thrilling effects), an anticipated crowd of one million, and a television audience of two hundred and fifty million.

And although we might expect millennial fever to run highest in America, youthful exuberance and a love of the big splash being national traits, it is in fact the more sedate and circumspect Great Britain where the fever burns hottest. They boldly advertise the largest celebrations in the world. The Millennium Dome

Sabbath-breakers, Atheists, Swearers, Blasphemers, Drunkards, Perjurers, Etc.

opens on December 31, 1999, the Millennium Wheel will turn in childish splendour just opposite the Houses of Parliament, and the Millennium Bridge will extend across the Thames, the first new bridge over the river since 1894.

If Britain boasts the biggest public displays, France can boast the most original—a huge ovum will drop from the great mother, the Eiffel Tower. On reaching the bottom, the egg will hatch revealing a multitude of television screens displaying millennial parties in progress around the world.

All of these celebrations are intended to excite their audiences with noise, light, and hubbub. They are all-inclusive and non-partisan—a secular feast, in other words. Yet something remains of the pagan and religious rites. All that noise might scare the demons away. All those paper horns—furling and unfurling—seem a bit phallic, a vestige of ancient fertility rituals. And all those hangovers might be a purgation, a symbolic harrowing of hell that leads to a morning-after resurrection.

When we look back to the beginning of the eighteenth century for records of celebrations, we see that the first day of 1701 received little publicity. It was noteworthy as the start of a new year, not the dawn of a new century. The *London Post* did note on December 31, 1700 that King William III travelled from Hampton Court to Kensington "where he is to receive the compliments of the nobility, tomorrow morning, at his leve, upon account of New Year's Day"—but no mention was made of any formal "new century" celebrations.

The same issue of the *London Post* also carried an advertisement for a "Parents New Years Gift"—a book entitled *A Choice Collection of God's Judgements and Mercies on Sabbath-breakers, Atheists, Swearers, Blasphemers, Drunkards, Perjurers, Etc.*—but again no advertisers hawked their wares with "new century" promos. Only across the Atlantic, in Boston, was the dawn of the eighteenth century welcomed with a public celebration of any note. There Samuel Sewall—who three years earlier had con-

WEDNESDAY, *January* 1. 1701.
A little before Break-a-Day, at *Boston* of the *Massachusets.*

ONCE more! Our GOD, vouchſafe to Shine:
Tame Thou the Rigour of our Clime.
Make haſte with thy Impartial Light,
And terminate this long dark Night.

Let the tranſplanted **Engliſh** Vine
Spread further ſtill : ſtill Call it Thine.
Prune it with Skill : for yield it can
More Fruit to Thee the Huſbandman.

Give the poor **Indians** Eyes to ſee
The Light of Life : and ſet them free ;
That they Religion may profeſs,
Denying all Ungodlineſs.

From hard'ned **Jews** the Vail remove,
Let them their Martyr'd J E S U S love ;
And Homage unto Him afford,
Becauſe He is their Rightfull L O R D.

So falſe Religions ſhall decay,
And Darkneſs fly before bright Day :
So Men ſhall G O D in C H R I S T adore ;
And worſhip Idols vain, no more.

So **Aſia**, and **Africa**,
Europa, with **America** ;
All Four, in Conſort join'd, ſhall Sing
New Songs of Praiſe to C H R I S T our K I N G.

Samuel Sewall's "My Verses upon New Century," published as a broadside appended to his *Proposals Touching the Accomplishment of Prophecies*, 1713.

fessed to wrongfully condemning nineteen "witches" to their death—took it upon himself to blast Bostonians out of their beds into the dark, wintry morning of a new century. He recorded this impromptu celebration in his diary:

> Jan 1, 1701.
>   Entrance of the 18th Century. Just about break-a-day Jacob Amsden and three other trumpeters gave a blast with the trumpets on the common near Mr. Alford's. Then went to the Green Chamber, and sounded there till about sunrise.

After this fanfare—which, Sewall grumbled, "cost me 5 pounds, 8 shillings, and 8 pence"—he gave a public reading of "Verses upon the New Century," a pious poem he wrote for the occasion in which he prayed that the "poor Indians" and "hardened Jews" would soon be converted.

A hundred years later, the new century provoked more interest. On January 1, 1801 the *London Times* ran the headline "First Day Of The New Century." An officer at the royal palace, it was reported, waved a white flag to signal a salute of guns, one that was immediately answered by another loud salute from the Tower of London, followed **42 pounders** by the ringing of church bells across the city. Even in Sheerness, a tiny city compared to London, officials marked the first day of the nineteenth century by firing a *feu de joie* salute and by deafening bystanders with cannons loaded with "42-pounders." But it was not just the first day of the nineteenth century that occasioned these noisy jubilations—the day also marked the union of Great Britain and Ireland, the birth of the United Kingdom.

The twin birth of the century and the union may also be why King George III chose January 1 to proclaim a nation-wide "public fast and humiliation" so that he and his subjects might "humble ourselves before Almighty God, in order to obtain pardon of our sins."

For His or Her part, the Almighty seemed to concur that the simultaneous birth of the United Kingdom and the nineteenth century warranted heavenly pyrotechnics, as recorded by a correspondent in London's *Gentleman's Magazine*:

> Dec. 31, 1800.
> At 7 this evening, was seen a very fine and brilliant meteor, at Camborne. It appeared in the south, and passed, with incredible velocity, the horizon, illuminating its tract with an immense glare of light, equal to the most vivid lightning, being in shape round, and emitting sparks in its *a vast variety of scintillations* progress; when it disappeared it seemed to explode in a vast variety of scintillations, like a sky-rocket, and presented to the spectators a most beautiful and magnificent effect. Its appearance seemed to impress the beholders with a sentiment of greater awe, as it happened on the evening which concluded the last day of the last year of the 18th century.

In America there were neither political unions nor heavenly showers to celebrate. What did receive wide publicity was the reception held at the White House by President Adams and his wife on January 1, 1801. Not only did the event mark the first day of the nineteenth century, it also established the tradition of the White House New Year's reception, an event that peaked in the late nineteenth century when Grover Cleveland exhausted himself by shaking hands with over eight thousand New Year's callers. But the reception held on the first day of the nineteenth century was a more exclusive affair, with only a few dozen patricians crowding into the oval room on the second floor of the brand new Executive Mansion. (The official banqueting hall in the east wing was not yet completed, though that did not prevent Mrs. Adams from using it to dry the family's laundry.)

Elsewhere in the United States, some civic officials feared that the advent of the nineteenth century was so exciting that it might incite citizens to dangerous excess. In Philadelphia, the Mayor's Office issued a proclamation in the *Aurora General Advertiser* on the last day of the *CAUTION* eighteenth century. "CAUTION," it began, "The evil and pernicious practice of firing guns on the eve of the old year has long been adopted by many of the indiscreet and thoughtless part of the community, to the great terror and annoyance of the citizens." Accordingly, continued the notice, "the legislature of this Commonwealth has deemed it expedient to pass a law forbidding, under severe penalty, the firing of guns in the City of Philadelphia, on or near any public high-way."

To the north, in what was not yet Canada, people managed to enter the nineteenth century without resorting to gunfire, but only because they didn't care that a new era had begun. On January 6, 1801, the *Saint John Globe*—a weekly, whose previous issue had appeared on the second last day of the eighteenth century—offered this glum admission:

> Nothing of moment has transpired since our last publication—neither arrivals by sea nor mails by land have furnished us any articles of intelligence—we are therefore obliged to amuse our readers with matter rather entertaining than new.

It would not be possible to ignore the dawning of the next century. The arrival of the twentieth century was the loudest and brightest the world *and noise that* had yet known. In New York the crowd around City Hall *wasn't music* numbered one hundred thousand and the din grew as midnight neared. The United German Singing Societies joined with Damrosch's Choral Union to form a choir of one thousand voices—but the boisterous crowd all but drowned out the singers. "There was music," wrote the *New York Times*,

> … and noise that wasn't music, tin horns and trumpets, drums and other din-evoking instruments. The latter were mainly manipulated by the small boys; the former came from lips and throats that were of the small boy once but are now more matured.

The president of the Council Chamber, Randolph Guggenheimer, climbed the stone steps and made a speech—or rather, as one reporter dryly put it, "was seen to move his lips as though addressing remarks to the gathering." Eventually, civic officials realized the absurdity of making speeches to such an obstreperous crowd and withdrew. The crowd barely noticed, and continued circling City Hall, swaying, singing, parading, and hooting. The decibel level increased as midnight approached, and then, as the hands of the clock on City Hall crossed at twelve, a roar split the heavens: "The lights flashed, the crowds sung, the sirens of crafts in the harbour screeched and roared, bells peeled, bombs thundered, rockets blazed skyward—and the new century made its triumphant entry."

FEAR THE NEW YEAR NOISE

PEOPLE "WITH NERVES" MAKE VAIN APPEAL TO MAYOR.

Ask That the Celebration Attending the Arrival of the Twentieth Century Be Prohibited, but the City Executive Declares That He Might as Well Try to Suppress the Din of the Fourth of July—Protest of the Physicians—S. J. Jones Wants Ordinances Enforced

Physicians with sensitive patients and people "with nerves" are viewing with alarm the noises that will usher in the new year and the twentieth century. With the expectation of an "unusual pandemonium" on Monday night some are sending letters to the Mayor asking that he prevent the noise and permit the new century to be born "under humanitarian conditions."

from the *Chicago Tribune*, December 29, 1900

In every city that celebrated the dawn of the twentieth century, it was the sound of the event that captured the attention of newspaper reporters. The *Boston Herald* reported that the city's civic officials reproduced the musical ceremony staged two centuries before by Samuel Sewall, though they prudently did not adhere to their forefather's "break-a-day" schedule. At midnight, as the clock tower sounded the hour, each stroke was answered by a chorus of four trumpet blasts:

the century will go out with a toot

> From the tower of King's Chapel there sounded the first stroke of midnight. The trumpets echoed in a long drawn blast. The second stroke fell. Again the trumpets echoed in lengthening cadences. The third came, and was repeated likewise, and afterward the others, until the whole 12 had been tolled off from the ancient meeting place and sounded again from the high porches of the hill.

As the twelfth blast of this solemn ceremony died away, the citizens of Boston took over where the trumpeters left off, and fulfilled the *Boston Herald*'s understated prediction from the day before that "the century will go out with a toot":

> It seemed at 12 o'clock as though the engineer of every locomotive in the city and its vicinity had tied the whistle valve wide open, while

from the harbor, every side of it, came the blasts, some long and some short, of whistles, ranging in volume from the shrill toot of launches to the more voluminous tones of the tugboats and the hoarse challenges of the great steamships. Add to this the report of

stuff their ears firearms and cannon crackers, which were audible in many localities, and you may make up a description
with cotton wool of the pandemonium which reigned for a few minutes in the quiet old city which, two centuries ago, welcomed the coming of a new cycle with little idea of the changes in many ways which the years have brought to pass.

A few medical experts feared, in all this audio, a health hazard, especially for "sensitive people" and victims of nervous disorders. The *Chicago Tribune* quoted a "woman physician" who informed the mayor that

> I have under my care two cases where noise is most distressing and where the critical brain condition requires utmost quiet. Would it not be well to suppress the usual midnight noise of New Year's Eve and usher in the new century under an entirely new regime—a more humanitarian condition?

Mayor Harrison replied that it would be "absolutely impossible" to prevent the din, but nonetheless issued a request that owners of factories urge their night-shift employees not to abuse the steam whistle. Anticipating that the mayor's half-hearted request would go unheeded, the *Chicago Tribune* advised overwrought citizens to "hide their heads under blankets or stuff their ears with cotton wool."

On the last day of the century, the bruit began in Chicago's business district around the dinner hour as hawkers sold their "leftover stock of

the banging election horns, squawkers, and noisemakers" to those leaving work. Throughout the evening the noise increased, moving
of torpedoes downtown. At a few minutes before twelve, reported the *Tribune*, "men stood on the street corners with a watch in one hand and a revolver in the other" and "at the stroke of midnight there was a burst of sounds." The revellers then made their way home, disturbing patients in hospitals and residents of the suburbs until the small hours of the morning.

In Toronto, one complaint against the noise had more to do with aesthetics than a good night's sleep. The reporter for the *Toronto Star* approved when the thousands gathered at City Hall silently gave audience to a majestic symphony of bells:

> The hush deepened as the moments grew fewer. It became intense—then the hour came. The heavy-toned giant boomed the midnight hour; a pause, and then twenty strokes rang in the new. To the southeast the chimes of St. James' could be heard, and from every quarter of the city bells uncounted took up the strain; many had impatiently begun already, and the silence of the waiting crowd had a silver edge of distant chimes.

CITY HAILS THE CENTURY.

Elaborate Electrical and Bunting Decoration on the City Hall.

If any one does not find himself in a proper twentieth century New Year's humor this morning he needs to go down town and look at the old City Hall and see how it has been coyly decked for the new century reception. All day yesterday and all last night decorators and electricians were working on the building, and the work will not be finished until 6 o'clock to-night.

from the *New York Times*, December 31, 1900

But then the moment of transcendence was disrupted by the vulgarity of the hoi polloi. "Less appropriately," lamented the reporter, "came the hoots of steam whistles and the banging of torpedoes and shot guns."

For the most part, however, the citizens of almost every city exulted in the clamour, the din, the making of a joyous noise for the new century: in Saint John, New Brunswick, where officials triggered fire alarms and crowds sang "God Save the King," in Los Angeles where men and women alike "blew tin noise dispensers till their lungs refused to do further duty," in Quebec City where ninety-nine cannons were fired from the Citadel, in London where the "silvery note" of Big Ben was followed by a "mighty shout from thousands of throats," in Sydney where half a million people gathered in the streets to cheer the new century and celebrate the birth of an independent Australia, in Paris where "even the quietest quarters were invaded by the horn-blowing, bell-ringing and shouting and singing revelers." And yet nowhere, it seems, did people dedicate themselves as wholeheartedly to producing a deafening racket as they did in San Francisco, the *ne plus ultra* of the new-century hullabaloo. As the *San Francisco Examiner* reported the events:

thousands of throats

> Early in the evening the crowds began to claim the big streets as their own. Each cable and electric car coming from the residence districts was crowded and clamorous. Men, women and children hung on as best they might until they could get into the swirl of the roistering throng. And every one of these men, women and children seemed provided with some instrument for making loud and unusual sounds. There was a deal of rivalry in the size of horns. In some were enough to have set a small tinsmith up in business, and they gave out noises as if blown by Stentor. Some were many-colored; some bedecked with ribbon. Occasionally a lad would struggle along blowing at a horn larger than himself, and puffing as if he expected to outdo the efforts of all the winds. Merchants of horns established

from *The Literary Digest*, January 5, 1901

themselves along the walks and did business which gave evidence of prosperity as well as joyous enthusiasm. One of these men sold a large wagon-load of noisy horns between the going down of the sun and 11 o'clock, when he said he wished he had another wagon-load *making night hideous* to sell … Here and there a bell would ring. Some boys dragged jangling tin cans up and down the streets, just to let people know that they considered themselves the real lords of the merry night. Again, a drummer would come rounding along, his martial music making the crowds fall unconsciously into step. The shrill fife occasionally sounded a war-strain. Cymbals clashed in vigorous bands. Through it all the motormen and gripmen clanged their difficult way. Everywhere was clang and clash and roar. And so the thousands upon tens of thousands paraded and laughed, shouted and made continuous din upon the streets ... Suddenly over all the city "The Examiner's" great siren sent its announcement that the new century had arrived. Half a million fire-crackers roared in their explosion at "The Examiner" building. Then all the bells gave tongue. Then all the whistles strained their throats. Pistol shooting was forbidden but the clamor of bells, rattles, horns and other instruments for making night hideous was appalling for hours.

Clamour for the ears, spectacle for the eyes—the new-century festivities battered every sense. In New York, forty lyddite bombs exploded in City Hall Park at the stroke of midnight:

Bombshells innumerable shot upward and, careening meteor-like across the sky, burst into myriad fragments, gyrating and squirming and falling earthward in showers of green and gold and red and blue ... showers of fantastically-shaped objects: balls of various colors, glittering arrowheads and sprays of silver and gold, red, and blue and spikes of prismatic lights, huge bouquets of flowers, like balls of silver foil opening out into blossoms of variegated colors.

The nearby towering skyscrapers—like the thirty-eight story Park Row building, the tallest in the world when completed in 1899—might have been expected to hinder the view, but as a reporter for the *New York Tribune* pointed out, they only augmented the dazzling scintillations:

Fountains of colored fires shot up from among the trees in the park and, from the tops of two skyscrapers in Park Row, cataracts of fire descended to meet them. The effect was highly attrac- *making the* tive and striking, and its beauty was not a little *darkness radiant* enhanced by the reflection of the thousand falling balls of color in the unlighted windows of the many other lofty structures which surrounded City Hall. These reflections would light up story after story of the windows as they swung slowly earthward, and thus multiplied the display a hundred fold.

But fireworks already belonged to a bygone era; as early as 1749, pyrotechnics were familiar enough that Handel wrote *Music for the Royal Fireworks.* Now, at the dawn of the twentieth century, a century which numerous editorialists had already dubbed "the electric age," a new spectacle was needed. That new spectacle was, of course, the light bulb, an innovation which allowed the *New York Times* to proudly claim that

it was a distinctly electric celebration in which the city indulged. Everywhere the shimmering gleam of electric lights shot their effulgence out over city and river and harbor, lighting up the thoroughfares with a noonday brilliance, throwing their deep reflection against the overhanging sky, making the darkness radiant.

City Hall was completely festooned with electricity, outlined with lights coloured red, white, and blue, while the exterior surfaces were studded with another two thousand untinted bulbs. The façade bore illuminated

PUNCH, OR THE LONDON CHARIVARI.

THE SPIRIT OF PUNCH "HIC ET UBIQUE"

from *Punch*, January 2, 1901

letters: "WELCOME 20th CENTURY." At two minutes to midnight, all the lights were turned off and, in the words of a *New York Tribune* reporter, "something resembling a hush fell upon the vast assemblage." For two minutes gloom and silence held sway—then, as the clock tower began to toll, the master switch was thrown and in an instant "every electric bulb was re-illumined, and the red, white, and blue globes lit up the building to midday brilliance."

In Austria, the drama of a momentary plunge into darkness was taken one step further: there, all of Vienna was in *tenebrae* thanks to the electrical company's overenthusiastic decision to cut the power to the entire city. At exactly midnight, power was restored and the sudden return of city-wide illumination was deemed by an American correspondent "supremely beautiful and decidedly impressive." ***Light up!***

But not only civic officials and electric companies played with the light switches—in San Francisco the *Examiner* exhorted all the city's residents to turn on, light up, and shine out:

> Surely this is the time for San Francisco to hail the new century and by brilliant illumination to give symbolic testimony to her expectations of a matchless future. Every home in San Francisco should be lighted, every office building, every factory, street, square, and public structure should be ablaze ... In all the big cities—Chicago, New Orleans, Omaha, Cleveland, Detroit, St. Louis, Los Angeles, and San Francisco—the motto of tonight will be, "Light Up!"

And light up they did. In homes across the city, as innumerable watches and clocks ticked out the last seconds of the nineteenth century, "from thousands of windows the honest light went out to greet the baby year." In Cleveland, the moment of illumination was synchronized perfectly thanks to a signal—an ear-splitting siren—from the fire department. In Los Angeles—appropriately for the city of angels—people re-lighted their Christmas trees, strings of electric lights having been introduced a few years earlier as a safer alternative to the traditional hanging candles.

All this excess of sensation, though, could be dangerous. In England, newspaper columnists fretted about what would happen in the streets of London on the last night of the nineteenth century. To allay the potential for rioting and hooliganism, civic officials tried to steer a middle course: they decided, in a rather spoilsport spirit, not to organize any official public celebration of the new century, but at the same time they did not deter the thousands of individuals who, on the night of December 31, 1900, spontaneously gathered around ***the age of the Hooligan*** landmarks such as St. Paul's Cathedral and Westminster Abbey. The potential for an all-out riot was real: the cathedral was circled by a strong force of police, who were in turn circled by the vast crowd. Within the crowd, national divisions were another powder keg. A large number of Scots, singing of course *Auld Lang Syne*, were irked when their anthem

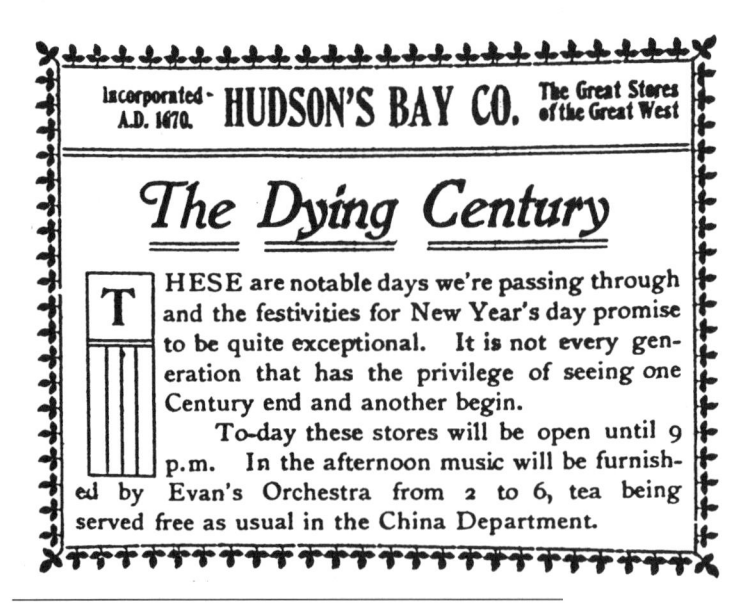

from the *Manitoba Free Press*, December 29, 1900

was drowned out by a surge of "English" songs such as *They All Love Jack* and *The Absent-Minded Beggar.*

Altercations did occur. The *London Times* reported that "the rougher element commenced to assert itself" around eleven o'clock and that "a number of women were borne down by the crush and trampled upon."

In North America too, civic officials fretted about controlling crowds larger than any that had gathered before. In Boston, the *Herald* reported that the last night of the nineteenth century drew more people into the streets than the Fourth of July—no mean feat in a city that sparked the American Revolution. In San Francisco, tens of thousands "overflowed the sidewalks and surged up and down the streets, always moving, ever seeking some new means of expressing pleasure at the death of the century." Cable cars inched through the masses, jammed with passengers unable to get out.

In New York, a hundred thousand people crammed the downtown. More than a thousand police officers ringed City Hall. The bridges teemed with pedestrians, and the ferries from Long Island and New Jersey were packed like canned asparagus. In Sydney, Australia, the city was so overwhelmed that many visitors found accommodation only on steamers anchored in the harbour. In Berlin, the city's downtown *strassen* were, in the words of an histrionic correspondent for the *Chicago Tribune*, "blocked with struggling humanity." Kaiser Wilhelm's decree that the twentieth century had begun one year earlier had apparently been forgotten.

The ugly incidents that did occur in North American cities were relatively minor. In Boston, where the cable car company was caught off guard by the size of the crowd, people were forced to hoof it back home after midnight, and Beacon Street became dangerously jammed. "Women," reported the *Boston Herald*, "were the chief sufferers, and many of them had experiences that they will never forget. Many were knocked down and others were crushed or had *their clothing almost torn off*." As pedestrians competed with hackney carriages for the street, some were pushed against coach wheels and were almost run over. In New York, a momentary panic occurred after midnight as people ran for the trains departing for Brooklyn and uptown New York. "Several women were badly frightened," reported the *Times*, "and two or three fainted. A small boy was also injured by being trampled upon." A New York police officer was also nearly killed by a man who "endeavored to scalp him with a pint flask of ready-mixed cocktails." According to the *Times*, the man was an habitual drinker, and "the demise of an entire century bore in upon him with such crushing force that he was forced to apply his antidote in amplified doses."

For the most part, though, the birth of the new century was everywhere a showcase of the best in human nature. In Los Angeles, people heading home on the crowded streetcars sang gospel hymns. In Toronto, "groups of three or more held hands at street corners and sang to the memory of happy days." In San Francisco, women, enjoying a brief interval of gender equality, "entered into the frolic with the wildest enthusiasm ... their eyes and teeth were *bright with laughter*. They threw off conventionality for the time being and let their folly have full fling."

Even in New York, according to the *Tribune*, police were able to claim that "they preserved order without having to use their clubs" because the crowd "was one of the best-natured that they had ever been called upon to handle." In Boston, the *Herald* admitted that "there was a good deal of drunkenness, as at any holiday time" but added that "most of it was of the sort meant when a man is described as better, not worse, for wine, and those whose legs wobbled scandalously did not allow eccentricities of gait to interfere with the serene current of their good nature." The civilized behaviour of the throngs was probably prompted by the numerous children in the crowds, a presence heartily endorsed by the *San Francisco Examiner:*

> This one night of all the year, this night which is to fade into the dawn of the new century, should be a night for the children. They will forego their beauty sleep for once and years hence will recall with joy the fact that they witnessed the incoming of the twentieth century.

An Entirely Unparalleled Renewal of this

Twentieth Century
Sale of Undermuslins

The greatest news of Muslin Underwear that ever we or any one else has had to tell.   Thousands of splendid garments have disappeared during the week for the smallest prices which such Underwear ever cost.   Now comes a freshening of this great January sale.

Many of the Garments for Less Than the Material Cost.

Quantities are even greater now than at the beginning of the sale, qualities not a whit lower, variety of choice as wide or wider.   Think of buying dainty Corset Covers for 4c., Drawers for 10c., Gowns for 24c., Misses' Drawers at 6c., Short Dresses at 24c., Long Slips at 6c.   Such prices for such values have never been matched anywhere—would not be possible here but for the fact that the purchasing of immense—75,000 garments in all—quantities brings to us the most notable trade opportunities.   Buy your year's supply—the first year of the new century can scarcely show such chance again.   Read on:

Muslin Underwear.	Corsets Under Wholesale.
2,400 Corset Covers at 4c.	**$1.00 J. B. Corsets at 45c.**
Masonville Muslin, high neck, felled seams, pearl buttons.	French Models, medium waist, short hip, black sateen trimmed with embroidery.

---

from the *New York Times*, December 30, 1900

Still, the party spirit was thwarted in some cities by the harsh cruelties of economics and climate. In Pittsburgh, where crowds gathered of their own accord, city officials nixed an official public celebration "ow-

-32°

ing to the refusal of the city treasurer to pay the bills that would be incurred." In Winnipeg, Manitoba, nature did the nixing—on the last night of the century, prairie thermometers dipped to a breath-taking -32°C (-27°F). As the *Manitoba Free Press* observed the next day: "No one in Winnipeg imagined for a moment that he was living in southern California."

There were other notable pockets of indifference. In Boston, the *Herald* noted that stockbrokers were oblivious to the significance of December 31, 1900: "It was a day of activity, like its predecessors, and, very likely, similar to what its successors will be. Speculation heeds not the centuries, the old

Melicans not make muchee New Year

or the new." And thanks to an unbendable temperance law prohibiting the sale of liquor after eleven o'clock, the downtown hotels in Boston also lacked new-century excitement. The *Herald* reported that, as midnight tolled, "an unusually dull time" was had at Parker's hotel, "a shroud hung over Young's," and "lethargy stalked in absolute control" at Quincy House. At the American Entomological Society, too, there was no buzz of activity. "This society will not celebrate the advent of the twentieth century," their spokesman declared. "We really have no excuse to celebrate at this time of year—it is not bug weather."

In Boston's Chinatown, the century likewise opened without fanfare, as the *Herald* reported in an item short in length but long in cultural clichés:

> Chinatown was practically deserted. "Melicans not make muchee New Year," said one almond-eyed celestial. The Chinamen have their new year some time in February, and they will usher in the century in their own peculiar way. The American New Year's Eve in Chinatown passed unnoticed.

There were many people, of course, who yearned to fête the new century but not with the plebeians in the downtown streets and public squares. To accommodate delicate temperaments, affluent parents hosted new-century "teen" parties, sparing no expense to ensure that junior entered the twentieth century intact. In Los *Miss Pansy Bloomer* Angeles, the *Times* reported on several such parties in its first social column of the twentieth century:

> Mrs. E. E. Crandall gave a New Year's party for her son Henry last night at her home, No. 123 West Thirtieth Street, entertaining a number of young people, who played progressive hearts during the early evening, the victors in the game securing prizes. A literary and musical programme was enjoyed and refreshments served. At 12 o'clock a display of fireworks was enjoyed, after which dancing was in order. The house was elaborately decorated with lilies, carnations, smilax and English ivy.

In Washington, according to the *Evening Star*:

> Mr. And Mrs. George C. Bloomer gave a beautiful dance last night for the associates of their daughter, Miss Pansy Bloomer. The reception room, ball room and supper room were each profusely adorned with palms, flowers and vines. The dancing kept up till the new century had dawned. Supper was served before the last hour of dancing.

In New York the elite Lakewood Golf Club managed "to usher in the twentieth century under the auspices of golf excitement" by hosting a two-day tournament on December 31 and January 1. Golf-*gay caricatures* ers could therefore claim to have played one tournament in two centuries. The *Tribune* also reported that in Buffalo a hundred and fifty members of the Sprudel Fishing Club closed the century by staging an imaginatively conceived allegorical pageant. Picture this:

> One exhibit was a dilapidated cart drawn by cows; this was followed by an outfit labelled "automobile," consisting of a wagon the front wheels of which were directed by an automobile steering gear, the

---

CENTURY POEM OF POET LAUREATE.

LONDON, Dec. 31, 3 a. m.—The Standard publishes a poem by Alfred Austin, entitled " The Passing of the Century," which is distinctively above the average of the laureate's work.   It contains six verses, the third of which is as follows:

> Dust unto dust; he is dead, though he
> Was the last of the centuried years that flow,
> We know not wherefor, we never shall know,
> With the tide unebbing of time and go
>   To the phantom shore of eternity.
>   Shadows to shadows, they flit and flee
> Across the face of the flaming sun,
> The vague generations, one by one,
> That never are ended, never begun.
> Where is the dome or the vault so vast
> As to coffin the bones of the perished past,
> Save the limitless tomb of oblivion?

The coming of the New Year, which Mr. Austin makes feminine, occupies the last two verses, the final one of which reads:

> Yet mind her, dawn of the dark, for she,
> She, too, must pass 'neath the lychgate porch;
> And give to her keeping the vestal torch,
> That may ofttime smolder and sometimes scorch,
>   But rebrightens and burns eternally:
>   The beacon on land and the star at sea,
> When the night is murk and the mist is dense,
> To guide us whither, remind us whence,
> The soul's own lamp, through the shades of sense.
>   She must tread the unknown the dead year trod
>   Though rugged the road, yet the goal is God,
> And the will of all-wise omnipotence.

---

from the *Chicago Tribune*, December 31, 1900

power being furnished by a skeleton horse, who pushed against thills fastened to the rear axle.

The fishermen themselves were dressed as "gay caricatures of the city's progress in the last one hundred years." Demanding less exegesis was the simple pageant performed at midnight at the Concordia Club in San Francisco:

> At one end was the 1900 post, past which the Nineteenth Century, represented by a boy, Norman Phillips, dressed as Father Time, was riding a bicycle. At the other post coming on the stage was a female representing the Twentieth Century riding in an automobile.

Club members could also forgo the clubhouse in favour of public performances. In Boston, the *Herald* gave star billing to a high-concept "Twentieth-Century Show" opening at the Nickelodeon on December 31, 1900:

> In order that the entrance to a new century might be properly observed, Mgr. Walker has prepared an extra long list of amusing features for this week. In the main curio hall will be seen for the first time on any stage Prof. Harry Hoppe's cat circus, the only genuine cat circus ever exhibited ... At the word of the Professor they go

through a military drill with great precision, perform various acrobatic feats, ride a bicycle, smoke cigarettes, and various other almost impossible performances.

In many cities, celebrations were provided for the poor and infirm so that they might cheerfully embark on a new century of indigence. In Berlin, the British ambassador spent the first day of his twentieth century hosting "about fifty chimney-sweeper boys at dinner in a hall hired for the occasion." On the same day, in London, the *Times* related how the Borough Polytechnic spent eighty pounds entertaining a large number of waifs:

wolf child

> A tea was given to 1,000 of the poorest children in the slum district of the Borough. A huge Christmas tree was on view, illuminated by electric lights, and adorned with 500 dolls, dressed by the lady members of the institute and the scholars of the Domestic Economy School.

A similar gala was arranged for the inmates of the Institute of the Crippled Children of the Poor in New York. Mrs. Arthur Elliot Fish reported that on the first day of the new century everyone was on their best behaviour, even the "wolf child," a young scamp who usually "took delight in tying the small cripples to the table legs."

Two hundred miles away in Washington, President William McKinley also greeted the new century. According to the *New York Tribune*, he entered the new era "surrounded by the cares of office and engaged in the drudgery of actual work." McKinley did, however, briefly tear himself from his drudgery just before midnight to join his wife and members of the cabinet in a nearby room. There, the president seated himself and turned his gaze to the clock on the mantle: "When the click of the weights announced the birth of the century, he jumped to his feet" and shook hands with all present. Revitalized by this presidential hootenanny, McKinley returned to his office and worked into the night.

the drudgery of actual work

If he did get to bed that night, President McKinley was awakened by a courier banging on the front door at 5:00 a.m. The *New York Journal* had dedicated its first issue of the twentieth century to the president, and made the delivery of that issue something of a promotional event:

> The first *Journal* to be printed in 1901 went immediately to President McKinley on a special train chartered expressly for that purpose, carrying no freight but that one newspaper, carrying no passengers but the courier with the *Journal* ... Before 5 o'clock this morning the first *Journal* printed in 1901 will be in the hands of the president.

Upon receiving the newspaper, McKinley would be in possession of valuable news, such as the *Journal*'s plan to send its first issue of the century to the president.

The *Journal* was hardly alone in marking the turn of the century with a stunt. In New York, the Dawn of the Century Open Speed Trial got

The Dawn of the Century Open Speed Trial

underway in the opening moments of the new century. The eight-mile course wound through the city, and as the *New York Times* reported, competitors could use any means to traverse the distance.

> When the first stroke of 12 o'clock sounded ... the roadway was crowded from curb to curb for the length of three blocks with motor vehicles, while bicycles filled in the interstices and athletes in running costume, with sweaters and overcoats covering them from the chill of the night air, thronged the sidewalks.

The winner of the race was a "steam motor vehicle" which clocked in thirty-nine minutes after departing, an astonishing twelve miles an hour.

The turn of the century inspired other competitions as well. In San Francisco, Hannah Martin and Joseph Israel made it onto the front page of the *Examiner* by being the last couple to be married in the nineteenth century:

> **Cupid was not left out**
>
> Down at the Occidental restaurant, on Bush Street—Peter Kline's place, where the best canvasbacks are served—the ceremony will be celebrated. The ceremony has been so timed that as the solemn words are spoken by Rabbi M. S. Levy of the Bush Street temple, the nineteenth century will flutter to its close and the twentieth century rise big with life and hope of promise.

Across the continent, in a chamber of New York's City Hall as a hundred thousand revellers created a mighty din outside, another couple hastened to become the first couple to be married in the twentieth century:

> Cupid was not left out of the celebration, nor bombs, nor red fire, nor ear splitting horns could scare the little god of love away. Sharp on the stroke of 12 Miss Maggie Kelleher, of No. 97 Central Park West, stood blushingly up beside Charles E. McCue, of No. 79 Tillary Street, Brooklyn, in the Aldermen's Chamber, and they were made man and wife by Alderman Seebeck, who finished the job in exactly one minute and twenty-eight seconds.

Across North America and Europe, thousands of other couples followed the McCues's lead and also exchanged vows on the first day of the twentieth century: in Chicago alone, the *Herald* noted that one hundred and forty marriages, a new record, were solemnized on January 1, 1901.

In Saint John, New Brunswick, the *Globe* reported that the local magistrate had devised a stunt of a different sort:

> The county jail will present an unusual appearance tonight. For the first time in very many years it will be entirely empty. The grating doors on the rows of cells will all swing wide open, every bolt and bar will be loosened, and no footfalls save those of the turnkeys will echo through its gloomy corridors.

TO BE THE LAST BRIDE
OF THE OLD CENTURY

XIXth. CENTURY

XXth. CENTURY

from the *San Francisco Examiner*, December 31, 1900

The magistrate reasoned that he should allow the prisoners to "begin the twentieth century anew." Most of the prisoners were delighted with their unexpected freedom, but one, Michael Collins, longed for his familiar cell. "He kept *every bolt and bar will be loosened* visiting the jail throughout the night, hammering at the door for admittance, causing much disturbance to the deputy sheriff."

While the magistrate in Saint John absolved his prisoners of "doing time," civic officials in Detroit commemorated the turn of the century by devising another way of triumphing over time:

> Mayor Maybury sealed a copper box, specially made for the purpose, which contains papers relating to the history of Detroit, in its social, religious, commercial, professional, and political character, written by men and women prominent in those walks of life. On top of these papers was a greeting from Mr. Maybury to the mayor or chief executive officer of the city in the year 2000. The box is 12 x 8 x 6 inches and on the lid is a silver plate with an inscription telling of the contents, when it was sealed, and saying that it is not to be opened until Jan 1. 2000.

The mayor and his friends were ahead of their time: it was not until the 1930s that Thornwell Jacobs popularized the idea of time capsules.

Officials in one other city also hit upon the idea of sending their successors a message through time. A "Century Ball" was held on the last night of the century in Kansas City, Missouri. The event was a tremendous success: fifteen thousand people attended, paying ten dollars each. Above

—————————◆—————————

GENERAL JAIL DELIVERY.

New Century Will Begin With a Clean Sheet.

The county jail will present an unusual appearance to-night. For the first time in very many years it will be entirely empty. The grating doors on the rows of cells will all swing wide open, every bolt and bar will be loosened, and no footfalls save those of the turnkeys will echo through its gloomy corridors.

The closing of the nineteenth century has been made a year of jubilee for those unfortunates who by too frequent use of alcoholic stimulants or by natural depravity or viciousness found their way into this place of confinement.

from the *St. John Globe*, December 31, 1900

the dance floor small light bulbs set in an hourglass pattern blinked out, one every minute until at 11:59 p.m. a single bulb remained illuminated. On the dance floor was another curiosity—a steel "Century Box" into which guests could stuff whatever message they pleased. When the ball ended, the box was to be sealed and not opened until the first day of the

the century box   twenty-first century. A few of the contributions to the Century Box were noted by a reporter for the *Kansas City Star*—the police chief, John Hayes, scribbled this note to a person he would never meet, someone whose grandparents were probably not yet born:

> To the Chief of Police, Kansas City, Mo., A.D., 2001.
>   Hope you may have success much as we are having at present. The weather is a little cold tonight, but we are having a delightful time. I hope there will be many changes in the police department in the way of detecting criminals and their treatment.

Someone else graced the Century Box with this anonymous rhyme,

> This century is done.
> We are having lots of fun.
> We wish you good luck,
> For twenty-hundred and one.

Perhaps the most meditative contribution to the Century Box was the lyrics to "A Hundred Years to Come," a choral piece sung earlier that evening by the Old Men's Quartette at one of the local churches:

TO 'TRIBUNE' MEN OF 2001.

MEMORIAL FORMULATED BY FAM-ILY AT ANNUAL DINNER.

Three Hundred and Twenty-five Pres-ent at Meeting in Auditorium Hotel and All Sign Document That Is to Be Kept Locked in Safety Deposit Vault One Hundred Years and Then Opened and Read—Short Talks Made by Guests and Members.

from the *Chicago Tribune*, January 2, 1901

We all within our graves shall sleep—a hundred years to come;
No living soul of us will weep—a hundred years to come;
But other men our lands will till, and others then our streets
  will fill,
While other birds will sing as gay, as bright the sun shine as today.
A hundred years to come.
Yes, yes, yes! A hundred years to come.

For many people living in the final days of the nineteenth century, the melancholy thought that in "a hundred years to come" they would be lying in their graves, unwept and nigh forgotten, did not inspire them to bang a drum, blow a horn, explode a firework, play progressive hearts, enter a midnight bicycle race, dance the night away, or even attend a performance of cigarette-smoking cats. Instead of indulging in such secular entertainments, these people tended to the welfare of their souls and spent the last night of nineteenth century in church. As the Reverend Dr. Thomas said to the congregation assembled in Toronto's Jarvis Street Baptist Church, "We are in an altogether unique position—none of us will ever again see the end of a century and we must make use of the time still left to us." Thomas's words were echoed in Toronto's *unto our knees* Christ Church by Reverend Sydney Chambers. "This night is one out of the common," he said. "We stand in a position where we never stood before, nor never will stand again … the new century is come. Unto our knees, then, and let us pray."

Such crowds swarmed the churches on the last night of the nineteenth century that many were turned away at the door. In some cities, such as Washington, several churches issued "cards of admission" to their regular attendees and barred others from entering. Even with these crowd-control measures, churches were packed to standing-room only: in Chicago's Holy Family Church, eight thousand faithful filled the pews. The same church had been busy from noon till the supper hour as hundreds waited in line to make their end-of-the-century confession to one of eighteen priests on duty. Some of the more evangelical churches closed the century with marathon services. The Methodist congregations of Los Angeles "spent nearly ten hours in devotions on the closing day of the century." Not to be outdone, the First Baptist Church held "a centennial conference during the last twenty-four hours of the nineteenth century and the first twenty-four hours of the twentieth century."

greet the author of time

For many denominations, the late-night services held on the last night of the century were an ad hoc innovation. New Year's Eve is, after all, a secular celebration. Still, as the *Boston Herald* noted, "many of the churches which have never taken notice of the passing of the year have specially prepared programmes for their services on the night of December 31 which will include music, brief addresses, and prayers." In Roman Catholic churches, permission to hold midnight mass on December 31— a Monday—had to be provided by Pope Leo XIII. The Pope, who had previously declared all of 1900 to be a holy year, issued a decree explaining his reasons for endorsing the end-of-century services. It was most appropriate, he said, that Roman Catholics should "in the depth of night rise, and greet the author of time."

In most Protestant churches, the last night of the nineteenth century was also the first time that late-night services had ever been conducted. Methodists were the exception: their "watch night" services had been held every New Year's Eve since John Wesley, their founder, had instituted them in 1740. Traditionally, Methodist watch night services commenced around ten o'clock at night and continued until ten minutes to midnight when the entire congregation fell to silent prayer until after the new year dawned. When these watch night services were adopted by all Protestant churches on December 31, 1900, it made for a striking contrast with the secular celebrations underway in public squares and downtown streets: outside, the stroke of midnight prompted a redoubling of an already deafening din; inside, the hands of the clock crossed amid meditative, prayerful silence.

End-of-the-century watch night services were varied and idiosyncratic, generally organized by individual congregations. An exception was the chain of non-denominational watch night services organized by one Frank D. Higbee, impresario, scoundrel, scapegoat—no one knows which. "My business," Higbee once told the *New York Times*, "is evolving ideas and selling them for entertainment, advertising, and other purposes ... as well as helping myself in a perfectly legitimate enterprise."

Leo XIII.'s Message to the Twentieth Century:

The greatest misfortune is never to have known Jesus Christ. Christ is the fountain-head of all good. Mankind can no more be saved without His power than it can be redeemed without His mercy.

When Jesus Christ is absent human reason fails, being bereft of its chief protection and light; and the very end is lost sight of for which, under God's providence, human society has been built up.

To reject Dogma is simply to deny Christianity. It is evident that they whose intellects reject the yoke of Christ are obstinately striving against God. Having shaken off God's authority, they are by no means freer, for they will fall beneath some human sway.

God alone is life. All other beings partake of life, but are not life. Christ, from all eternity and by His very nature, is "the Life," just as He is "the Truth," because He is God of God. If any one abide not in Me, he shall be cast forth as a branch, and shall wither, and they shall gather him up and cast him into the fire, and he burneth (John xv. 6).

Once remove all impediments and allow the spirit of Christ to revive and grow in a nation, and that nation shall be healed.

The world has heard enough of the so-called "rights of man." Let it hear something of the rights of God.

---

excerpt from Pope Leo XIII's "Message to the Twentieth
Century," *Catholic World*, January 1901

Higbee came up with his idea in the final months of 1899. His scheme was to coordinate a series of "mammoth watch night meetings" in six of the largest cities in the United States: New York, Brooklyn, Philadelphia, Boston, Washington, and Chicago. Higbee intended to charge people one dollar to attend his events and, if hundreds of thousands attended, he would rake in a tidy profit. His first problem, though, was how to persuade people to pay for a watch night meeting when, at almost any nearby church, there was sure to be one for free.

Higbee needed a carrot, something people couldn't get anywhere else, and came up with this one: he would get the one hundred most prominent people in the world to write "greetings" to the twentieth century—their thoughts, in other words, about what the new era promised—and he would not unseal these greetings until the last night of the nineteenth century. Then they would be read to the audiences at his gatherings.

Higbee's second problem was how to persuade the one hundred most famous or powerful people on the planet to write the new-century greetings for him. For help, he turned to Clara Barton, the president and founder of the American Red Cross. On August 9, 1900, Higbee sent a letter to Barton outlining his scheme and offering to give her organization half of all his profits; in return, he would be given "credentials" as an

A salutation-speech from the Nineteenth Century to the Twentieth, taken down in short-hand by Mark Twain:

I bring you the stately matron named Christendom, returning bedraggled, besmirched and dishonored from pirate-raids in Kiao-Chow, Manchuria, South Africa & the Phillipines. with her soul full of meanness her pocket full of boodle, and her mouth full of pious hypocrisies. Give her soap + a towel but hide the looking-glass.

Mark Twain

New York, Dec. 31, 1900.

Mark Twain's new century greeting, as printed in the *San Francisco Examiner*, January 1, 1901

ambassador of the Red Cross. Barton agreed and Higbee crossed the Atlantic to begin soliciting greetings from "kings, potentates, and men of eminence."

For the most part, Higbee had great success in rounding up the new-century greetings, though occasionally he did run into snags or get himself into hot water. Kaiser Wilhelm, for example, wanted to be

A pocket full of boodle

included on the "top one hundred" list, but had painted himself into a corner by declaring one year earlier that the century ended on December 31, 1899. The frail Queen Victoria, on the other hand, played hard to get because the too-bold Higbee had tried to approach her directly, instead of going through the British ambassador to the United States.

His worst gaffe, however, involved Mark Twain, who happened to be returning to North America on the same ship as Higbee. Twain responded enthusiastically to Higbee's request for a new-century greeting, and sent one off a few days after he arrived home. Proud of having coaxed a contribution from the famous Twain, Higbee bragged about his success to

NEW YEAR'S WATCH IS OFF

F. D. Higbee's Greeting to 1901 for the Red Cross Fails.

PROMISED TO RAISE $300,000

Promoter of Scheme Explains His Connection with Meeting as Purely Business.

The New Year's watch meeting at Madison Square Garden under the auspices of
the Red Cross Society at which it was intended to read greetings from potentates,

from the *New York Times*, December 25, 1900

curious reporters, and let it slip that Twain—a vocal opponent of American imperialism—had submitted a politically contentious greeting. Twain
had entitled his brief contribution "A Salutation speech from the Nineteenth Century to the Twentieth, taken down in short hand by Mark
Twain":

> I bring you the stately matron named Christendom, returning be-
> draggled, besmirched, and dishonored from pirate raids in Kiachow,
> Manchuria, South Africa and the Phillippines, with her soul full of
> meanness, her pocket full of boodle, and her mouth full of pious
> hypocrisies. Give her soap and a towel but hide the looking-glass.

When reporters besieged Twain's home, clamouring for an advance
copy of this "greeting," Twain became annoyed with Higbee and suspi-
cious of his scheme, as he expressed in a letter to the entrepreneur dated
December 3, 1900:

> Dear Sir:
>   Please send me a complete list of the names of contributors of
> the sentiments which are to be read on your Red Cross watch night.
> I wish it for publication. The list thus far issued by you *a circus poster*
> contains only vague generalities, and one definite *in a graveyard*
> name—mine—"Some kings and queens and Mark
> Twain." I am not enjoying this lofty and sparkling solitude and dis-
> tinction which has not been authorized by me, and which makes
> me feel like a circus poster in a graveyard, or like any other adver-
> tisement improperly placed.

To this, Higbee responded with a placating letter vaguely assuring Twain
that the greetings of many other worthies were in transit. This stonewall-

ing irritated Twain further, whose next letter of December 12 was more terse:

> Dear Sir—
> I was quite sure you could not furnish the list, and it turns out that I was right. You have neglected to return my "greeting" to me. Please send it without delay and remove my name from your list.

Still stalling for time, and perhaps genuinely ill from the stress of his increasingly teetering scheme, Higbee sent word to Twain via his secretary that he was temporarily indisposed. The humorist was not amused and sent a final letter to Higbee:

> Will you return my "greeting" to me and strike my name from the list? This correspondence is wasting my time quite unnecessarily. I am an enemy of your scheme.

Higbee then returned the "Salutation speech" to its author, but not before the greeting was reproduced, in Twain's own hand, on the front page of several American newspapers.

But Higbee's troubles were only beginning. He had succeeded in acquiring a hundred new-century greetings, but the logistics of coordinating mammoth watch night meetings in six major cities, and a few other smaller ones that signed on late, were beginning to overwhelm him. He learned that the city of New York was planning a rival new-century celebration outside City Hall, with free music and fireworks. He also learned that he did not have enough cash on hand to pay for Sousa's band, which he had booked for Madison Square Gardens.

Faced with these problems, he cancelled his watch night celebration in New York. Then he called off assemblies in Boston, Washington, and Philadelphia for similar reasons. The watch night meeting in Chicago went ahead in the Coliseum, but to a smaller crowd than expected: hundreds turned away

proclaimed himself a new Messiah

when they arrived at the building and learned that they would be charged one dollar to enter. The meeting in Chicago was also marred—as the *Herald* reported the next day—by a bizarre occurrence that took place as the audience bid farewell to the nineteenth century with "Old Hundred," a hymn based on Psalm 100:

> All were pausing for the exact moment which would mark the century's close when suddenly attention was distracted by an incident. An old man with grizzled beard and roughly clad rushed to the space in front of the audience, and, stretching out his arms to represent the cross, proclaimed himself a new Messiah. As the strains of "Old Hundred" died away, he sang a hymn and started upon a recitation of passages from the Bible. At that moment, F. M. Lewis, one of the audience, seized the old man and threw him across the railing into one of the boxes. Men and women gathered around him, forgetting all about the moment upon which they had intended solemnly to fix their attention. Then, with a crash, a salute of twenty-

FUNERAL OF A CENTENARIAN.

William Scott, Who Lived in Three Centuries, Will Be Buried To-day.

WILLIAM SCOTT.

from the *Chicago Tribune*, January 3, 1901

five guns fired simultaneously rang out in the rear of the auditorium and the assemblage awoke to the presence of the new century.

For the American Red Cross, their association with Higbee and his end-of-the-century scheme ended up a near disaster. Their half of the profits amounted to $379—rather less than the three hundred thousand dollars Higbee had initially promised them. Worse, as one board member lamented, "we are threatened with law suits and all sorts of trouble on account of debts created by our agent Frank D. Higbee."

Perhaps worst of all, few of the hundred "new century" greetings that Higbee had solicited were anything more than bland platitudes, probably written by mere assistants to the "kings, potentates, and men of eminence." The uninspired message from Queen Victoria was typical:

> The Queen is deeply interested in the great work of humanity which the society has undertaken, and sends her best wishes for the new century to the American Red Cross.

Others greetings, such as the one contributed by Clara Barton herself, who probably entered the new century regretting that she had ever heard of Frank D. Higbee, almost collapse under the weight of their grandiloquent rhetoric:

> The great nineteenth century, the century of centuries, like a tired giant after a monster day's work, lies down to rest. Sleep, grand old

---

Will See His Third Century To-morrow.

Special to The New York Times.

UTICA, Dec. 30.—Abraham E. Elmer will to-morrow witness for the second time the birth of a new century and attain the distinction of having lived in three centuries. Mr. Elmer was born in Warren, Herkimer County, Jan. 26, 1782, and on his next birthday he will be 119 years old. He is in good health, his only affliction being blindness. He is still able to walk about his home and has a good appetite. Mr. Elmer uses tobacco freely and liquor in moderation. He ascribes his long life to heredity and regular living. Events which took place early in the closing century still remain fresh in his mind.

Will Have Lived in Three Centuries.

PATERSON, N. J., Dec. 30.—Mrs. Harriet De Hart, a negress, and her small circle of friends are making preparations to celebrate the unusual event of a person living in three centuries. Mrs. De Hart, who lives with Mrs. Lottie Benjamin, also colored, on Graham Avenue, claims the age of 100 years. She is yet keen of eye and quick of action, and her voice is firm and clear. She says life is still sweet to her, and she hopes to greet many another year.

---

from the *New York Times*, December 31, 1900

century, while the bells of the world toll your honored requiem, and History, with her pen dipped in living gold, stands on tiptoe to write your name at the top. What shall she write? Thou hast chained lightning, and bade it speak like a prattling child. Thou hast yoked the steam, and bade it draw your burden like the willing ox. Thou hast struck the shackles of human slavery, and the bound walked free— the toiling slave is a man. Thou hast said to science, "Rise, fair-eyed daughter, and go forth to bless and to heal the world." Thou hast said to woman, "There is place for thee, my hitherto timid, shrinking child; go forth and fill it, that in thee mankind may be doubly blest."

More honest and moving than any of the hundred greetings coaxed out by Higbee was this last item from the *New York Times*. It reveals, perhaps, the heart-felt sentiment that may indeed motivate new-century celebrations, both then and now:

Charles Contrell fell into ill health during the final weeks of the nineteenth century. Because he was eighty years old, he accepted the prospect of death with equanimity, and yet he yearned for one thing: to live long enough to see the twentieth century. On the night of December 31, 1900 he had his wish: Contrell "closed his eyes just as the clamor that greeted the new century began." Barely audible over the tin horns and sirens piercing the streets, Contrell spoke a final sentence to his son. "I am content," he said. "It is the beginning—it is the end."

Chapter Three

Letters and Diaries
A Private View

LETTERS AND DIARIES begin with a date; it is our door into the text that will follow. We read *Thursday, the 5th of May* or *4 a.m., Sept. 19* and instantly conceive a setting: the room is chill or thick with the scent of lilacs; outside war is brewing or Napoleon is about to be defeated or a volcano to erupt. Like notations about the weather, a date drops a pebble into the waters—details accumulate, a world is being made. We, from our seat in the future, look back through the thickets of history to the precise moment when the writer, marking the time on the top corner of her journal, looked blindly forward.

Sometimes a date is so significant in itself that the diary entry consists of nothing more than its inscription, the numbers slyly encoding a secret kiss, an unnamed loss, a momentous public event the writer *Malone ill* expects never to forget. On January 1, 1900, Lady Gregory, *with his leg* patron of the Irish drama and dramatist herself, opened her journal with the notation "Jan 1,1900" and said nothing more. Perhaps her intent was simply to try out the new digits of what Henry James called "this monstrously numbered century."

On the first day of the nineteenth century, rung in at midnight by every bell in every church in London, the British secretary of war, William Windham, took the trouble to sit down, sharpen his pen, and inscribe the date in his diary—yet all he wrote beneath was "Malone ill with his leg." He had nothing to say about the state of the world, no retrospective to perform on his own life, no vision of the future to impart. Still, his singular attention to the health of a friend cannot but charm us.

For James Jenkins, a Quaker residing in England, the dawn of a new century was less an important milestone than a handy touchstone, a peg to hold a bit of local history in place. On January 1, 1800 he wrote:

> On the first day of the new year and of the new Century died Sam Bevington of Grace Church Street, Brass Ingot, and tin warehouseman, and Willm. Kinder, Stock Broker,—I well knew them both, but was not intimate with either.

Writing to Thomas Poole on December 31, 1799, Samuel Taylor Coleridge also felt the need to note, if not annotate, the occasion:

> Being so hurried for time I should have delayed writing till to-morrow; but to-day is the last day of the year, and a sort of superstitious feeling oppressed me that the year should not end without my writing, if it were only to subscribe myself with the old words of an old affection.

Like Coleridge, we too may feel impelled to mark the end of an era, to inscribe ourselves on a closing page of history—but what do we say? Do we have the time or strength of character to review the past year, much less the past century? Journalists and feature writers must contrive tidy end-of-the-century summations, but in the private space of the diary or letter we are not bound by expectations or tradition. Our New Year celebrations are a familiar secular ritual, but new centuries are infrequent and their celebration must remain essentially ad hoc, never achieving the momentum of ritual, or that comfortable sense of "Oh, this is how it's always been done." How, then, do we mark this rare occasion? Do we take the conventions of New Year's Eve and multiply them by one hundred (or is that ninety-nine)? Do we make huge resolutions and turn our worlds upside-down? Do we destroy the past, as Siegfried Sassoon did, making a bonfire of his childhood fort, and carry on into the new century unencumbered? Or can we just make a note of the weather and get on with our day?

a sort of superstitious feeling

Observations about the weather are frequent in end-of-the-century jottings and, to a certain kind of mind, compelling. Because most of our documents were written in the northern hemisphere where January teems with weather, we find many references to the climate and its quirks. Some of our predecessors found meaning here, or at least portent: clear weather boded well, wild wind and rough seas swept away the past and promised a fresh start or, on the contrary, erased all comfort. But even when the weather stands for nothing but itself, its mere mention invigorates the imagination.

In the diary he kept for more than forty years, James Woodforde, country parson in England's Norfolk county, omitted any mention of the turn of the century, but he *was* interested in the weather. Like many pastoral diarists, he meticulously recorded his dinner menu and often its constitutional effects, as on Sunday, December 28, 1800 when his entrée of "fryed Codlings, and a boiled Bullock's Kidney" made him "but very so-so today—nervous." On January 1, he wrote:

> Anno Domini 1801, Union with Ireland, January 1, Thursday.
> We breakfasted, dined, &c. again at home. The New Year began with very dark, cold, windy and very wet Weather indeed. Dinner today, Giblet-Soup & rost Rabbit. Briton at Weston House in the Evening, supped there, stayed till 10.

NEW CENTURY WEATHER.

Probabilities

Manitoba — Fair and cold.

Minnesota and North Dakota—Fair, continued cold, Tuesday and Wednesday; variable winds.

The Temperature.

Observations of the weather bureau, taken at 7 o'clock last night, Winnipeg time:

Winnipeg	.—14	Battleford	.—22
Edmonton	.— 0	Duluth	.— 6
Minnedosa	.—18	Helena	.— 2
Prince Albert	.—24	Qu'Appelle	.—22
Swift Current	.—29	St. Paul	.—'2
Kamloops	.27	Buffalo	.36
Chicago	.8	Cincinnati	.30
Jacksonville	.70	New York	.40
Philadelphia	.38	St. Louis	.16
Sault Ste. Marie	.2	Montreal	.34

MARINE NEWS.

OCEAN STEAMSHIPS.

Dec. 31.	Arrived At.	From.
American	.. .. ..Halifax..	Liverpool
Dec. 30.		
Corinthian	.. .. ..Halifax.	Liverpool

from the *Manitoba Free Press,* January 1, 1901

Another country parson, William Holland, noted the clarity of the frosty Somerset air:

> Wednesday December 31, 1800
> The last day of the year. The ground is covered with snow. The sun shines clear and the horizon looks keen for frost. Thus concludes the year.

Weather surrounds Joseph Farington's final diary entry of the eighteenth century like a chilly set of parentheses. Farington, a leading member of the Royal Academy of Arts, had recently lost his wife and his sorrow was deep—in attending to the state of things outside his window, he seemed to find some *a real cold day but clear & calm* diversionary solace. Between his opening, "Much snow last night," and his closing, "Much snow on the ground," Farington lays bare his most private suffering:

> Wednesday Decr 31st
> Much snow last night. A fine clear morning. Thermometer in my bedroom 34—In the open air 28. This day concludes the year 1800—a year in which I have suffered the greatest trial of my fortitude that I have had in this world.—By application in the daytime to the study of books on the subject of religion, I have for a considerable time past got through the day as well as I could expect, endeavouring to

establish a foundation for hope and composure on that best of all basis, trust in God and in the mediation of our Lord Jesus Christ, whose promises to the penitent are unlimited.—But I still labour under the anxiety caused by the shock to my affections, and which, as a Man, I feel incessantly.—The early part of the mornings I often pass under the greatest oppression of spirits. A thousand tendernesses are remembered, and a thousand omissions and imperfections on my part are recollected.—My mind is much worn down by such distressing thoughts, but I hope the humility and caution which they occasion, will render me still more fit to receive these holy impressions which I am daily seeking for in the Scriptures ... I employed myself in making extracts, & afterwards rode out towards Tetbury.—Much Snow on the ground.

On another continent clear cold weather also closed the eighteenth century but here the consequence of the frigid temperature was tragic. In the diary of Archibald McLeod, fur trader, we read:

Wednesday 31st December 1800.
A real cold day but clear & calm.

Thursday 1st January 1801.
Still Colder than yesterday, Hoole & La Couture arrived from Swan River, & Le Mire with them, the latter brought me a keg of H. Wines, the two former brought two pieces the 3d they left at Mr Perignes, I gave all the people in the Fort a dram which they took, three qts. Rum (reduced) to effect, after that I gave them fourteen Quarts among them, there were people from Fort des Prairies, Red River, Swan River, Free Men, & Iroquois, in all 38 Men including my own men I likewise gave them 1/2 Foot Tobaco each man, they danced & sang all day & night, but had no quarrels ...

Friday 2d.
Cold, & Blowy, nobody went off Today; early this morning one of the old women, who are in a Small Lodge at the Fort gate was found frozen to Death. Somebody had given her a little Liquor & it's supposed she laid down to Sleep, but the very intense cold siezed her & carried her to her long home, the people put her body on a scaffold as the ground is so hard frozen as not to admit of digging a hole to put her in;—Several of the Men wanted to buy rum, but I refused them all.

For other authors, the weather that blows out a century is not just a chilly fact but a portent of cosmic or social revolution. In his notebook

all the forces in nature
entry for the last day of the eighteenth century, Coleridge makes a mundane weather report his stepping stone to an eschatological comment about the "blab" that will fill the air on the real "last day," the one that will end the earth:

The last day of the century the weather was clear. All the World seemed to play except the Galley Slaves who, for being becalmed, were forced to ply their Oars. At the last day 'twill be nothing but Blab.

A hundred years later, a stormy close of the nineteenth century seemed to portend global upheaval. Compton Mackenzie, who went on to spy for the British secret service and publish more than a hundred novels, was seventeen years old at the time:

> The nineteenth century went out on New Year's Eve in the south of England to a savage gale, so savage that one of the megaliths of Stonehenge was blown down upon that night; I have always felt this was an omen of how much of the past the twentieth century would destroy.

In London, ninety miles from the tumbling slab at Stonehenge, Queen Victoria experienced the same end-of-the-century tempest:

> 31 December 1900
> A terribly stormy night. The same unfortunate alternations of sleep and restlessness, so that I again did not get up when I wished to, which spoilt my morning and day.

> 1 January 1901
> Another year begun, and I am feeling so weak and unwell that I enter upon it sadly. The same sort of night as I have been having lately, but I did get rather more sleep and was up earlier.

She died three weeks later at half-past six in the evening on January 22, 1901. For many of Victoria's four-hundred million subjects, the death of the monarch who had ruled over them for more than sixty years is what brought the nineteenth century to its definitive close.

As Queen Victoria knew well, in the northern hemisphere the season of the New Year brings with it a surplus of complaints, viral and otherwise— influenza, colds, pneumonia, pleurisy and, if the sufferer re- ***the dates of*** covers, an ensuing depression of spirits. Reading through ***our deaths*** eighteenth and nineteenth-century diaries and letters, we enter a damp world of sickbeds, coughs, death and angst. This, at least, was the world of novelist Leo Tolstoy as 1899 gave way to 1900:

> December 20, 1899, Moscow.
> Health not good. Mental condition good, I'm ready for death. A lot of people in the evenings—I'm tired. *Resurrection* didn't appear in No. 51, and I was sorry. That's bad. I'm thinking over philosophical definitions of life.

> January 1, 1900, Moscow.
> I'm sitting in my room, and everybody is here, celebrating the New Year. All this time I've written nothing in my diary, I've been unwell. There's a lot to note down ... I was riding along in a horse-drawn tramcar, looking at houses, signboards, shops, cabmen, and people driving or walking by, and suddenly it became so clear to me that all this world, including my life in it, is only one of an innumerable number of possibilities of other worlds and other lives, and for me only one of innumerable stages through which it seems to me I am passing in time.

Stricken with a lung disease and only three years from death, the novelist George Gissing was plunged into more pessimistic musings by the chilly turn of the century, as he revealed in a letter to his friend Edward Clodd:

> My dear Clodd: December 30, 1900 Paris
> ... I know you are very busy just now, so will not write more. In 1901, we shall meet, I hope, but not early in the year, as I cough consumedly, & dare not travel in any but safe weather. All good things be with you! You have a much better chance than I of seeing the century out of its teens, for you are one of the men who live long & enjoy life to the end.

Even many in better health than Tolstoy or Gissing were afflicted with *it's a hard fact* morbid speculations as the nineteenth century came to its close. Arthur Balfour, soon to become the first British prime minister elected in the twentieth century, wrote gloomily to Lady Elcho on January 2, 1901:

> I meant to write to you yesterday on the first day of our new century but I felt too languid. I don't at *all* like the idea that not *one* of us, can possibly live into the next century, it's a hard fact, not an idea and must be accepted as such.

Sigmund Freud, too, was reminded of the inevitability of death as he stepped into the century that would first revere, and then disparage, his work. He wrote to his friend and colleague, Wilhelm Fliess:

> Vienna, January 8, 1900
> The new century, the most interesting thing about which for us may be that it contains the dates of our deaths, has brought me nothing but a stupid review in the *Zeit* by Burckhard ... It is hardly flattering, uncommonly devoid of understanding, and—worst of all—to be continued in the next issue ... I do not count on recognition, at least not in my lifetime. May you fare better! At least you can address yourself to a more respectable, educated audience, at home with ideas. I have to deal in obscure matters with people I am ten to fifteen years ahead of and who will not catch up with me. So all I seek is quiet and some material comfort. I am not working, and there is silence in me. If the sexual theory comes, I shall listen to it. If not, then not.

Sorrows deeper than sickness are linked to the end of the year. The son of Erasmus Darwin found himself unable to balance his yearly accounts, and on December 30, 1799 he drowned himself in the river that flowed at the bottom of his garden. His father, the grandfather of Charles Darwin and a prominent scientist in his own right, poignantly reveals his sorrow in a dutiful letter to his publisher ten days later:

> Dear Sir:
> You will please to do as you please about the Aphidivorous larva with the aphis in its mouth. A few strokes would give it, as in the

drawing, which I shall stick on the paper below ... My great affliction for the sudden death of my beloved eldest son, who used to call at your house, has prevented me for a while from sending Bennet's work, but shall be done soon.

But grimmer still is a letter whose contents we shall never read: on the last day of the nineteenth century, as then reported in the *Los Angeles Times*, a suicide pact was carried out in New York City:

> A man and woman who went to Courtney's Hotel on Fulton Street and Manhattan Crossing, Brooklyn, Saturday night, were found dead in bed today. Two unlighted gas burners were turned on full. There was nothing leading to the couple's identity, except a letter, which is in the hands of the Coroner.

For those at or beyond middle age, shaped by the century they leave behind and comfortable in its numerals, a new century often evokes anxiety because it seems a country of exile, a place where they will always be strangers. Rudyard Kipling, exactly half way through *there was a gloss* his life at the turn of the century, said: "It's a great shame because if I had been born twenty years later I might have seen and understood the drift of the new century." Nearly sixty years old in 1799, Hester Thrale—better known as Mrs. Piozzi and now chiefly remembered as the biographer of her friend Samuel Johnson—observed that as she herself had aged, the dawn of another year had lost its dazzle, its "gloss":

> Saturday night December1799.
> I shall feel glad this year to see December close upon me, which for some time has carried with it a sensation more awful than pleasing. When the sand was high in the hour-glass, I well remember longing for a New Year as if it had been a new gown; there was a gloss on every 1st January *then*, as if all misfortune would slip over and not stain it.

With fifty-six years and eighteen novels under his belt when the century changed, Henry James likewise felt impelled to turn his gaze from an unknown future to the solace of the familiar past:

> January 1, 1900
> My dear Rhoda Broughton,
> I am sadly afraid that my silence and absence, so ungracefully persisted in, have nigh cost me your esteem—or at least ranked me, for you, with those who appear perversely to desire to be *so monstrously numbered* forgotten: in which case you will, no doubt, unstintedly have obliged me! ... This dreadful gruesome New Year, so monstrously numbered, makes me turn back to the warm and coloured past and away from the big black avenue that gapes in front of us ... I want to give you my fervent wishes for the dim twelvemonth to come. It looks to me full of goblins, to be deprecated by prayer and sacrifice—and my incense rises for your immunity, of every kind, not less than for my own.

THE DYING CENTURY.

THE peace of Autumn, ere late winds have blown,
　　Is on the woodland glory, deepen'd now
　　　　To auburn hue. O'er yonder mist-cloud brow
The swallows—last of *thine*—have southward flown.

'Tis calm for thought betwixt the summer's breath,
　　Laden with richness of the season's prime,
　　　　And that storm toss'd, distressful aftertime
Which comes adown the valley shade of death.

Pause now—the years have passed, and there is given
　　A time for thought, a holy hour of peace.
　　　　The deeds are done ; the history must cease;
'Tis written how thy sons have lived and striven.

The bracken browns upon a thousand slopes,
　　The squirrel gambols on his merry round,
　　　　The ripen'd chestnut drops to mossy ground.
When in the waking spring thy youthful hopes

Were wont to whisper, " That which failed last year
　　This summer shall the promise all fulfil,"
　　　　Crept there a forecast shadow cold and still
Of when there was no more to hope or fear ?

In the long afterwards again will come
　　The season's sweetness ; other eyes will see
　　　　The orchards laden ; but 'tis not for thee,
Old Century, will sound that Harvest Home !

---

from *Gentleman's Magazine*, December 1900 (and opposite page)

Lionel Muirhead, friend of the poet and editor Robert Bridges, likewise turned to the pleasures and comfort of memory:

> My dear Robert,
> … Well here we are at the end of the century both having had a far larger slice of health and happiness than has fallen to the lot of many we have known. I dont understand life in the least and dont now seek to do so: the puzzles in it are quite insoluble and must be left to be cleared up in the *saecula saeculorum* of which my portion of the twentieth century is but the narthex. But it is a thing to be grateful for that the years have planted in one's mind a garden of clipped hedges and sheltered nooks where all sorts of pleasant memories of people and scenes and books and things that cannot be enumerated bloom perpetually. It is my hope that if sight should fail they will still be visible. You have helped me to plant this garden, and will I am sure accept my thanks.

The consolations of age and nostalgia are not always needed companions. John Burroughs, American essayist and naturalist, was over sixty at the turn of the century but he nonetheless entered the new era in a felicitous mood, pleased that he had finished a poem, pleased that he had had a good walk:

A hundred golden autumns went before
  With air as light, with woods and wealds as brown ;
  But when *these* ling'ring leaves shall flutter down,
They are the last of *thine* for evermore.

I stand beside a newly open grave—
  A grave now holding ashes of the dead—
  Dust wrapp'd to decency in sheeted lead,
Hiding decay.   The world may try to save

The hero's memory, but secret sleep
  Guards the unwritten truths of life and love,
  Which never shall discordant Fame remove
From sanctu'ry of shadows dark and deep—

Truths which perchance have bound a firmer cord
  To life divine ; links of a fairer chain
  Than that of mighty deeds which live again
On Hist'ry's page of famous deed and word.

    •   •   •   •   •   •   •

The winds have blown, and low the rotting leaves
  Lie at the black wet trunks of oak and beech ;
  The wail has died away.   A sigh for each
Thro' the bared branches now the night air breathes.

White gath'ring clouds hide out the waning moon,
  Thro' the long night they veil the winter sky.
  A shroud ! a shroud ! for such as have to die !
The open grave must have its tenant soon.

Open and waiting !   Silently to-night,
  Perchance, they hither bring thy winding-sheet,
  Cover thy hoary head and helpless feet,
And lay thee low, away from mortal sight.

                           E. M. RUTHERFORD.

January 1, 1900.
  Good bye 1800 and all thy progeny! We have grown old together.
Thy end has come, but I stay a little longer. I have looked upon thy
face all my life. My father looked upon it all his life, my grandfather
more than half of his. Now the door I shut and we shall see thee no
more. Welcome to thy successor! But he is a stranger, a new-comer,
and it is hard for the old to make new friends; we become ac-
quainted, but not wedded. The new days can never be to us what
the old were. In our youth the days become part of us; they mingle
with our blood; they take on the very color of our souls; but in age
they hardly touch us; they come and go like strangers. Only youth
can live in the present and the future. In youth we constantly pay
tribute to the future, and, to make the account even, in age we
constantly pay tribute to the past.

Jan. 1, 1901.
  Finish Bluebird poem in morning. Lunch with Dr. Cleghorn. We
walk to Boston and back. A good start on the new century.

We can sense that Burroughs's buoyant welcome to the new century
was prompted by an habitually sanguine temperament, not merely by the

occasion. But even in those of a melancholy disposition, the prospect of a fresh new era could transform the blues into manic excitement: "I want to live faster," wrote author Maxim Gorky, who had grimly contemplated the end of things only a few months before:

> June 1899
> How am I? The same as ever, Mariia Zakharovna—restless … On the whole I live a difficult and joyless life. I work a lot, I am tired, my health has suffered … I am still the same as always, just as ridiculous and just as foolish … The past is better than the present, although I say so perhaps only because I am already thirty years old, I have worked a lot, I have climbed high and am tired.

brighter, faster

> January 1900
> Happy New Year!
> I am living as absurdly as always and feel desperately overwrought. I shall be going to Yalta at the end of March or in April, if I do not fall ill before that. I really want to live differently somehow—brighter, faster—the main thing is faster … Truly, the time has come when we need something heroic: everyone wants something stimulating, something bright, something which is not like life, you know, but more elevated, better, and more beautiful. It is quite essential that the literature of today should start to embellish life a little, and as soon as it starts to do this, life will embellish itself, i.e. people will start to live more quickly and brightly.

The new-century vigour that raised Gorky's spirits also raised many a glass in parlours and dance halls. Accounts of *fin-de-siècle* parties and balls abound in the closing days of the eighteenth and nineteenth centuries, from backyard picnics in wartime or an outdoor camp on the fur trade to elegant house parties, elaborate balls and royalty.

England's King George III showed a lackluster sense of occasion at the end of the eighteenth century, sweeping his guests out of the royal residence even before the tolling of the midnight bells. No doubt his more fun-loving son, the Prince of Wales, later George IV, had additional plans for later in the evening. His sister, Princess Augusta, wrote to him:

> December 30, 1799
> The Queen has no objections to your bringing or sending Lord Robert & Lord Charles Manners, & she will be very happy to see Arthur Paget. We shall dine at Frogmore precisely at four o'clock & you will order the *beaux* to be there a little after seven o'clock as the King wishes the Ball to be over before supper.

Peter Mark Roget, creator of the great thesaurus, also attended an end-of-the-century party, one that began early, but which, to his glee, lasted well into the brand-new nineteenth century:

> We were invited for five in the afternoon—this was ridiculously early for a dance that was going to pass the century. We went, my cousins, Sam, my aunt, and I, at six. I saw several friends from Edinburgh. We

A FAREWELL.

TIME, who devours his children, now claims thee,
  Poor dying Century ! With eager pace
  The New Age hurries on to take thy place,
And thou goest forth into the Darkness. We,
Who knew and loved thee, turn reluctantly.
  To the new comer's unfamiliar face,
  Look in his eyes and strive in vain to trace
Thy likeness in the features that we see.

In vain ! What there is shown none may descry.
  But we can smile though skies be overcast,
  Can front the future as we faced the past,
And bear a light heart with us till we die,
  Can find a laugh for the New Century,
  And just one tear at parting with the Last !

from *Punch*, January 2, 1901

commenced to dance at 7; at 11 we supped for half an hour. We danced during the rest of the century and continued until 4:30 a.m.! There is something that surpasses by far Annette's ball! I did all the dances except one. Admire, if you will, how I can dance nine hours running and have myself on my feet afterwards. I had engaged a bed at a tavern

we danced during the rest of the century

across from Uncle's in Pratt Place. They had promised to wait up for me, but no matter how I knocked no one opened. I continued to walk in the snow in front of the door during a half hour before someone opened the door for me. The next day I was very tired.

While Roget narrowly avoided freezing to death in the snow, one of the guests at another end-of-the-century ball was not so fortunate. Mrs. Trench, an English matron whose autobiographical writings were collected by her son as *The Remains of the Late Mrs. Richard Trench,* lived in Germany from 1799 until 1801:

Went to a ball at Mad. Angestrom's, the Swedish Minister's wife. Every one seemed to partake in the design of finishing the century with festivity and cheerfulness. The company was the elite of the Berlin society, and the ball was unusually animated and brilliant. I had just danced one dance with Mr. Caulfield, and was resting myself during the second in an outer room, when I heard that M. d'Orville, a young officer just one-and-twenty, had fallen down in a fainting fit in the dance. After some moments he was removed from the ball-room into Mad. Angestrom's boudoir, where all the common remedies of salts, essences, cold water, and fresh air were tried without effect. Still no one was much alarmed. However, a physician and surgeon were called in. They exhausted in vain all the resources of their art; he was irrecoverably gone, and afforded an awful example of the uncertainty of human life. Mad. Angestrom, whose nerves had been lately shaken by the death of a favourite son, was affected in a dreadful way. She fainted, and on her recovery knew nothing of what had passed, but was impressed with the idea that something had happened to her children. Her husband went to their apartment, and brought them to her from their beds, wrapped in large cloaks ... At first she did not know her children, and she continued to utter such incoherent rhapsodies as were both shocking and pathetic. *The shrieks, faintings, tears,* and hysterics of every woman who either had really weak nerves, or who wished to display her feelings, completed the horror of the scene. I wished to escape. Lord Carysfort and Prince Radziwill offered me their carriages, but I refused one, and there was a mistake about the other. At last the contagion of the scene spread to me. I wept violently, and remember no more than that I was wrapped up by Mr. Ridley and Mr. Caulfield, who both showed infinite good nature, in a large cloak, and put into a carriage; that Mr. Ridley accompanied me home, where Mr. Kinnaird and he remained with me till a few minutes past twelve, that I might not be left to begin the new century a prey to melancholy reflections.

shrieks, faintings, tears, and hysterics

A few weeks later, a letter followed from Prince Adolphus, offering a dubious cause of death for young M. d'Orville:

> The shocking accident of which you were a witness on the 31st of last month will, I am afraid, have made a deep impression on your mind. It is at least very difficult for a person of your feelings to forget immediately such an event, and as it happened at a ball, all dancing parties must for a time recall that accident to your remembrance. I do sincerely pity M. d'Orville's fate, and I wish he may serve as an example for other young men, that they may not likewise fall victims to their dress.

In India, the British celebrated the end of the eighteenth century with elegant house parties and marked the midnight moment by "drinking a bumper." Had they been in England when the century turned, the party might have been more modest than this one recorded by William Hickey, a self-styled "prodigal rake"—we imagine a great flurry of servants behind this lavish account:

> Having invited Sir Henry Russell and his family to end the year and the century with me at Chinsurah, after having arranged the business of entering upon the new Shrievalty, Mr. Thoroton kindly undertaking to attend to the duties of the office during my absence, on the 23rd of December, 1800, Sir Henry Russell, Lady Russell, a young lady then recently arrived from England who resided with them, the sweet little infant Rose Russell and her nurse Mrs. Ryan, an uncommon fine woman, set off in my boat for Chinsurah, which place we reached by two o'clock in the afternoon; being there joined by Major Holmes of His Majesty's 10th Regiment, Captain Eames of the same Regiment, Mr. Robert Ledlie, and Mr. James Simpson, Barristers of the Supreme Court, all of whom I had requested to join us for a few days. This company with

we all drank a bumper

Mr. Birch's family, and some other neighbours that occasionally added to our number, made the house very gay and cheerful. Time glided away in the utmost harmony and good-humour. Both Sir Henry and Lady Russell have often declared since that those were amongst the happiest days of his life. On the 31st of December I had a particularly jovial company with a merry dance in the evening. At the moment of midnight the church bells struck up a peal, and we all drank a bumper, standing, to the new century.

Other colonies, other lives. How different from Hickey's festivities in Chinsurah was the celebration recorded by Alexander Henry, a fur trader camped near the Red River on the last night of the eighteenth century:

Sunday, Jan 1st, 1801.
The new year was ushered in by several volleys, which alarmed a camp of Indians near by. The men came running in armed, having ordered the women to hide themselves. But they were agreeably deceived, and got a share of what was going—some sherub and cakes. Every woman and child was soon at the fort; all was bustle and confusion.

A hundred years later, gunfire again startled some new century revellers, though this time the locale was South Africa and the weapon—an armament called a "Sanna"—was aimed not in the air but at the celebrants. The occasion was recorded by Solomon Tshekiso Plaatje, a black South African who published several novels and translated Shakespeare into Tswana:

Monday, January 1, 1900
The first day of the first week of the first month in 1900. Not at all a lovely morning. The distant pop of the Mauser distinctly shows that there is no holiday for poor beleaguered us. I tried to go to town but "Au Sanna," going strong, caused me to come back and take shelter ... In the afternoon David stood watching a *merry maidens* train of merry girls, amidst who were Meko's sisters-in-law in the best of millenaries, celebrating the New Year with jolly games. All of a sudden a "Sanna" came round and spoiled the whole thing. Mr. Briscoe's garden is an intolerably near spot for 94 pounds of mortar to burst while a train of giggling girls are enjoying the first day of the first year of the twentieth century near Bokone—particularly when they were under the impression that it was directed to town. It sent nearly all the merry maidens in different directions. Some lay flat on the ground—it was for dear life—and "Sanna" fairly put them in memory that their lives were dearer and more expensive than their New Year's dresses.

While the maidens in South Africa ducked for cover, two teenage brothers back in England welcomed the new century by devising a conflagration of their own. One of them, Hamo Sassoon, was later killed in the First World War; the other, Siegried Sassoon, went on to become one of the great antiwar poets of the century. Their deliberations are recorded in Siegried Sassoon's memoirs:

During December, my brother Hamo and I celebrated the advent of the new century ourselves by making a big bonfire. To begin with, I had opposed the idea because it meant pulling down the fort, which had enough tarred timber in it for a very fine blaze. I was fond of the fort, and at first I did my best to save it. Hamo, however, was determined to destroy it, for he thoroughly enjoyed strenuous occupations, such as chopping or digging. He had built the fort affectionately, and was now longing to tear it down again; in fact he'd already borrowed the garden hatchet and crowbar for the purpose. "Anyhow," I said, "you can't do it without my permission; it belongs to me just as much as it does to you, and Michael ought to be asked about it as well." "What'll you take for your share?" he asked dourly. Knowing that he had ten bob, I became irresolute, and after a brisk haggle, agreed to take 7s. 6d. It went without saying that he was entitled to his share of any chocolates I bought with the money … Thus, between tea and dinner on a dry frosty evening, the fort went up in flames and in brief glory was consumed. In the heat of the moment I was too busy and excited to connect the conflagration with anything except the new century. But even if I'd stopped to meditate, I don't suppose I could have realized that the sparks were flying upward from those few years of the departing century which I was able to remember … This being so, I might well have fed the bonfire with many another relic of the past, such as our dapple-grey rocking-horse, and the babyish books from which I had first learnt to read, and the old Ariston organ, whose muffled grunting music had expired several years ago when the handle came off and nobody bothered to get it put on again.

a very fine blaze

The librettist W. S. Gilbert preferred something a bit more splashy in his tribute to the dying century:

My dear Dorothy—
… I'm making a lovely lake, 170 yards long and 50 yards wide, especially for you to bathe in. I said to myself: "What would Dorothy like better than anything else?" And the answer was a Lake, because her mother was one once. We are going to turn the water on at midnight on the 31st Dec.'99.

Eleven years later, after a long and illustrious career, the seventy-five-year-old Gilbert would suffer a fatal heart attack in this lake, while attempting to save another young woman from drowning.

Some, however, like Henry James, preferred to avoid all the fuss and retired to bed:

December 30, 1900

My dear Gosse,
I come up on Monday tomorrow again (I've been here a week,) but perversely, wretchedly, I'm afraid I shall be unable to join you in your midnight mirth. I've accepted an invitation from the George Lewis's—& that means midnight mirth there. I shall escape thence at the earliest hour, but it can only be to convey my poor old bones to bed. I shall convey them to your door on the earliest other occasion. Don't meanwhile break

convey my poor old bones to bed

yours, or any one's else, in your rush for the infant favours of the new century—but keep them sound, all of you, for the longest possible stretch of the same. Yours, all, always Henry James

The philosopher and theologian Schleiermacher attended none of the many parties in the German town where he lived but preferred to spend his time reflecting on them. He wrote to his sister:

> During the last night of the century my thoughts were much with you and the congregation in general; indeed they always are during the first hour of the new year and on the first Easter morning, being drawn towards you by the remembrance of the beautiful and the most appropriate manner in which festivals are celebrated among you. Of your illuminations, the effect of which was not, I dare say, impaired by the moonlight, I drew in my mind a most agreeable picture. Here the night was not celebrated with any solemnity; there was neither the ringing of bells nor firing of cannon, and most people made the transit while drinking, gambling, or dancing, for on all sides I heard of balls and punch parties. I had only to preach in the afternoon of New Year's Day, and was therefore able to go in the morning to the Cathedral, which was much fuller than usual, and where the whole court was present.

In the diaries of Ruth Slate, a working-class girl brought up in a Nonconformist Christian household, we find that a good night's sleep also took precedence over whooping it up:

> Monday, 31 December 1900. 2:45 p.m.
> Here I am, on the last day of the last year of this century. We were nearly at our wits' end getting ready for Christmas, and the endless number of parcels, letters and telegrams seemed wonderful. At last I was free to go home … This evening, to please Grandma I went to bed quite early. I was wakened by the village band, which paraded the street, and hearing through the wall our neighbour's clock strike twelve knew that the new year and century had begun.

For many young women, the twentieth century would open new doors and new paths in life for them to choose. Two women in particular began their adventures on the last night of the century. Paula Becker, later to become the art- *a new world arising around me* ist Paula Modersohn-Becker, travelled to Paris, leaving on the eve of Germany's new century:

> Dear Mr. Modersohn:
> I am returning your Pauli lecture to you with many thanks. Reading it in Lilienthal during the half hour I had to wait for the omnibus shortened the time most agreeably. New Year's Eve, at half-past one, I begin the great journey. That will be a lovely little moment when I shake the dust of Bremen from my feet. Hurrah! Right now my poor head is in chaos: packing, saying adieu, talking about Fitger!!!, my plans in Paris, and Mozart arias which my sister is singing in this very room. And so for now, very happy New Year's greetings to you and your dear wife. And in the new century when I am in Paris, the

the cover from *Ladies' Home Journal,* January 1901

great pit of sin, I shall often think of your sweet and peaceful little house.

The next day in her journal she wrote:

> I am in Paris. I departed on New Year's Eve. I listened to the New Year's bells from our dear old rooftop overlooking the Weser in Bremen. Then my family accompanied me in a great procession to the station. My trip lasted seventeen hours. And now I am living here in the bustle of this great city. Everything rushes and swirls around me in a damp and foggy atmosphere. It's filthy here, very filthy—an inward filth, way down deep inside. Sometimes it makes me shudder. It seems to me as if I needed more strength than I have to live here, a brutal strength. But I feel that only sometimes. At other times, I feel blissfully clear, and serene. I can feel a new world arising around me.

Isabelle Eberhardt, writer, cross-dresser, tax collector and adventurer, also wanted to see the new century dawn in Paris but could not rest in one place long enough. Instead she left Livorno at midnight on December 31, 1899 and arrived in Sardinia the next day:

> Le 1er janvier 1900.
>   I am alone, sitting facing the grey vastness of the shifting sea …
> I am alone … alone as I've always been everywhere, as I'll always be throughout this delightful and deceptive great Universe … alone, with a whole world of disappointment and disillusion behind me, and of memories growing daily more distant, almost unreal.

There are more inward forms of adventure—so many women's diary entries are concerned with self-improvement that we can expect the reforming spirit of New Year's, not to mention the coming new century, to intensify this. Margaret Sloan, a southern belle and avid diarist, began the century newly married, optimistic and in love:

I want to be a better girl

> Sunday Dec. 30—1900
>   This is the last Sunday of 1900, the last of the 19th Century! No one living today will see the close of the next century! This is a solemn thought, and makes me feel that I am doing nothing for my Saviour while the years are flying so rapidly. I am going to try to be better and do some good in the World.

> Tuesday—New Years day. Jan 1st. 1901.
>   This is the first day of the year, and the first day of the Century, we are in Batavia N.Y. and Willard didint get today off, but he comes home to dinner, so the day dont seem so long. Last night we didint retire till 10 o'clock then it didint seem long till mid-night and I was awake when the bells begun to toll the death knell of dear old 1900. Willard folded me in his arms and wished me a happier year, and we decided that we should be happy since we were all in all to each other, so the old Century died and the new one was born in perfect love to us. He caressed and kissed me often while unconscious, and a wife appreciates affection every time if she loves her husband. The

whistles blew, bells rang, and many were up watching in different ways something none of us will ever see again. It was solemn, and how I hope Willard will be brought to Christ this year! This morning he said, "I love you, of course I do, my little girl is all the World to me!" This makes me happy, to feel I am his all, I make his happiness. I have written home today and it has been a quiet day yet I have been rather happy in spite of the loneliness! I want this year to be better spent, and I want to be a better girl.

Nice empty days. For some, the world does not seem open to change, new century or not. Maud Berkeley, the matriarch of a late Victorian household, took time to record her children's daily activities in both words and drawings, but devoted only humdrum scribblings to what the future promised:

> First year of the new century. What will it bring? Nothing in particular. Dorothy and Maurice growing steadily. Jim and I bumbling along as usual.

Even Charlotte Perkins Gilman, political analyst and author of the feminist landmark "The Yellow Wallpaper," gave more end-of-the-century attention to housework and self-improvement than social speculation:

> Wed. Dec. 27, 1899
> Nice empty days.
> Lovely weather. Arrange things gradually.
>
> Saturday 30
> Clean room—sweep, scrub, & oil. Enjoy it. Take walk p.m. with Miss Quick & Jennie.
>
> Sun. Dec. 31, 1899
> Finish answering all letters on hand. Slept ill—feel badly … Try to rest p.m. Take walk with several. Still tired. Must go alone more.
> Notes for 1900. Get well—get well—get well. And do good work! Pay all debts if possible.

Kartini, the Indonesian feminist, bubbled with enthusiasm for the new century:

> My own dearest Mevrouw,   Japara 1—1—1901
> To you both and to your trio in Europe, our heartiest good wishes for the new year and the new Century. What a world of thoughts fill my brain in writing down those words: the new Century! What will it bring Mankind? But no, let me now not dream, I want to cheerfully chat with my dear angel.

For Jane Cunningham Croly, an activist for women's rights who dedicated her *History of the Woman's Club Movement* to "the Twentieth Century Woman," the end of the nineteenth century also promised a renewed society:

> The woman of the past has especially been crammed up, bound around, and blindfolded by her special form of belief, by her tradi-

tion, by her social customs, by her education, by her whole environment; and the effect will remain stamped more or less upon her individuality long after the predisposing causes have passed away and better influences have taken their place. But the present is full of encouragement. The new life has begun: the woman is here—not the martyred woman of the past; not the self absorbed woman of the present, but the awakened woman of the future.

But in a letter to her friend Caroline Morse, Croly revealed a gloomier side. A fractured hip and consequent illness that would take her life in 1901 soured her thoughts on the closing century:

> We go to-morrow, and begin a new chapter in this most disastrous of years. So many things seem to culminate toward the close of the century—good fortune for some, evil fortune for others; hopes dashed at the seeming moment of realization, as if all the forces in nature were aiding to make an end of the century's efforts ... For my part I feel as if I had been forcibly brought to a standstill. In a few days I shall have reached the milestone: I shall be seventy ... As it is, I feel a little tinge of regret that my annihilation last June was not more complete; that I did not leave, along with my dear friend, Mrs. Demorest. Not that I am wholly unhappy; I only feel somehow brought to an unfinished close; left in a state of animated suspension. I seem to see everything from a distance; separated by my inability to participate in the goings and comings, the doings and pleasures of others. I feel the wall that stands between those who still live and those who have passed from this world.

New life and evil fortune, flames and fountains, nice empty days and friends with sick legs—considering the vagaries and diversity of human experience, perhaps the best advice for a new century is that offered by children's author Hilaire Belloc to his friend E.S.P. Haynes:

> You are rather gloomy about what you facetiously term the New Century ... God bless you! You take things too hard, especially great whacking things like centuries. Note you: I would be the last to speak ill of a century. I snap my fingers at 99 years; but between that and a century there is *great whacking things like centuries* all the difference ... I have discovered a 1s. 6d. luncheon at a place called Villa-Vita where I will take you when I am absolved from my present bout of work. It is palatial. That is a wholesome, practical, sensible, materialist discovery to start the century with.

Chapter Four

Looking Backward

MIDNIGHT, NEW YEAR'S EVE—that threshold between past and future (like every moment, you say)—just before crossing over, we look back. Some praise, some moan, some catalogue bests and worsts, some look for the place we went astray. "No one ever regarded the first of January with indifference," wrote Charles Lamb, the nineteenth-century essayist. "It is the nativity of our common Adam." When Lamb heard the clock strike midnight on the last night of the year, his mind was tugged back by time:

> I never hear it without a gathering-up of my mind to a concentration of all the images that have been diffused over the past twelvemonth; all I have done or suffered, performed or neglected—in that regretted time.

Lamb was fonder of looking backward than forward. "I am naturally," he said, "shy of novelties." Rather than imagine the future, he preferred to drift down a river of memories, even sorrowful ones:

> I would scarce now have any of those untoward accidents and events of my life reversed. I would no more alter them than the incidents of some well-contrived novel. Methinks, it is better that I should have pined away seven of my goldenest years, when I was thrall to the fair hair, and fairer eyes, of Alice W——n, than that so passionate a love-adventure should be lost. It was better that our family should have missed that legacy, which old Dorrell cheated us of, than that I should have at this moment two thousand pounds in banco, and be without the idea of that specious old rogue.

The play of memory: it is a human impulse, and it most especially thrives when things seem to be coming to an end. As the editor of England's *Annual Register* wrote at the end of 1800:

> It is natural, on the expiration of any period of time, to pause, and look back upon its most prominent features, or events—those that recur oftenest to the mind, on the survey, stand forward on the canvas, and throw other occurrences in the background.

John Bowles wrote much the same thing in his *Reflections on the Political and Moral State of Society at the Close of the Eighteenth Century:*

> A change of century is calculated to fill every considerate and feel-
> ing mind with emotions, which it is impossible to describe ... Such
> a change brings together, in one point of view, objects so vast, that
> the concerns which ordinarily engage our most anxious solicitude,
> dwindle, upon comparison, into almost total insignificance.

Unlike looking forward, retrospect is bound by fact. There are real events and real objects to work with and, like bricks and gravity, they constrain the architect's imagination. But at the same time memory is never static. We re-arrange and re-imag- ***a peg to hang one's thoughts on*** ine lost time, changing the filters so that sometimes it is "warm and coloured" as Henry James said, and sometimes it just reveals the sinister beginnings of all the trouble we now find ourselves in. But the stories we conceive from our histories do more than explain or justify us; they are our identities, both personal and social. So, if New Year's Eve is a time for private reflection, the turn of a century yields a larger public stock-taking. It is the nativity of a whole civilisation of Adams.

To some, it may seem absurd that a simple number should provoke such reflection. "Why make a fuss about the first of January 1, 1901?" wrote the editor of *The Nineteenth Century and After.* "This is a mere arbitrary point of our own fixing, in the whirling cycle." The reason, as the same author went on to muse, is that

> it's a peg to hang one's thoughts on ... here is a point that we have
> marked for ourselves in the flux of time. It suggests to us, inevitably,
> fresh wonderment at the flux which is carrying us all.

Frederic Harrison, a prolific exponent of the philosophy of logical posi- tivism, remarked upon the same irony, the paradox of an arbitrary number prompting meaningful contemplation. "The habit of treating a century as an organic whole," he began, skeptically, in an essay entitled "The Eight- eenth Century,"

> is the beaten path to superficial comparison. History, after all, is not
> grouped into natural periods of one hundred years, as different from
> each other as the life of the son from that of the father. Nor, what-
> ever the makers of chronologies may say, does mankind really turn
> over a new page in the great Record, so soon as the period of one
> hundred years is complete ... And as men are not born at the begin-
> ning of a century, and do not die at the end of it, but grow, flourish,
> and decay year by year and hour by hour, we are ever entering on a
> new epoch and completing an old one, did we but know it, on the
> first day of every year we live, nay, at the rising and the setting of
> every sun.

And yet, Harrison continued, the act of "constructing" a century at its end, of looking back and remembering, has genuine worth. It imposes order on the chaos of event:

> But though a century be an arbitrary period ... we must for conven-
> ience take note of conventional limits, and fix our attention on

special features as the true physiognomy of an epoch. History altogether is a wilderness, till we parcel it out.

And parcel it out they did. The fund of public retrospectives that appeared in the closing weeks of the eighteenth and nineteenth centuries was enormous. The December 30, 1900 issue of the *Boston Herald* was typical, featuring articles with headlines such as these: "Greatest Men of the Century," "Century's Wars: A Complete Record from Napoleon's Campaigns to the Trouble in China," "Arts and Sciences: Wonderful Progress in the Past Hundred Years," "Women of 1800: Ways and Work of Wives, Sisters and Sweethearts a Century Ago," "The Old and the New: Interesting Comparisons of Conditions and Customs in 1800 and 1900," "Portraits on Our Postage: Complete List of Stamps Issued by Uncle Sam up to End of Century." Other newspapers, from Paris to Vancouver, followed suit, prompting the *London Times* to observe on January 1, 1900 that "Moralists, with the century as well as the year behind them, are making a week of it. Everything is reviewed, from finance to football."

Everything is reviewed

In spite of their disparate subject matters—finance, football, postage, war—such retrospectives shared one assumption: their authors conceived of the turn of their century as not just a still point in time, but as an almost physical standpoint from which they could gaze back serenely on the preceding hundred years. The tropes and metaphors these authors employed, implicitly or explicitly, were spatial. The turn of a century is a threshold, a door through which we walk into another life. Or it is a mountaintop from which we see both backward and forward. As Virginia Woodward Cloud put it in an elegant sonnet written for the first day of the twentieth century, that "one white moment" between the centuries is a gate through which humanity must pass, though not without pausing to throw a contemplative glance back:

the watershed of this coming midnight

At the Gate

Nay: on thy lip a warning finger place
And stay thine eager steps. One moment wait
On hither side; one moment turn thy face
(Before thou shalt pass in and close the gate)
Back to the path by trembling Doubt made Sweet.
When yonder latch is lifted to thy hand,
The farthest limit pressed by thy glad feet,
And in the temple of thy dreams they stand,
Thou'lt long for what uncertainty made dear,
And know that Pain, not Joy, hath made thee wise.
Above each gate flames Duty's sword; 'tis here
The radiance of thy one white moment lies.
Then linger to enshrine it; stay thy feet,
And live this hour by trembling doubt made sweet!

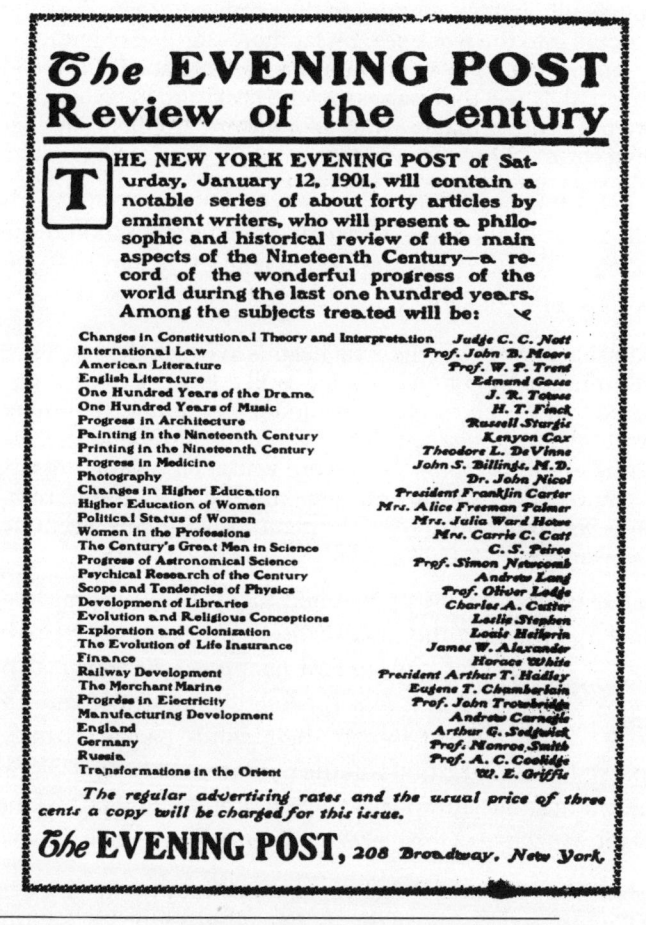

advertisement for the *Evening Post* of January 12, 1901

Ian MacLaren, a nineteenth-century novelist and minister, also gave the century-moment a physical form: for him it was like Pisgah, the mountain in Deuteronomy from which Moses could look back towards the slavery of Egypt and forward toward the milk and honey of the Promised Land. Another biblically-minded writer, the Dean of Windsor, employed this trope in the sermon he delivered at St. Paul's Cathedral on the first day of the twentieth century. "Standing on the threshold of a new century," he said, "we are in precisely the same position as the children of Israel. We cannot go back, and we cannot stand still. Whether we would or not, the irresistible sweep of time compels us to go forward." A secular version of this topographical metaphor appeared in an editorial in the *Boston Herald* on the last day of the nineteenth century:

> It is a startling feeling that comes over one when standing on the Alpine ridge which constitutes the watershed dividing between the rise and destiny of the Rhine and Danube rivers; the one to pursue

its course till finally it empties in the northern ocean, the other its till it pours into the Black sea. Yet far more startling ought to be the experience of millions, as, standing on the watershed of this coming . midnight, they feel themselves looking backward in review over the record of a century that is dying, and forward prophetically over the coming career of one new born.

Even in regions characterized by utterly flat topography—the Canadian prairies, for instance—essayists instinctively compared the turn of the century to a soaring promontory. On January 1, 1901 the editor of the *Manitoba Free Press* observed that

> Looking backward from the great heights to which the steady ascent of the nineteenth century has led is like looking from a plateau which stands far above the ever mounting foothills that mark the gradual uplift of the range. Turning to look into the future, we see towering ahead of us the vast ascent whose far off summits, rising with the century, will be crowned with the glory of the new day towards which the progress of humanity is advancing, ever onward and upward.

While the turn of a century inspired many, like this prairie editor, to peer ahead and imagine the mountainous prospects of an unknown future (as subsequent chapters will show), it provoked others of a less speculative and more reflective temperament to cast their minds backward to what had already passed. One of the first was the poet Samuel Taylor Coleridge, who wrote the chemist Sir Humphry Davy on January 1, 1800, asking him to include a retrospective of the eighteenth century in a book he was writing:

a series of dreams by an old lady

> I wish in your *Researches* that you and Beddoes would give a compact compressed History of the Human Mind for the last Century … Or if you won't do it there then do it for me and I will print it with an Essay I am now writing on the principles of Population and Progressiveness.

Davy was too busy to write the essay Coleridge desired, but as it turned out he needn't have worried. A similar project had already been undertaken by Hester Thrale, the friend and biographer of Samuel Johnson. "I could make a pretty book," she wrote in her diary, "to bring out on the last Days of 1799 or the first of 1800 could I get materials cleverly around me, and time for study: as anecdotes of the late century—not a history." Within a year, the scope of her book had grown, as she again recorded in her diary:

> Wednesday 20. Jan. 1796. Brynbella.
>   This day I determined on a project my brain has long been hatching—that of getting a book ready for publication this time five years if possible to come out early in 1801—containing a summary of events, general ideas of what has happened in the world during those centuries … I must make the title of it *Retrospection* … if by

God's mercy the volumes should be completed, they may be really useful to some, and entertaining to others, and may bring me in a thousand pounds first and last.

Mrs. Thrale believed her idea to be so original, and so theft-worthy, that she swore her own daughter to secrecy. She published her book on the first day of the nineteenth century as *Retrospection: or A Review of the Most Striking and Important Events, Characters, Situations, and Their Consequences, which The Last Eighteen Hundred Years have Presented to the View of Mankind.* Over a thousand pages long, and riddled with typographical errors because of the rush to have it out for the turn of the century (imagine!), *Retrospection* was dismissed by *The Critical Review* as "a series of dreams by an old lady." It sold only 516 copies.

While Mrs. Thrale boldly attempted to review eighteen centuries of world history, others writing at the end of a century attempted more limited retrospectives. When novelist Arnold Bennett looked backward on the last day of 1899, he reviewed only his own literary output, though his meticulous number-crunching seems more befitting an overzealous accountant than a man of letters:

> Sunday, December 31st, 1899.
> This year I have written 335,340 words, grand total, 228 articles and stories (including 4 instalments of a serial of 30,000—7,500 words each) have actually been published. Also my book of plays—*Polite Farces.* I have written six or eight shorts stories not yet published or sold. Also the greater part of a 55,000 serial—*Love and Life*—for Tillitsons, which begins publication about April of next year. Also the whole draft (80,000 words) of my Staffordshire novel *Anna Tellwright.* My Total earnings were £592 3s.1d., of which sum I have yet to receive £72 10s.

Bennet was proud, even smug, about what he had accomplished over the past year. That pride was writ large in most of the writers who reviewed their entire century in the closing weeks of 1800 and 1900. After all, the old century belonged to those writers, and they to it—one of its years had witnessed their birth. Writing in *deemed a madman* the January, 1801 issue of the *Gentlemen's Magazine*, one century reviewer sounded like a doting parent as he claimed that the intellectual accomplishments of the eighteenth century—*his* century—surpassed those of any other in world history:

> To prove that the eighteenth century is unequalled by any of the preceding ones, especially in England, we need but remark that it boasts a Newton, Locke, Johnson, Handel, Wren, Chambers, Reynolds, Henway, Howard, and many others.

The editor of a rival magazine, *The Oracle*, agreed, saying that the eighteenth century "may be fairly considered as the most important of any that history has related since the downfall of the Roman Empire." A columnist

Greatest Men of the Century

CENTURY'S WARS
Complete Record from Napoleon's Campaigns to the Trouble in China.

GOOD-BY TO KINGS
Con Ethan Allen Thinks There Will Be None at End of Next Century.

A ROSY FORECAST
Most Thoughtful Men of the Day Outline Great Things for New Century.

SPHERE OF WOMAN.
How It Has Broadened Told by Leading Women, Who Are Very Hopeful.

LABOR'S OUTLOOK
Edwin Markham and Others See a Bright Future for the Workingman.

Good Man's Fall, By Holman Day.

A WAR ON BRYAN
United Effort to Oust Him and Regenerate the Democratic Party.

SONG BY E. S. FOGG
Pretty Melody. "The Old Schoolhouse by the Brook." Words and Music.

CLASSIC STONE.
Carrara's Marble Quarries in Italy May Pass Under Yankee Control.

HOOLIGAN MOBS.
Julian Ralph Tells of Their Supreme Contempt for Police of London.

BEAUTY SUPREME
Pan-American Exposition, First of the New Century Will Be a Wonder.

from the *Boston Herald*, December 30, 1900 (and opposite page)

for *Bell's Weekly Messenger* went further, proposing that the achievements of the eighteenth century had outstripped all previous centuries put together: "The elapsed century has exhibited unparalleled phenomena, ideas, and deeds, that cannot be traced in all the mental combinations nor in the most extraordinary acts of our ancestors." The poet Matthew Prior upped the ante yet again when he asserted that the eighteenth century would not even be surpassed by the centuries to come: "Nothing went before so great, And nothing greater can succeed."

We can imagine the chuckles Prior's confident claim might have provoked a hundred years later when the nineteenth century drew to its close. "We know," wrote the editor of the *London Times*,

> that the nineteenth century surpassed the most extravagant fancies of the eighteenth. The man who on January 1, 1801, should have set forth a plain tale of even the half of what is realized and is commonplace on January 1, 1901, would inevitably have been deemed a madman.

The same editor then made a bolder declaration, unaware, no doubt, of the similar claim a hundred years earlier. "It has been said," he wrote, "and truly, as we believe, that the nineteenth century surpassed the sum total of all the eighteen that had gone before in the Christian era." His assertion was echoed in *The Outlook* where a contributor stated that

the actual gain made in the realm of science in the nineteenth century is really comparable, not with the eighteenth or any one century preceding, but with all recorded history.

A contributor to the *Spectator* then rounded out the glowing assessment of the nineteenth century by assuring his readers, as Matthew Prior had done before, that even future centuries would pale in comparison to the one just ending:

> But, so far as one sees, no coming century can ever bring about so vast an advance in our conceptions of the material universe, of the world we live in, and of our own bodies as the one that is now running swiftly to an end. The advance from the all but zero of 1800, in the majority of the sciences, is greater in proportion than any advance from our present state can be.

Not satisfied with these vague boasts, one author attempted to demonstrate the pre-eminence of the nineteenth century more methodically. In *The Wonderful Century*, published slightly prematurely in 1898, Alfred Russel Wallace—who collaborated with Charles Darwin in developing the theory of natural selection—compared the discoveries and inventions of the nineteenth century with those of all previous centuries. "We find," he concluded, "only five inventions of the first rank in all preceding time—the telescope, the printing press, the mariner's compass, Arabic numerals, and alphabetical writing." To this list of five

the uses of dust

Wallace added, after further reflection, two more—the steam engine and the barometer—making a list of seven important discoveries for all time before the advent of the nineteenth century. In contrast, Wallace asserted, the nineteenth century itself could claim twenty-six major discoveries or inventions, including railways (#1), the telegraph (#2), Lucifer matches (#5), the velocity of light (#17), the uses of dust (#18), and germ theory (#26). Dust may seem an odd inclusion, but nineteenth-century scientists had learned that atmospheric particles helped turn water vapour into precipitation.

Wallace had proven that the nineteenth century was four times as great as the rest of history, because it could claim nearly four times as many scientific achievements: "Both as regards the number and the quality of its onward advances, the age in which we have lived fully merits the title I have ventured to give it—The Wonderful Century."

Wallace's American counterpart was the indefatigable Henry Davenport Northrop whose *Grandest Century in the World's History*—one of twenty-six books he published between 1899 and 1901—found grandeur in everything from battles to agriculture to *the world's greatest sons* "the sublime triumph of electricity." "Such a Century Plant," he wrote, "unfolding its wonderful blossoms, has not been seen before in the history of man." And like Wallace he revealed a few quirks of his own; whereas Wallace condemned the relative neglect of phrenology, Northrop devoted a full chapter to the origin and growth of Mormonism.

Many reviewers borrowed Wallace's ranking approach, and sifted the accomplishments of the nineteenth century into tidy lists of the "top ten" or "top hundred." (As familiar to us as late-night television, these "century lists" were new: no one at the end of 1800 had attempted to systematically rank the deeds of the eighteenth century.) One such list appeared in the *Boston Herald* on December 30, 1900. Entitled "The Fifty Greatest Men of this Century," the two-page spread was bordered by fifty portraits of white, bearded, sober faces. "Who are the world's greatest sons?" began the piece—

> What made them great? What influences have they left upon the present generation? With the sun of the twentieth century breaking through the grey of the dying year, it may not be out of place, perhaps, to take a backward peek at the celebrities who have made the last hundred years notable.

The men in the list included Johann Wolfgang von Goethe, Honoré de Balzac, Walt Whitman, Sir Walter Scott, William Thackeray, Charles Dickens, Lord Byron, Heinrich Heine, Lord Tennyson, Robert Browning, Friedrich von Schiller, Samuel Taylor Coleridge, Victor Hugo, Alexandre Dumas, Nathaniel Hawthorne, Henry Wadsworth Longfellow, and James Russell Lowell—as well as dozens of others now forgotten by most late twentieth-century readers. The inclusion of each worthy was justified in a

GRANDEST CENTURY

IN

THE WORLD'S HISTORY

CONTAINING A

FULL AND GRAPHIC ACCOUNT OF THE MARVELOUS ACHIEVE-
MENTS OF ONE HUNDRED YEARS

INCLUDING

GREAT BATTLES AND CONQUESTS; THE RISE AND FALL OF NATIONS;
WONDERFUL GROWTH AND PROGRESS OF THE UNITED STATES;
FAMOUS EXPLORATIONS, DISCOVERIES, ETC., ETC.

SUBLIME TRIUMPHS OF ELECTRICITY

REMARKABLE INVENTIONS; PROGRESS OF SCIENCE, LITERATURE, ART
AND AGRICULTURE; CELEBRATED MEN AND WOMEN
OF THE CENTURY, ETC., ETC.

By HENRY DAVENPORT NORTHROP
Author of "Gem Cyclopedia of Universal Knowledge," " Queen of Republics," Etc., Etc.

Profusely Embellished with a large number of
Phototype and Wood Engravings

NATIONAL PUBLISHING CO.
PHILADELPHIA, PA.

Title page from Henry Davenport Northrop's *Grandest Century
in the World's History*, 1900

pithy sentence or two: Goethe because he possessed "the most universal
mind that the world has ever produced," Whitman because he was the
poet of "athletic democracy, of jubilant health, and the creative powers of
mankind."

Other newspapers and columnists devised rival lists of the greatest
men of the century. The list in the December 1900 issue of *The Outlook*
included Georg Hegel, Giuseppe Mazzini, Immanuel Kant, Hermann von
Helmholtz, Friedrich Schleiermacher, and Herbert Spencer. In *The Dial*,
social critic Jackson Boyd proposed a list including Karl Marx, Jeremy
Bentham, and Leo Tolstoy, a selection that prompted one respondent to
fight back with a counter-list that named Edgar Allan Poe, Honoré de
Balzac, John Ruskin, George Meredith, Robert Browning, and others.

Some list-makers tried refining their criteria by selecting not the greatest men of the century but the greatest books. One such list of titles appeared on January 1, 1901 in *The Dial* and included page-turners such as Charles Lyell's *Principles of Geology*, Hermann von Helmholtz's *Tonempfindungen*, Friedrich Froebel's *Education of Man*, Franz Bopp's *Comparative Grammar*, Henry Maine's *Ancient Law*, and Barthold Niebuhr's *Römische geschichte*. Of course, none of the dozens of lists included exactly the same selections as any other; the principles of selection were entirely subjective. Edward Everett Hale, an American clergyman and popular author, included John Ruskin's *Modern Painters* on his list simply because he felt that book had "sent young men and young women out from their houses into the open air and made them read clouds, trees,

the master dogma of the century
vapours, and mountains as they had not read them before." Hale included novels by Victor Hugo for an even more peculiar reason: "For myself, I do not read Victor Hugo. But people do read him in France and Germany, and I think he made a good many dead men take up their beds and walk."

Although each list was idiosyncratic, there was one book that appeared in almost all of them, and usually near the top: Charles Darwin's *Origin of Species*, first published in 1859. Most list-makers shared the sentiment expressed in *The Dial* on January 1, 1901:

> The book of the nineteenth century, beyond any possibility of a successful challenge to its pre-eminence, is *The Origin of Species*, by Charles Darwin ... It is doubtful if any other book, in all the history of modern thought, has been so far-reaching in its influence, or productive of such immense intellectual results.

Even reviewers of the century who despised Darwin's theory could not deny the influence it had on the nineteenth century. Jackson Boyd noted that because of the theory of natural selection,

> Men are asking, Why hesitate in consigning to a lethal chamber all idiots, lunatics, and hopeless incurables? And in the larger field of national politics, why should we show any mercy to the weak? Might becomes right.

It was frightening implications such as these that led Boyd to affirm grimly that Darwin's "doctrine of evolution ... may be regarded as the master dogma of the century."

Besides Darwin, the names that recur most often as greats of the nineteenth century are Goethe and Hegel. There is not, as we might expect, any mention of Freud, but there are indications that many already realized the significance of Marx. As a contributor wrote in "The Great Books of the Century," published in *The Dial* on January 1, 1901:

> The propaganda of socialism has become so marked a feature in the political life of most of the civilized nations that it cannot be ignored

in any survey of the tendencies of nineteenth century thought, and credit must be given to the book which, more than any other, has been responsible for this movement. That book, it need hardly be added, is the *Kapital* of Karl Marx.

Although many of the list-makers managed to select individuals or books whose reputations have continued to flourish in the twentieth century, others—like the author of "The Century's Progress in Education and Literature"—were far less prescient:

> What new material the nineteenth century has given to fiction has been furnished by American writers. Joel Chandler Harris, George W. Cable, William Dean Howells and others have taken fresh materials and dealt with them with the genius of artists. Their work will live when much that is now popular of the writings of Englishmen will have been entirely forgotten.

Although Harris (the creator of Uncle Remus), Cable (the author of *Old Creole Days*), and Howells (a columnist for *Harper's*) still merit a paragraph or two in American encyclopaedias, it would be a stretch to say their works still "live." On the other hand, some authors seem conspicuously absent from the lists, at least from our late ***their work will live*** twentieth-century perspective. None of the lists, for instance, includes Herman Melville (who published *Moby Dick* in 1851) or Mark Twain (who published *Tom Sawyer* in 1876 and *Huckleberry Finn* in 1884). Anton Chekhov and Lewis Carroll are also not mentioned. Henry James is cited on a single list.

Perhaps to avoid risking the ridicule of posterity, some authorities attempted to sidestep the issue of "the century's greatest." That was the strategy employed by William Watson, a specialist in writing poems about the deaths of other poets, when he was put on the spot by *Harmsworth Magazine*:

> You ask me to say what I consider to be the finest poem of the nineteenth century. I could as easily tell you what flower I consider to be the most exquisitely perfumed, what woman's face the loveliest, what mountain peak the most majestic that I have ever seen … There are no rivalries in Art.

Without exception, these end-of-the-century lists comprised only men—their names, their inventions, their books, their deeds. Also without exception, these lists of "the greatest" were compiled by men. Women, in the closing weeks of 1900, indulged in the retrospective impulse, but they did not systematically catalogue and rank as they looked backward over the preceding hundred years. Instead, they simply lauded the nineteenth century for effecting social transformations in the sphere of women. For these writers, the nineteenth century had put an end to all manner of primitive and oppressive assumptions. Writing in the opening days of the twentieth century, Ida Husted Harper, suffragist, scorned "the

from the *Boston Herald*, December 30, 1900 (and opposite page)

sad-faced widow and sour-visaged old maid of a hundred years ago whose only vocation was to eke out an existence with sewing or teaching or to

sour-visaged old maid of a hundred years ago

cumber another's home." She despised, too, "the dainty first-of-the-century maiden who burst into tears upon the slightest occasion and swooned at the sight of a mouse." She laughed to think that a hundred years earlier a renowned physician, Dr. Gregory, had advised young women to "simulate such sickly delicacy as is necessary to keep up the proper female charm."

Now, Harper proclaimed, in 1900, there were new models for young women to emulate: the "end-of-the-century golf-girl" who stood "muscular" and "stoutly shod," or the "bright-eyed business woman of today, forging a way for herself among the world's gainful occupations." These were "strides worthy of a hundred years."

In her first syndicated newspaper column of the twentieth century, Margaret Sanger, founder of the birth control movement, said that women of the early nineteenth century "took cold if exposed to a shower" because they "had not our strong health nor our immunity from nervous irritation." While the women of 1800 "could not walk over a frosty meadow because of their thin kid shoes," Sanger's readers—whom she affection-

ately addressed as "my girls"—could traipse about "without the slightest inconvenience in our short skirts and thick boots." For Sanger, the nineteenth century had been, in short, the "wonderful century" because it had witnessed the evolution of women:

> Young women a century ago fainted with ease, and frequently dissolved in floods of tears if vexed or reproved. I hope that my girls neither faint nor weep, except for very grave reasons. Then, too, the mother of the twentieth century girl does not lace her daughter till breathing is anguish ... Nor does she caution her girls against too much exercise, nor blush at their healthy appetites, this sensible mother of the period.

The perception that the women of the early nineteenth century had been weepy, breathless creatures was almost a commonplace. Writing in the *Atlantic Monthly* in 1901, journalist Elisabeth Bisland—who in 1889 had affirmed women's independence by racing Nellie Bly around the world in less than eighty days—also lampooned the neurotic women of her great, great grandmother's generation:

> Tears were always flowing ... A "delicate female" was a creature so finely constituted that the slightest shock caused hysterics or a swoon, and it was useless to hope for her recovery until the person

guilty of the blow to her sensitiveness had shed the salt moisture of repentance upon her cold and lifeless hand, and had wildly adjured her to "*live*," after which her friends of the same sex, themselves tremulous and much shaken by the mere sight of such sensibility, "recovered her with an exhibition of lavender water," or with some of the cordials which they all carried in their capacious pockets for such exigencies.

Of course, not everyone saw the changes in the sphere of women as progress. Writing in *The Independent* in the opening months of the twentieth century, Henry T. Finck longed for "the good old times" when women were "flowers" instead of "vegetables"—that is, when they were "ornamental" instead of "useful." Similarly, in the January 1901 issue of *The Contemporary Review*, someone calling himself "Rusticus" lamented the "decay of domesticity" and censured the nineteenth century for having allowed women to forget their wifely duties:

> Women used to be able to make their husbands' shirts. Give nine cottage women out of ten nowadays a couple of dozen yards of calico, and they could no more turn it into shirts than they could turn a lump of pig-iron into a dinner-knife.

Rusticus sounds more like a crank than a thoughtful social critic, but he was not alone in looking backward and faulting the old century. There *a tangled mass of larvae* was, in fact, a minority of authorities and writers who voiced such dissent, employing the turn of the century not as a metaphoric mountain-top from which to extol the preceding hundred years, but as a soap-box from which to decry every aspect of it. The novelist Emile Zola—who as a young man had suffered such poverty that he was forced to eat sparrows trapped in his attic—was scathing in his social retrospective. His review of the preceding hundred years was solicited by the *Chicago Tribune*, which asked him "Has the century brought happiness?":

> Has the telephone, electric lights, or the telegraph diminished the hunger of the hungry? Civilized? Not yet! Despite our self-satisfied bumptiousness mankind is still piteously groping after real civilization, like a tangled mass of larvae tumbling and crawling out of some dark, slimy cavern toward the light that will give them wings ... Our brains are still befogged; our private and public life is still based upon vile, exasperating ignorance. Reason, now proclaimed by a hundred prophets in every country, has everywhere the greatest trouble to penetrate through the thick folds of inane prejudice.

Writing in the January 6, 1900 issue of *Literature*, novelist George Gissing also diagnosed a weakening of moral fibre, linking it to the single-minded pursuit of scientific achievements that had dominated the nineteenth century:

> Physical science, which vaunted so large a promise, stands bankrupt before the human soul; it has quickened hunger, yet offers no

food; it has stung the multitudes with a base ambition, and smirched the ideal even of those who try to hold aloof. The man of science has allied himself with the man of the shop.

For Frederic Harrison, writing this time an essay entitled "Christianity at the Grave of the Nineteenth Century," what had debased the values of the old century was self-evident—the press:

> We fell more and more under the rule of the newspaper press; and the press grew more and more noisy, braggart, bustling and smart. It got so furiously up-to-date that it even announced events before they had happened, and smashed books before they had been read.

Literary authors, too, said Harrison, had been complicit in undermining public decency by turning to the streets for dialogue:

> In prose and in verse, the favourite style is the Cockney slang of the costermonger, the betting ring, and the barrack canteen. The reek of the pot-house, the music hall, the turf, the share market, the thieves' fence, infects our literature, our manners, our amusements, and our ideals of life.

Andrew Lang, the renowned translator of Homer, elaborated Harrison's attack on the press by tracing a decay in the public's reading habits that had occurred in the course of the nineteenth century. Entitled "The Decline of Intellect," Lang published his essay in *The Critic* in December 1900. "Our intellectual interests have ***wild and vain theories*** descended in the course of 1800–1900," he said. A century-long "process of degeneracy" had transformed most British citizens into mere "sixpenny readers"—readers of those cheap novels that we now call pulp fiction. "The sixpenny reader," said Lang, "does not want to understand. He is in a state of abject intellectual indolence," spurning serious literature and books about history, "complaining even of references and footnotes." In locating the nineteenth-century root of this intellectual decay, Lang was bizarrely specific: "Our intellectual degeneracy, I trace—to Sir Walter Scott."

> Before 1814, the birth year of *Waverley*, novels were mere objects of contempt among the world of educated readers. By 1832, the year of Scott's death, Bulwer Lytton could seriously state that no literature but novel-writing had any pecuniary reward.

According to Lang, Scott's historical novels had adulterated the public's mind and instigated a "period of rapid degeneracy"—people had turned to baser and baser reading materials:

> Then arose railways, with railway bookstalls, and scrap periodicals; and photography, and flimsy picture books ... then the whirlpool of anecdote, interview, fustian, and police romance.

Such attacks on the old century were hardly new. A hundred years earlier, in the December 1800 issue of *The Gentleman's Magazine*, a sour

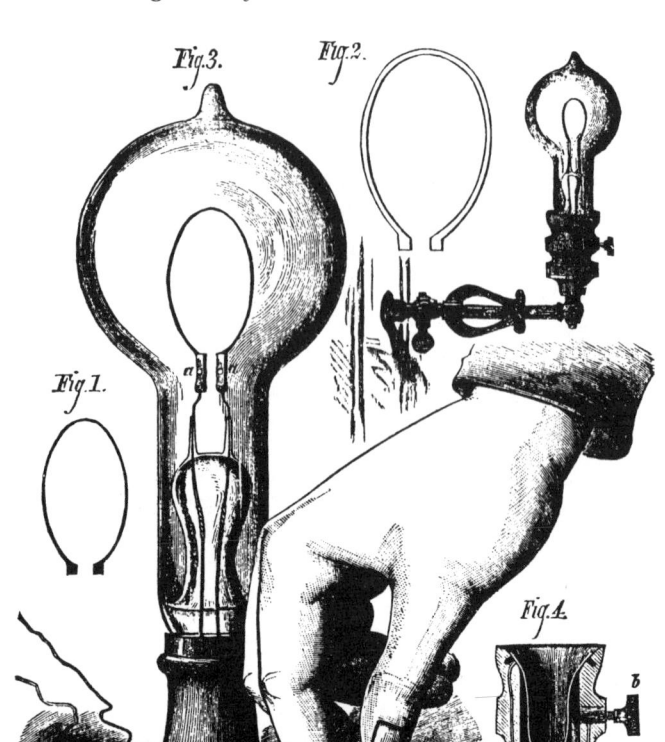

EDISON'S MARVELLOUS INCANDESCENT LAMP.

from *Grandest Century in the World's History* by Henry
Davenport Northrop, 1900

contributor had acknowledged the scientific advances of the eighteenth
century, but only as a warm-up to disparage their effect:

> Whilst one century has produced all these changes, we do not say
> (though knowledge has extended) that wisdom and good sense have
> increased; nor, though riches and wealth have multiplied, do we
> presume to decide as to real happiness; and we are sorry to see a
> general disposition to despise what is ancient, and to shew a con-
> tempt for the wisdom of our ancestors, which leads to wild and vain
> theories, and conducts men to those experiments, which end in
> unhappiness and confusion.

John Bowles was no less incriminating in his *Reflections on the Political
and Moral State of Society at the Close of the Eighteenth Century*. The very
foundations of society, he claimed, were never "in so calamitous or so
perilous a state" as in 1800, "this awful juncture." The upper classes, he
wrote, had abandoned the countryside for the "dissipated metropolis"

where they could pursue "voluptuous indulgences" and "expensive and enervating pleasures." The middle classes had "turned their minds from the attainment of competence to the acquisition of wealth." And even the "lower orders" had begun to "entertain notions of independence, alike injurious to themselves and to society at large."

It was the terrible eighteenth century, Bowles said, which had overseen this destruction of the class system, but something else had actually effected it: the press, already exerting the evil influence for which it would again be maligned a century later. For Bowles, however, the press included not just the "red writing" of news-hungry journalists, but novels, book reviews, grammar textbooks—anything, in short, that could be read:

> Other means are certainly resorted to for the same detestable purpose; but none is so much calculated for the universal circulation of bad principles as the press, which is incessantly employed, at once to corrupt the fountains of science, and to stimulate the lower orders to tumult and insurrection. To these baneful effects it is made subservient by every mode and species of publication ... by novels teeming not only with allurements to vice, but with the horrors of blasphemy, by new Annual Registers, by Monthly Magazines, and Critical Reviews, by cheap tracts, and Jacobin Newspapers—and even by reports of Parliamentary Speeches.

As they looked backward in both 1900 and 1800, what appeared to be a "wonderful century" to some reviewers clearly appeared to be "unhappiness and confusion" to others. Still others, however, refrained from explicit moral judgements, and merely noted that the completion of a hundred year cycle had an existential impact, for better or worse, on the human psyche. Annie Russell Marble was one such, remarking in *The Dial* on February 16, 1901, that

> Critics have noted that the period at the meeting of centuries, arbitrary rather than logical in division of time, is often marked by unrest, contradiction, and transition. Whether such symptoms are psychological or pathological, it is not our part to discuss.

Others commented, again without passing judgement, on how the preceding hundred years had altered humanity's conception of the universe, making it seem both a smaller and a bigger place. One author, looking back from the vantage of 1800, was *it is not our part to discuss* amazed that the eighteenth century had pushed the boundaries of outer space far beyond anything imaginable in the year 1700: "Optical glasses opened a vast and unbounded theatre to our perception, and promised to carry our views still farther and farther into the universe." At the same time developments in communication—simple things like an improved postal system and the use of optical telegraphs— made the world seem more tiny. The *Annual Register* for the year 1800 noted that "There was no preceding period when so great a portion of the human race conversed with one another, verbally or mentally, and with so much facility." The Reverend Charles Backus, in a sermon delivered on January 1, 1801, likewise observed that "the inhabitants of the earth have had more mutual intercourse within the last century, than in any former period." And a contributor to *The Gentlemen's Magazine* contrasted the "diffuse" world of the early eighteenth century with the tightly-bound one of the year 1800:

> Now it is different ... All the learned men in different countries correspond with each other, and communicate information; and it is a circumstance, perhaps the most honorable of any recorded of the human race, that in matters of general utility, whether in what is conducive to health, to plenty, or general happiness, arising from discovery, the world is but as one family, and whatever is known is as freely communicated.

A hundred years later people again looked backward and again felt that the world had simultaneously expanded and contracted. As a contributor to the *Los Angeles Daily Times* wrote on January 1, 1901, the microscope had extended the limit of the known universe far beyond anything imaginable a century earlier:

> Perhaps the most marked characteristic of scientific research in the nineteenth century, has been its study of the infinitely little. It has been an age of inconceivably minute and accurate measurements. Each branch of science has turned microscope or spectroscope to seek for some primal cause, the atom, the molecule, the cell, the microbe, the number of lines in the spectrum, the number of vibrations of light or heat. The micrometer has played the part that the mariner's compass did in the age of discoveries.

And yet if the microscope and spectroscope had expanded the limit of the observable universe, other innovations had again made the planet seem far smaller than it once was. In a column entitled "The Shrinkage of the World," a contributor to *The Review of Reviews* noted that

> The reduction of the duration of the Atlantic passage from twenty-six days to less than six, is no small achievement for a single century ... It is a curious reflection that Louis XIV, whether on sea or land, could not move more rapidly than Julius Caesar ... But the Nineteenth Century has changed all that ... Man mounts a bicycle, and trebles his speed; climbs into a locomotive, and swoops across the country for hundreds of miles on end at over a mile a minute. At sea he has more than doubled his speed. The result is, that although space has not been abolished, every one is nearer neighbours with every one else. The world has become perceptibly smaller. Nations are to one another now almost as parishes were in the last century.

A literary version of the same sentiment appeared in "The Shrinking Earth," a poem published in *The Chatauquay's* last issue of the nineteenth century:

And then a strange thing came to view
That set the wise to thinking:
As man in skill and wisdom grew,
The earth kept shrinking, shrinking.

The steamships throbbing o'er the deep,
The cables creeping under,
Contracted all the seas that keep
The continents asunder.

A hundred miles became as ten
Where iron steeds went rushing,
And myriads, soon, of angry men
For ampler room were pushing.

Looking backward on December 31, 1999 (or 2000), we might make very similar declarations about the twentieth century. Our universe has extended far beyond what anyone could have imagined in 1900, beyond Pluto, beyond the galaxy, even beyond the cluster of galaxies to which the Milky Way belongs; it *the world looks before and after* has extended, too, to include both a subatomic universe and a universe that Freud began to map—the unconscious. And yet the same hundred years has also contracted the universe in a way that could not be fathomed by Wallace, or Northrop, or Rusticus. We can turn on the TV and see camps of Armenian refugees as if we are looking out a window. We can log on to the Internet and view—live—a colleague in Paris or a heart operation in Miami. Add to this other claims that recall those of our turn-of-the-century predecessors—the twentieth century has pushed technology further than all centuries before, the twentieth century is more immoral than any previous century, the twentieth century has pandered to a debased media—and we see, wearing different costumes and holding other props, ourselves.

And perhaps, too, we are like our predecessors in our ability to simultaneously belittle and believe in the regenerative power of a new century. As a contributor wrote in the January, 1901 issue of *The World's Work*,

> No one expects the figures on the dial of the centuries to work any immediate changes ... And yet the imagination is touched. There is solemnity in the sounding of the fateful hour. The world looks "before and after" ... And where the imagination is touched, there may well be, in some subtle way, an effect upon human action.

Chapter Five

Looking Forward
Fear and Trembling

"I got drunk on the mornin' of the new century y'r honor," explained Tuffold Knutt, "to drown my sorrer."

"What was there about the new century to fill you with sorrow?" asked the magistrate.

"I got to thinkin' that mebby I wouldn't live through it, y'r honor."
—*Chicago Tribune*, January 2, 1901

THE PAST MAY MAKE US quake with shame or weep for all that we've lost but at least it stands there solidly behind us, knowable and done with. We are not in a trembling state of expectation when we think it over—there's no suspense in looking back. We enjoy the lists and catalogues of what we have lived through—"100 Best Novels of the Century" or "Great Infamies of the Past Hundred Years"—because they are familiar. In the face of the millennium, that excess of futurity, we need to hear about the old days. Like children wanting to hear the same story again and again, we are comforted by going over what was. Repetition soothes us.

But the unknown piques our imagination and quickens our hearts, either with excitement or anxiety. To some, as we'll see in the next chapter, *same as ever it was* a new century is an undiscovered country that inspires radiant hope. To others, as we'll see in this chapter, it is a *terra incognita* that provokes "sorrer" and fear—fear of death, fear of degeneration, fear of apocalypse—and even, paradoxically, the fear that nothing at all is going to change.

Throughout the last year of the nineteenth century, a Russian playwright toiled away on a rather mirthless drama called *The Three Sisters*: in its closing scenes, a drunken doctor fails to help the victims of a fire and a young lover is killed in a duel. Yet despite its grim plot, Anton Chekhov called his play a comedy, a claim perhaps prompted by the aloof transcendence that sometimes characterizes intellectual life at the end of a century—it's as if the century's end is a pinnacle so high that, looking down, all the triumphs and catastrophes of humanity blur into laughable insignificance. Viewed from the distant perch of futurity, human activity is reduced to the scurrying of ants. That, at least, is the cosmic, and perhaps comic, perspective of Tuzenbach, one of the central characters in Chekhov's *fin-de-siècle* play:

> VERSHININ: Life, what will it be like when we're dead, imagine it in two or three hundred years' time.
>
> TUZENBACH: We're dead and gone, people will be flying in balloons, fashions will have changed, a sixth sense will be discovered and developed perhaps, but life will be, in essence, the same: difficult, very mysterious, and happy. In a thousand years' time people will still be crying: "Life, life is hard," but they'll fear dying and run from death just as they do now ... Two or three hundred years, a million years pass, and life is still the same as ever it was. It doesn't change, it's constant, it follows its own laws.

Many echoed Tuzenbach's scepticism. "Life to come will be much like life that has been, an admixture of good and evil," wrote Rabbi Voorsanger in the *San Francisco Examiner*'s first issue of the twentieth century. It was a dour sentiment shared by the editor of the *Boston Herald:* "What a fine thing it would be for this merry world," he wrote on January 1, 1901,

same old mitten

> had it sloughed its skin with the old year, and started in today young and fresh again, the glamour of sophistication extinguished in the clear light of regeneration. But, on the contrary, here we all are, and just as badly off as before we stepped across the border into this untried territory of time.

This end-of-the-century *weltschmurz* was expressed poetically as well. On the second last day of the nineteenth century the little-known Marie Nelson Lee published this in the *Chicago Tribune:*

Something of a Sameness

Same old winter,
 Same old year,
Same old dying,
 Same old bier.

Same old New Year,
 Same old boy,
Same old watch-meet,
 Same old joy.

Same old jokelet,
 Same old rhyme,
Same old whiskers,
 Same old Time.

Same old leaf turned,
 Same old make
Same old promise—
 Same old break.

Same old fellows,
  Same old call,
Same old bid to
  Same old ball.

Same old music,
  Same old whirl,
Same old tryst with
  Same old girl.

Same old question—
  Same old give
Same old mitten,
  Same old live!

Marie Nelson was perhaps whistling in the dark—along with Rabbi Voorsanger, Tuzenbach, and the editor of the *Boston Herald*—in claiming that the new century would bring with it nothing worse than nothing at all. Others—either more fearful or more forthright—proclaimed that big, bad changes were coming down the pike. That at least, was the portent of the new century for many when it dawned in 1901 and, to a lesser extent, in 1801.

"The worm shall feed sweetly on us," James Dana told his New Haven congregation on the first Sunday of the nineteenth century. "Soon the grave, which waits for us, will be our house." Reverend Charles Backus, also in Connecticut, was equally blunt in the sermon he delivered a few days earlier on January 1, 1801. "We must die," he said to his listeners, pausing dramatically, not knowing that he himself had but two more years to live. "There is not one now on earth," he continued,

expect to be numbered with the dead

> who took an active part in the concerns of life when the last century commenced. There are very few individuals on this globe, who were born a hundred years ago. We meet on an occasion which is new to us all. Before the return of another such day, every one of us must expect to be numbered with the dead.

Dana and Backus, along with Tuffold Knutt who took to drink, were of course stating the obvious: we are mortal. Nonetheless, it is a startling thing to be reminded—out loud and in front of your friends and neighbours—that you will shortly be dissolving in your grave. But for eighteenth-century sermonizers the fact that death is fearsome is what makes its prospect wholesome: it prompts reflection on the existential choice facing all humanity—live it up and go to hell, or fear the Lord and go to heaven.

That, at least, was the message Dana and Backus went on to deliver, as did Charles Gildersleeve in a sermon preached near the end of the eighteenth century to his congregation at Midway, Georgia:

frontispiece from *Forecasts of the Coming Century by a Decade of Writers*, Manchester: The Labour Press, 1897.

Let us look forward through a century to come, and ask, where will you be at the close of it? Objects awfully solemn here rise into view. All swept off the stage of time—launched on the boundless ocean of eternity—not one will be left—your fathers, who left New-England one hundred years since, are gone—not one of them remains. The same will be said of you, one hundred years hence. You must then either be stinking from gulf to gulf in hell, under the pangs of eternal death; or towering from glory to glory in Heaven, in beatitude divine.

Of course, sermons on fire and brimstone have been liturgical showstoppers since the Middle Ages: the closing days of the eighteenth century merely provided a convenient peg from which clergymen could dangle visions of eternal torment recycled from countless sermons preached long before the century's end. But even among the laity—ordinary people—it appears the end of the eighteenth century inspired a melancholy fetishizing of death. In the *Gentleman's Magazine* for December 1799 an unnamed contributor brooded upon the whereabouts of all those worthies who had breathed their last in the eighteenth century:

> There is something awful, and improving, in the thought that we cannot be admitted to a communion with those elevated spirits who have gone before us, but by passing through the vale of death ...
> As we wander through the mansions of the illustrious dead, the inquisitive observer naturally demands, "What is become of the minds that once informed these bodies?" The eye that sparkled with intelligence, the heart that beat with generosity, now lie mouldering in the dust.

One hundred years later, the closing hours of the nineteenth century again provoked "grave" thoughts, variations on Freud's glum observation that the new century contains the dates of our death. Newspaper editors, the secular heirs of the last century's sermonizers, were especially prone to such melancholy meditations. The editor of the *Manitoba Free Press*, for example, solemnly reminded his readers that "We have the best of the dying century, but the next one will vanquish all those who now see the birth of the new." The editor of the *Chicago Tribune* assured his more excitable readers that "those who indulge in tonight's riot of noise will be gone before the twenty-first century comes in." The editor of *Puck* sighed that "few of us will see all of this century," adding the feeble consolation that the new era would probably turn out "worse than I hope, but better than I fear."

not more than seventy-five

A reporter for the *New York Times* attempted a more scientific tally of the new century's anticipated death toll. After some hasty calculations, the reporter concluded that "Not more than seventy-five people now living in the United States will behold the dawn of the twenty-first century." He could not have imagined how medical advances would extend the human lifespan: in fact, on the first day of the twenty-first century, more than fifty-thousand U.S. citizens—frail but quite alive—will be able to place their birthday in the nineteenth century.

Other writers committed their intimations of mortality to verse. In the December 1900 issue of *The Gentleman's Magazine*, E. M. Rutherford published "The Dying Century," a poem in which the nineteenth century and all who were born within it are marching forward to the crypt:

> White gath'ring clouds hide out the waning moon,
> Through the long night they veil the winter sky.
> A shroud! a shroud! a shroud for such as have to die!
> The open grave must have its tenant soon.
>
> Open and waiting! Silently tonight,
> Perchance, they hither bring thy winding sheet,
> Cover thy hoary head and helpless feet,
> And lay thee low, away from mortal sight.

WANTED TO GO TO THE BOTTOM.

——x——

John Haslam, a carpenter, aged 48, living in Hackney Road, Shoreditch, was charged on Monday with attempting to commit suicide.

Constable Patrick Weldon, 46 J R, gave evidence that at a few minutes to twelve on Monday night he saw the prisoner make a rush for the canal bridge in Queen's Road, Dalston. Witness caught him as he was in the act of jumping over, and asked him what he meant to do. He said " I want to finish up with the old century. I want to go to the bottom." Witness took him to the station.

His wife said they had been in distressed circumstances, and that worried her husband.

The magistrate remanded him to gaol for a week.

---

from *Mercury*, January 5, 1901.

In the pulpits, in the papers, in bad poems and good—one gloomy Gus after another reminded the public that the grim reaper awaited them in the twentieth century. For many, it was overkill, at least until the incessant brooding on graves and death became, like the century squabble, the *the last minute of the last hour of the last day* target of satirists, as in this fictitious anecdote from the *Chicago Tribune*'s first issue of the twentieth century:

> Shortly before 12 o'clock p.m. December 31, a shaggy-haired man with a large red nose and a large red mouth stationed himself at a prominent corner downtown and proceeded to harangue the crowd passing by.
>
> "We are standing, my fellow citizens," he said, in a powerful voice, "at a momentous period of the world's history. This is the last minute of the last hour of the last day of the last month of the last year of the last century that many of us will ever—"
>
> A big snowball took him in the mouth, the clock in a neighboring tower struck twelve, and he passed sputtering and swearing into the twentieth century.

For some, the anxiety provoked by the end of a century centred not on their individual mortality, but on the loss of the accomplishments of their entire generation—they, collectively, would be consigned to the dustbin of history. "Future generations," predicted James Dana in his sermon preached on the first Sunday of 1801, "will run over the history of our age with like rapidity and indifference as we do that which preceded us." One hundred years later, a contributor to the *Overland Monthly* fretted over the same prospect: "At the birth of the new century it is usual rather than banal that we should look about and wonder what our progeny will say about us." His prognosis: that he and his contemporaries would be reviled as "flippant, irreverent, and rough" by people looking backward at the end of the twentieth century.

we will be forgotten

To Canon Mason—whose sermon at St. Paul's Cathedral on December 31, 1900 was recorded in the *London Times*—the most humbling forecast was that the great men admired by his congregation—the poets, politicians, scientists of the day—would be little more than quaint footnotes to the people living at the end of the twentieth century. "Darwin will look to them as Newton looks to us," said the Canon. "Wordsworth and Tennyson and Browning will be as shadowy and remote as Pope and Gray are to us." A contributor to *The Review of Reviews* went even further: in the thirty-eighth century, he wrote, looking very, very far forward, posterity would have as little connection with people born in the nineteenth century as his readers now had with the ancient Romans.

Another author, writing in *The Ladies Repository*, posed the question "What will people think of us a hundred years to come?" and mused that the peculiar citizens of the late twentieth century might be horrified by "our present system of choking the life out of criminals." The author then joked that there was really no need to fear that future generations would consign the nineteenth century to oblivion:

> Will they be as much amused at our habits, costume, and language as we are at those of the people of the last century? Surely this will not be! Are we not the greatest people the world ever saw? Do we not live in the most remarkable era of the world's history? Does anyone suppose that the people of the next century will know more than we of this progressive age? How can this be when we have so far outstripped all who have gone before us that further progress seems impossible? We have steam and lightning harnessed to our chariot. How can the twentieth century beat that?

In his own lifetime, the author of this piece—the Reverend James Midwinter Freeman—achieved some renown as the author of *A Handbook of Bible Manners and Customs* and *The Use of Illustration in Sunday School Teaching*. Today, Freeman is all but forgotten.

While some people pondered their own mortality, and some bemoaned the eclipsing of their generation, others looked forward at the turn of the century and foresaw something still more catastrophic: the annihilation of humanity. Visions of "the end" have arisen, of course, in every decade

FREE
Frolie
Fortune-
Telling
Calendar
For 1901

AN AMUSING GAME

The Frolie Fortune-Telling Calendar is the Most Interesting of all Parlor Games

THIS unique Combination Calendar and Fortune Teller is a distinct art production of 16 pages, 6x6 inches, beautifully printed on heavy cardboard in 14 colors. At once the handsomest calendar and most amusing and interesting game for everyone. Sent on receipt of 5 cents in stamps for mailing.

Address Department "C"
The AMERICAN CEREAL COMPANY
CHICAGO, ILL.

advertisement from *The Chautauquan*, December 1900.

of recorded history: Nostradamus, for example, began making his prophecies not at the end of his century, but smack in its middle—1547. Still, despite the perennial nature of apocalyptic prophecies, they do seem to have surged in the closing days of the eighteenth century. In the sermon he delivered on January 1, 1801, *we live in the last days* Charles Backus noted that "divines have of late bestowed more attention upon the prophetic writings than has been known for several ages."

One of those divines was Backus himself. "We live in the last days," he told his congregation. "Events of vast magnitude are brought into existence in quick succession ... The work which the Lord hath been carrying on for ages, by the course of events, hath been brought into clear view within the last few years, as streams become broader and deeper in their near approach to the ocean." Backus was somewhat vague about which "events of vast magnitude" heralded the promised end of "this disorganizing period." He pointed toward empires that had recently arisen "amidst violent commotions," he condemned the growing acceptance of "deism and atheism," and he even blamed the decline of "gentle and amiable manners." "Painful as these events are," he concluded,

> they establish the truth of divine revelation, which predicts "that in the last days perilous times shall come" when the wicked are given up to selfishness, covetousness, boasting, pride, and blasphemy.

The "Ad" Column of the Future.

WANTED : Young millionaire as office boy in department store. Salary, $360,000 per week.

LOST : One billion dollars will be given for return of mongrel pup answering to name of Rubberneck. 41144 Fifth Avenue.

PRIVATE SCHOOL : Dr. Mushem's private school for infants. I fit all scholars for college by the time they are three years old. None admitted over four months of age. Send $100 in stamps for catalogue.

SHEENEY'S THEATRE : Mr. Noses Isaacstern presents Miss Maudine Fleshanblood, the highest type of dramatic art. Generations of breeding have produced in Miss Fleshanblood the largest legs and the smallest cranial capacity of any living star. Popular prices, $400,000, $500,000, $730,000.

SUBURBAN PROPERTY : If you are looking for a home, go to Grassdale. Only 800 miles from town. Four minutes to City Hall. This week lots on two million each, $400,000 down.

---

from *Life*, May 9, 1901 (and opposite page)

Some found very specific correlations between present events and biblical prophecies. In a speech made to the Irish House of Commons on June 7, 1800, Francis Dobbs argued that the proposed union of Great Britain and Ireland—a union which was to take effect on the first day of the nineteenth century—was a precursor to the second coming of Christ. In Dobbs's mind, the independence of Ireland was divinely ordained: in the Book of Daniel, said Dobbs, God had revealed his intention to fragment the Roman Empire in the year 408. Subsequent misguided attempts to restore the Roman Empire—by Charlemagne, by Emperor Charles V, and by others—had all failed because Ireland had never been forced to give up its political independence. By seeking to unite Ireland and Great Britain, the British prime minister—according to Dobbs—was defying the will of God. The result, he predicted, would be the second coming of Christ:

the immediate coming of the Messiah

> I have before given you some reasons why we are to expect the immediate coming of the Messiah. In my opinion, that bill that now lies upon your table proves that it is at hand. What is the British Minister now attempting to do? He is attempting to annihilate Ireland as a Kingdom, though it has remained distinct from all others time immemorial ... As well might he enact that from the day this Union is intended to take place, the snake, the viper, the adder, and the toad should thenceforth live and thrive in our land—for each is equally contrary to the will of God.

"We are not living in ordinary times," he told them. "We are living in the most momentous and eventful period of the world."

A NEW HISTORICAL NOVEL : Read "When England was in Power" by EdgarAmphere Volster. Written by the new electric process. 81 thrills in 200 pages. Only $98,000.

NOTICE TO PHYSICIANS : Under the new law, just passed, all new diseases discovered by physicians are not patented. I am a patent lawyer with a pull and will get your papers in double quick time. Address Marks, Room 800,258, " The Skyscraper."

CROOK'S TOURS: Billionaires and all people in moderate circumstances should avail themselves of our extraordinary offer. Party leaves New York on 10th, returning on 15th, making trip around world. Single tickets, $486,257,823. Steward's tips, $400,000 extra.

WANTED, PENSIONSERS : The population of this Empire is now only eight billions. Of these only seven billions nine hundred millions are drawing pensions. Do not delay, but send in your application to the government at once.

FOR SALE : A copy of the Bible, a celebrated folk-lore book of ancient times, in good condition. Price reasonable.

Some of Dobbs's ideas struck even his contemporaries as peculiar: one reviewer was alarmed by his views on reincarnation, remarking that "Mr. D. indulges in a singular opinion that all men who live now *I tremble* have lived before." Nonetheless, Dobbs's peers seem to have *whilst I write!* accepted his essential argument, namely, that the end of the eighteenth century would herald the end of everything, the whole shebang. Benjamin Farnham, also writing in the closing months of the eighteenth century, asserted that "I am of the opinion that many of the prophecies are at present fulfilling, by the present revolutions of the world." J. Lawrence concurred in his book entitled *Remarkable and Recent Predictions! Of Many Great and Astonishing Events that are to Happen Before and at the Close of the Present Century.* Edward King jumped on board with his *Remarks on the Signs of the Times,* first published in 1798 but then reprinted in both 1799 and 1800. "We approach the latter days," he wrote. "I tremble whilst I write!"

Particularly distressing to King was a prophecy from the Book of Revelation which describes how the contents of a seventh vial will be poured out into the air. In King's mind, this apocalyptic prophecy had been recently fulfilled "by the strange and novel invention of the air balloon, which took place at a time perfectly coinciding with the very first outline of the emblematical description."

One hundred years after Francis Dobbs warned of the divine wrath that would be unleashed by the union of Ireland and Great Britain, and one hundred years before the International Astronomical Union discovered that Asteroid XF11 might be on a collision course with Earth, the nineteenth century closed with apocalyptic predictions of another sort. This time doom came not from above—from neither Heaven nor the

Possible Growth of Our Population

Year.	Computed Population.
1900	77,472,000
1910	94,673,000
1920	114,416,000
1930	136,887,000
1940	162,268,000
1950	190,740,000
1960	222,067,000
1970	257,688,000
1980	296,814,000
1990	339,193,000
2000	385,860,000
2100	1,112,867,000
2500	11,856,302,000
2900	40,852,273,000

from "Possible Growth of Our Population" by H. S. Pritchett, reprinted in *Current Literature*, January 1901.

heavens—but rather from within society itself. For the British, especially, problems in the outreaches of the Empire provoked a bitter pessimism toward the future. In an address called "The Day of all the Dead" delivered to the Positivist Society on the last day of the nineteenth century, the ubiquitous Frederic Harrison observed that the century was closing

everything is going wrong

> in a time of widespread ruin, misery, and death ... From tens of thousands of homes in every part of the Empire there rises up the sound of mourning and despair. Our Indian Empire has been desolated by plague and famine. Vast districts of China are the scene of plunder, murder, and savage slaughter. South Africa is a wilderness of chaos, ruin, and race hatred ... All around us are signs of loss, waste, and death.

George Bernard Shaw concurred. "As the centre of the empire, this island is done for," he wrote at the end of 1900 in *The Humane Review*. He predicted that England would soon lose its international influence and degenerate into a mere "park for holiday tours," with a "head ranger" instead of a prime minister.

The *London Times* was equally pessimistic. "Went Out In Gloom" was the headline for an item about the last day of the century. "Floods were clapping their hands north and south and west," reported the item. "Birmingham Canal was breaking loose in Staffordshire and causing great havoc. The war news was bad." On and on went the litany of hard luck and bad planning, in newspaper after newspaper. "The impression created by columns of croaking and foreboding," wrote one commentator in the *Times*, "is that everything is going wrong."

But what, precisely, was the problem? To find out, several newspapers polled politicians, divines, authors, actors—anyone, in short, who might help diagnose the social ills that threatened the future well-being, and perhaps the very survival, of humanity. In the *New York World*, the question "What is the chief danger confronting the new century?" elicited a variety of responses. "Evil desires and covetousness" was the rather medieval diagnosis made by the Bishop of Hereford. His peer, the Bishop of Llandaff, disagreed, citing "infidelity and anarchy" as the predominant menace to the future. "The chief social danger is drink," asserted Frederic Farrar, the Dean of Canterbury, while Ellen Terry, one of the most popular actresses of her day, cited "the growing artificiality in our social life." Arthur Pinero, author of the play *The Second Mrs. Tanqueray*, feared that the growth of trade unions would doom future generations, while Joseph Arch, the founder of the National Agricultural Labourers' Union, declared that humanity would be increasingly threatened by "a large accumulation of wealth on the one hand and a large increase of pauperism on the other." Samuel Gompers, the founder of the American Federation of Labour, feared that western economies would soon be undermined by "Oriental competition," while publisher W. T. Stead predicted that the ethical foundation of "Christendom" would be destroyed by the continued exploitation of "one fourth of the human race which is born in a yellow skin." Arthur Conan Doyle, creator of Sherlock Holmes, anticipated that the new century would succumb to "an ill-balanced, excitable, and sensation-mongering press," a fear echoed by fellow author Max Beerbohm, who identified "jumpy journals" as a growing social evil. The most ominous response to the question about the new century's chief menace came from Frederick Temple, the Archbishop of Canterbury. "I have not the slightest idea," he said.

jumpy journals

In *Popular Science Monthly*, H. S. Pritchett, the President of the Massachusetts Institute of Technology, used recent census information to extrapolate the population of the United States in coming centuries. Knowing that his nation had a population of 77,000,000 people in the year 1900, Pritchett estimated that there would be about 385,000,000 Americans in the year 2000 (rather more than the current estimate of 275,000,000). Pritchett was not troubled by this part of his population projection, because he realized that a nation the size of the United States could easily support 385,000,000 people. However, when he extrapolated further, he concluded that the population of the United States would be nearly twelve billion in the year 2500, and more than forty billion in the year 2900. Needless to say, Pritchett found this prospect, distant as it was, somewhat alarming:

Standing Room Only

TIME'S ·APPEAL.

from *Punch*, January 2, 1901

How great a change in the conditions of living this growth of population would imply is, perhaps, impossible for us to realize. Great Britain, at present one of the most densely populated countries on the globe, contains about 300 inhabitants to the square mile. Should the present law of growth continue until 2900, the United States would contain over 11,000 persons to each square mile.

Other demographers writing at the end of the nineteenth century realized that a civilization would self-destruct long before it achieved a population density of 11,000 people per square mile. J. Holt Schooling, also writing in the last month of the nineteenth century, made the assumption that a maximum population density for the entire planet was one thousand people for each square mile of land. At that point, he said, "the earth will be so densely populated as to bring about conditions akin to those that cause a crowded theater to display the legend *Standing Room Only.*" Extrapolating from current birth and death rates, Schooling concluded that the planet would reach its maximum population density in the year 2250. "The world will be full," he predicted, adding that this was a situation of "vital and international importance."

Although Pritchett and Schooling had serious concerns about the increasing population of the earth, they were not, like Edward King a century earlier, "trembling whilst they wrote": their worst case scenarios were, after all, still hundreds of years in the future. As far as most people were concerned at the end of the nineteenth century, a much more immediate threat to civilization was the prospect of a world war. Preaching in Westminster Abbey on December 31, 1900, Dean Farrar predicted that "early in the coming century England would have to meet a combination of European powers." Rudyard Kipling, writing to the editor of *The Spectator*, John Strachey, on January 2, 1899 casually alluded to "the Great war between 1905 and 1915" as if it were an inevitability. And on the last Saturday of the nineteenth century, the *Chicago Tribune* carried an article that made a huge military conflict seem certain:

a great world war shall be fought

> In the present one may see on all sides the disposition of the world's people toward blood ... The whole world is restless, suspicious, and is building and equipping for war ... In the shipyards and arsenals of the civilized world men are working as they never have worked before, turning out arms and armaments. Is the century to go out in a world war? Only time may prove it. And if it should, that war will have had its numerous prophets.

For a London minister named Dr. Forsyth, it was not the stockpiling of armaments, but rather the rise of amoral individualism that made world conflict in the twentieth century inevitable. Writing in the last month of the nineteenth century in *Sunday at Home* Forsyth predicted that this terrifying ideology would be embodied in what he called "the anti-Christ of the coming age":

> A type of man that looms masterful in the coming time is the man of keen, prompt, and aggressive force, of indomitable, ungenerous, un-ideal will, without ethical, historic, or imaginative culture, of passionate egotism and insolent speech, of great resource and narrow, vulgar ambitions, of boundless prosperity without and invulnerable self-confidence within, of unscrupulous business, non-moral principles, and unspiritual joys. I speak of a spirit which may find its incarnation in the coming age.

Forsyth's description of the "indomitable, ungenerous, un-ideal will" echoes the "primal slaying will" to which O'Neill Latham gave voice in a poem published in the January, 1901, issue of *Cosmopolitan*. Entitled "A.D. MCM" Latham's poem foresaw that the war-mongering that closed the nineteenth century would devastate the human race in the twentieth:

> I am the Soul of Battle,
> The primal slaying Will.
> Spirit of Hatred, I. Hear my cry!
> I drive you forth to kill,
> I drive you forth to die.
>
> I cheat you with a banner, and I fool you with a name;
> You shout some windy legend till the hoofs are on your face.
> I spread a dream before you while I bring you all to shame—
> Till I am full with raven and diminished is your race.

Jumpy journals, a packed planet, world war—these were frightening and not inaccurate forecasts of the twentieth century. None of them, however, provoked as much hand-wringing as one other impending woe: degeneration. Humanity, it was feared, was regressing. Charles Darwin had shown that all species either adapted to new challenges and evolved, or, failing to adapt, vanished into extinction. Was it possible that *Homo sapiens* were devolving, reverting to their simian ancestry?

diminished is your race

William W. Ireland argued just that in his essay, "Degeneration," published in *The International Monthly* in the last year of the nineteenth century. With statistics, Ireland showed that in the United Kingdom "the number of suicides is increasing," there was "a serious augmentation of the numbers of the insane," and even the "number of idiots" appeared to be on the rise.

The cause of this manifest degeneration, said Ireland, was modern life itself. Common labourers were being shrivelled by factory work and urban squalor into stunted scarecrows:

> While the country people are big and well knit, with broad chests, muscular limbs, and agile step, the children, healthy and rosy cheeked, with bright eyes, the dwellers in the foggy atmosphere of the manufacturing towns seem of a different race; they are short of stature, with narrow chests, pasty complexions, and a worn out, faded look. They often have a distinct stoop, and bowlegs are common.

THE NATIONS ALL DREW NEAR, AT THE CLOSE OF THE XIX CENTURY,

AND MADE GOOD RESOLUTIONS FOR THE COMING YEAR.

BUT THE OPENING OF THE XX CENTURY IS LADEN WITH DISAPPOINTMENT.

from *Life*, May 9, 1901.

Newfangled ideas about the sexes were also promising to undo two thousand years of western civilization. "The natural calling of both classes," warned Ireland, "is being sapped by the shad- *the Indian rubber* owy myth of female rights and independence, and the *sucking bottle* future is being sacrificed to pure selfishness." He blamed in particular the replacement of "the nursing mother" with "the Indian rubber sucking bottle." This "artificial feeding," he asserted, "explains the deplorable condition of teeth in most people, a condition which seems ever to be getting worse."

Similar concerns were expressed in the February 1900 issue of the *International Monthly*. There, a Professor Erb of Heidelberg reported that modern life was leading to "an increase in nervousness." In contrast to the old days, he said,

> We live a faster and more restless life, and the pull upon the brain is more exacting and more constant. We indulge more in stimulants and drugs which excite or lull the intellect and the senses—tea, coffee, tobacco, opium, chloral, cocaine. An increasing proportion of our population now lives in large towns instead of in villages and the open country. There is a great deal more travel. Railway journeys even of a few miles have a jarring effect upon the nerves, and indispose for steady application and calm enjoyment. We may thus reasonably expect that, with this increased strain, nervous exhaustion and breakdowns should be more frequent.

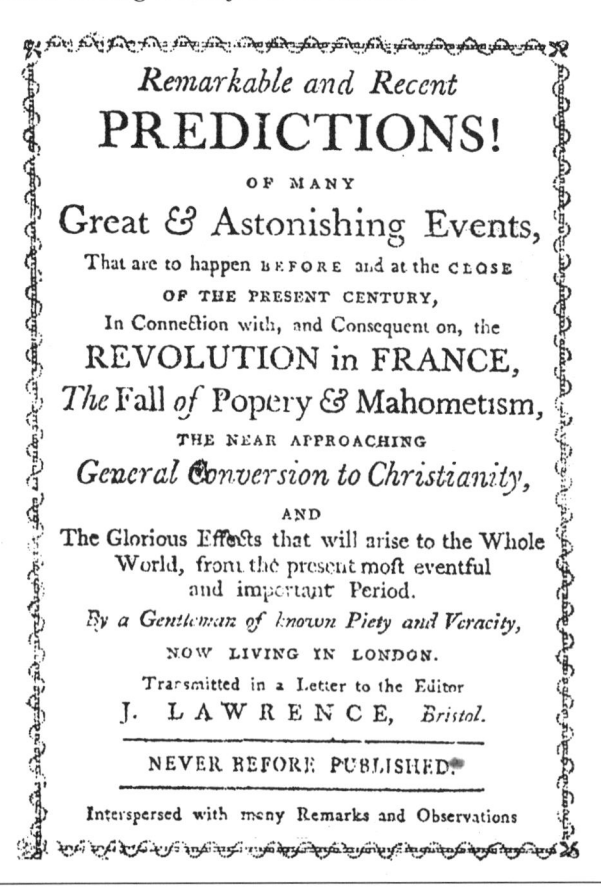

Remarkable and Recent

PREDICTIONS!

OF MANY

Great & Astonishing Events,

That are to happen BEFORE and at the CLOSE

OF THE PRESENT CENTURY,

In Connection with, and Consequent on, the

REVOLUTION in FRANCE,

The Fall *of* Popery & Mahometism,

THE NEAR APPROACHING

General Conversion to Christianity,

AND

The Glorious Effects that will arise to the Whole
World, from the present most eventful
and important Period.

By a Gentleman of known Piety and Veracity,

NOW LIVING IN LONDON.

Transmitted in a Letter to the Editor

J. LAWRENCE, *Bristol.*

NEVER BEFORE PUBLISHED.

Interspersed with many Remarks and Observations

title page for *Remarkable and Recent Predictions ...*, Bristol: J. Lawrence, 1794.

While Ireland and Erb fretted about the moral and dental decay of the western world, August Forel focussed on the shrinking human brain. In *the positive idiocy of humanity* his essay "Human Perfectibility in the Light of the Facts of Evolution," published early in the first year of the twentieth century, Forel asserted that "we are today in the presence of human brains which are not only not appreciably increasing in either strength or size, but many of which are deteriorating and degenerating." Considering that humanity's grey matter was already withering, "What will happen to our civilization in another hundred years?" he asked. "Shall we find it possible to prevent the universal deterioration, degeneration, the positive idiocy of humanity?"

The solution for the next century, said Forel, was simple: urge "the most highly organized brains and bodies to reproduce themselves as much as possible, while forcing the inferior and incompetent ones in the opposite direction." Only this proto-Nazi policy would save human civilization from impending degeneration.

Fortunately, Forel and the other prophets of degeneration were checked by the same force that helped end both the century squabble and the outpouring of morbid newspaper editorials: satire. In the December 29, 1900 issue of *Pick-Me-Up*, an unnamed humourist asserted that it was not the British public that was degenerate, but rather the British intelligentsia with their outrageous theories and absurd proposals:

corsets for boys

> Just lately the question has been asked, "Are we as a nation degenerating?" We point with pride to the valour of our lads in khaki and say most emphatically, "No." Then we take up our Daily Mail and find prominence given to a letter, the writer of which seriously advocates corsets for boys. And small wonder if we begin to doubt whether there isn't something rotten in the state of Denmark, after all. The British Boy in a corset!

Pick-Me-Up's chief rival, *Puck*, went even further by deriding not just the Chicken Littles of degeneration, but all the *fin-de-siècle* voices of doom, depicting them as apocalyptic loonies:

> The chronic unbeliever warns us of impending chaos. If he belong to the church, the demon of unreligious commercialism is to finish us presently. If he be a worker, the masses are about to destroy the classes. The Women's Christian Temperance Union sees drunkards' graves dug for us all, from the President down. The vegetarians behold a destroying angel upon us in the specious guise of a broiled beef-steak. The doctors of medicine see us being gnawed away by voracious microbes. Dr. Parkhurst expects the Lord to send another deluge almost any day, because we golf on Sundays. And a far-seeing humanist in Wichita, Kansas, begs *Puck* to give warning of the frightful loss of life that must ensue "when these here big airships gets to running into each other thousands of feet above the earth." He says that none of the other papers will pay any attention to him.

a broiled beef-steak

Although satire is more often cynical than sanguine, there is a profound hopefulness at the heart of these pieces from *Puck* and *Pick-Me-Up*: they refuse to believe that the troubles at hand are as bad as others make them out to be. Thomas Hardy expressed the same unlikely belief—hope in the midst of apparent desolation—in a poem he wrote on December 31, 1900, originally called "At the Century's Deathbed," and later retitled "The Darkling Thrush."

Pausing at a gate, Hardy looks out upon an empty, cold, and bleak landscape that he equates with "the century's corpse." Everything, everyone, lacks passion and pulse. But then, out of nowhere, he suddenly hears the "full-hearted" evening song of a thrush. The old, gaunt, "blast-beruffled" bird has as "little cause for carolling" as the poet and the blighted world he inhabits. And yet it sings.

So little cause for carollings

I leant upon a coppice gate
When Frost was specter-gray,
And Winter's dregs made desolate
The weakening eye of day.
The tangled bine-stems scored the sky
Like strings of broken lyres,
And all mankind that haunted nigh
Had sought their household fires.

The land's sharp features seemed to be
The Century's corpse outleant,
His crypt the cloudy canopy,
The wind his death-lament.
The ancient pulse of germ and birth
Was shrunken hard and dry,
And every spirit upon earth
Seemed fervorless as I.

At once a voice arose among
The bleak twigs overhead
In a full-hearted evensong
Of joy illimited;
An aged thrush, frail, gaunt, and small,
In blast-beruffled plume,
Had chosen thus to fling his soul
Upon the growing gloom.

So little cause for carollings
Of such ecstatic sound
Was written on terrestrial things
Afar or nigh around,
That I could think there trembled through
His happy good-night air
Some blessed Hope, whereof he knew
And I was unaware.

With Hardy's magnificent poem in mind, we turn to those who looked
forward to a new century with zeal, vigour, and glee.

Chapter Six

Looking Forward
Cheerful, Fast, and Bald

DREAD-INFECTED VISIONS of the future don't seem to date as quickly, or as comically, as cheerful ones. Somehow our exultant techno-dream always ends up looking silly. Maybe it's those one-piece outfits—they're all wrong for the post-adolescent figure (and so is that hair, which looks suspiciously store-bought). Or maybe it's that Pollyanna visions of the future leave too much out—all the coarse and accidental qualities of existence, that make up more than their fair share of life. Miserable visions are less laughable because they include so much that is eternally human—sorrow and death, for example.

But we ought not to be smug when we look back at looking forward. The future we imagine can never transcend the times we live in, and in conceiving it we expose the linearity of our imaginations, how bound we are by our assumptions, how difficult it is to escape the semiology of our own days. One hundred years from now our thrilling predictions about the World Wide Web will look absurdly off the point. And while past-imagined futures can be endearing and quaint—like coming upon a basket of kittens in a space station—our present-day projections about Mars colonies, organ replacements, cloning, smart bombs and weather control are not entirely utopian. At best, they promise us an uneasy comfort—perhaps we can cheat death, or fool the aging gene; perhaps we can have a war where only the bad guys die (assuming *What a wonderful world this will be in the year 2000!* they are not us); or perhaps if the earth gets too inhospitable, we can eke out an existence on the dark side of the moon. At the end of the twentieth century, we are too circumspect, too self-conscious, to forecast anything like an Age of Aquarius, a New Jerusalem, a Shangri-la, Xanadu, or El Dorado.

But at the end of the nineteenth century, especially in North America, many people indulged in buoyant, unbridled dreams of a new era, confident that the world was going to get better and wiser, brighter and faster. As the editor of the *Manitoba Free Press* proclaimed at the end of 1900:

> Judging the future by the past, the new century should witness many strange events, discoveries, inventions and improvements beneficial to the material prosperity of the world ... the achievements of humanity in the past are but the stepping stone to still greater achievements in the future.

The editor of the *Boston Herald* was just as excited: "Oh, yes, a great many things are going to happen during the new century," he exclaimed. "What a wonderful world this will be in the year 2000!" "There is today," he continued, "a mass and momentum of justice, mercy, enlightenment and chivalrous humanity that are at once the promise and the potency of a noble work for the whole human race." The editor of the *Chicago Tribune,* without a trace of irony, could even hail the return of a golden age:

> Perhaps the change will come in the twentieth century. The purely material may claim less attention and Mammon come to be less regarded. The commercial spirit, always destructive to art, may give place to a renaissance of art in its varied forms, and in the new cycle even greater apostles of beauty may appear. The world may have less of the useful and more of the beautiful. The intellect of mankind, tiring of the material, may turn towards the higher things, and with the advantages of increased education and deeper knowledge of science and nature, become notable for grand and diversified achievements.

In New York, where the century closed with millionaire developers competing to build ever higher and higher skyscrapers, it probably seemed self-evident that every new century would surpass its predecessor in excellence. That was the confident credo put forth by the editor of the *Tribune:*

> From the old century to the new. From great achievements to greater. From the sum of progress in nineteen centuries to the sum in twenty; remembering that the rate of progress is one of geometrical progression, so that each new century may exceed in greatness not only any of its predecessors, but all of them together ... All that was worthy of death in the past will be buried with that past which now is dead. But all that was good and true and worthy of life will survive, transferred and transplanted into the new life of the new century, and so perennially transferred into the new life that perennially arises above the ashes of the past.

This sense of "geometrical progression" was shared by the editor of the *Los Angeles Times*, who predicted that the twentieth century would unfold marvels beyond the comprehension of his present-day readers:

> The things we imagine will be but folly to the things that the coming century is bringing to us. And as each wonder is born to the world and takes its place among the wonders created in the nineteenth

from *En l'an 2000*, a series of illustrated cards by Jean Marc Côté, published by toy manufacturer Armand Gervais, Lyon for the 1900 festivities in France.

century, the people of that day will accept them as we accept the electric light, the submarine boat, and other marvels, with the blasé matter-of-course complacency so characteristic of the age. Then, while things border on the regions of the miraculous, the spirit of old Jules Verne, once considered the champion liar of nineteen centuries, will hover in the air and whisper triumphantly, "I told you so."

Machines to nurse the babe that's born

"We are impatient for what the coming century may bring," concluded the editor. "Impatient as the child who longs for daylight in order see what Santa Claus has placed in his stocking."

The marvels of the twentieth century were anticipated in song as well. In 1899 E. Spencer published his folk song, "A Hundred Years From Now," a sanguine, if robot-driven, forecast of the future:

> I'd like to see this earth again
> A hundred years from now
> And walk and talk with living men
> A hundred years from now
> I'd like to see how farming's done
> How business is and how it's run
> How votes are cast and office won
> A hundred years from now
>
> Of course there'll be no wood to burn
> A hundred years from now
> There'll be some tricks of trade to learn
> A hundred years from now
> There'll be big towns and steeples high
> And buildings that will scrape the sky
> And stores where all the world could buy
> A hundred years from now

There'll be machines to shuck the corn
A hundred years from now
Machines to nurse the babe that's born
A hundred years from now
Machines that fly and walk by day
Machines that work, machines that play
Perhaps machines to preach and pray
A hundred years from now

Machines to shuck corn, to nurse babies, to preach and pray—a strange collection of gadgets, but undoubtedly in Spencer's mind these devices *the entire problem of existence* would have one thing in common: they would all be powered by a force which seemed poised to transform the world: electricity. Such was the prediction of Henri de Blowitz, renowned correspondent of the *London Times*, writing in December 1900:

> My conviction is that there is a force, whose real scope and power remains unsuspected by men, for it is as yet hardly wrested from the enigmatic obscurity in which it lurks. I refer to electricity. It is my conviction that the task of revealing the full meaning of this demiurgic force is to devolve upon the twentieth century, and that then, the question solved, the entire problem of existence on this globe will be seen to have been solved as well.

With this new power, the living conditions of millions would improve *the miseries of gorged streets* enormously. While steam power, as E. P. Powell noted in his essay "Farming in the Twentieth Century," concentrates labor, and therefore population, the easy transmission of electricity would allow people in the new century to spread out comfortably over a wide area, as they had before the industrial revolution:

> The electric age will put an end to the packing of people like sardines in tenement-houses. It will take the people to the food, instead of carrying all the food to the people. Instead of factories, home life will be emphasized. Work will not need to be done so exclusively at great centers. The miseries of gorged streets and the problems of municipal misrule will steadily lessen. But electricity will do more.

More? Was Powell off his electric rocker? What else could electricity possibly accomplish? "When our homes are heated by *persons bred in vulgarity* electricity," the visionary continued, "consumption and many other diseases will wholly disappear—not in a day or a single year, but as certainly as yellow fever disappears before a frost." Electricity would also transform the household, solving, among other vexations, the problem of finding and keeping good servants:

> It is growing more and more difficult to secure for our households competent assistance, while the need of good help is greatly increased. It is impossible to build the ideal home simply because we must as a rule admit freely into our houses persons bred in vulgarity, or our wives must do work that stands in the way of higher work,

DREAMS OF MEN OF SCIENCE.

Mr. Frederick Dolman has been interviewing for the *Strand Magazine* some of the leading men of science of the day as to the dreams of the nineteenth which may become the realities of the twentieth century. The following were the answers received :—

SIR NORMAN LOCKYER. (South Kensington.)	The prediction by means of sun spots of famine in India and drought in Australia.
SIR W. H. PREECE. (Inventor with Marconi of wireless telegraphy.)	The unexpected which happens. A flying machine if based on some entirely new principle altogether out of our ken at present.
SIR JOHN WOLFE BARRY. (Engineer of the Tower Bridge.)	Storing of rain on Ben Nevis or other mountains which would give an immense amount of hydraulic pressure and be one of the best ways of dealing with the problem caused by the increased cost of coal. Rolling platform for congested streets. An Irish tunnel.
SIR WILLIAM CROOKES.	A great multiplication of " twopenny tubes." Universal house to house extension of the telephone. Phonograph in common use. Aerial navigation.
MR. J. H. SWAN, F.R.S. (Electrician and inventor.)	Chemical production with consequent cheapening of electricity, and extension of its use.
M. BERTHELOT (Sec. to French Academy of Science.)	Chemical manufacture of food, and consequent disappearance of cook and restaurants.
SIR HENRY ROSCOE. (Former President of the British Association.)	Same as M. Berthelot, but less sanguine. " The harnessing of many Niagaras." The application of science to the benefit of humanity in general.
MR. THOMAS BRYANT. (President of the Royal College of Surgeons.)	The cure of cancer and consumption by means of the study of bacteria. The prevention of malaria. The greater use of the Röntgen rays and hypnotism in medicine.

from *The Review of Reviews*, January, 1901.

culture, rest, and enjoyment. The advent of a power that can wash our dishes, wash our clothes, do our cooking, churning, sewing, and that without noise or dirt, is to be hailed with acclamations of joy … Electricity will help us to get rid of the invasion of our homes by a purely menial class.

Also writing in 1901, the science-fiction novelist H. G. Wells—who, as we'll see, made speculation about the new century into a mini-industry— agreed that electricity would take the drudgery out of housework, transforming it into a diverting recreation:

With a neat little range, heated by electricity and provided with a thermometer, with absolutely controllable temperatures and proper heat screens, cooking might very easily be made a pleasant amusement for intelligent, invalid ladies.

And the money that electricity would save! "Coal bills and oil or gas bills will be abolished," prophesied Powell. "Fuel and light will be so lessened in cost as to be practically, like education, free." Best of all, he added, electricity would nourish the human soul even as it took out the garbage:

> As electricity abolishes superfluous heat and dirt and waste of fuel, it introduces the beautiful. The electric fountains at the Columbia Exhibition—who will ever forget them? Decorative lighting of our houses and lawns will produce effects beyond our imagination at present to picture.

Of course, electricity had its rare sceptics as well. Frederick Dolman was one, as he made clear in an article published in *Strand Magazine* called "Science in the New Century":

> I have no doubt that the use of electricity in industries, both large and small, will be much extended. But I don't think it likely that it will be found advantageous for, say, cleaning the windows and scrubbing the floors of our houses, as imaginative writers have suggested, although a few people may choose to employ it as an exquisite way of having such things done. Nor would I dare to commit myself to the opinion that, in the next century, electricity will entirely supersede gas as an illuminant.

If Dolman was wrong in predicting the limitations of electricity as an illuminant, so was the editor of *Current Literature* when he predicted in January, 1901, that the twentieth century would see the "electro-mobile" displace its chief rival—the "steam-driven machine":

> It seems fair to say that the greatest promise of future usefulness is today held out by two types of automobile—those operated by electricity and those using steam as a motive power. The latter class have important advantages of radius of operation and lightness of construction, but with this is coupled the very serious disadvantage of complex construction, disagreeable exhaust and perhaps certain legal restriction as to operation. The electric vehicle, on the other hand, is exceedingly simple and perfect in its regulation and docile in its habits, but its radius of operation is small and its weight and cost are at present necessarily high. Notwithstanding these drawbacks, it has made for itself a place and will doubtless hold it in the future as against all competitors.

docile in its habits

Arguing the opposite but equally mistaken case was Edward Murphy. In the *San Francisco Examiner*'s last issue of the nineteenth century, Murphy carefully explained why the automobile of the future would be steam-powered:

> The automobile of the future—the ultimate automobile in its most practical form, as foreseen from this distance—will, it seems likely, depend upon steam for its motive power. The simplicity of steam propulsion must sooner or later come to be regarded in automobile construction as superior to every other consideration.

Although Murphy went on to acknowledge the existence of gasoline-powered automobiles, he hardly considered them a genuine threat to the ultimate ascendency of steam. Here Dolman agreed, shrugging off gasoline-vehicles as a mere toy of the sports enthusiast:

LES TUBES — GARE DU TUBE DU SUD A PARIS

A pneumatic commuter tube as depicted by Albert Robida in *Le vingtième siècle*, first published in 1883; reprinted Geneva: Slatkine, 1981.

The gasoline vehicle will probably continue to be used on the race track, but present indications do not seem to point to its extended use either as an instrument of pleasure or as an accessory of business. It has certain faults which apparently nothing can remedy, among these being danger, bad odor and jerky and unpleasant movement.

As off-target as the predictions of Murphy and Dolman turned out to be, they were not nearly as peculiar as some of the more energetic forecasts made by George Sutherland in his *Twentieth Century Inventions: A Forecast.* The chief rival of the prolific H. G. Wells in forecasting the twentieth century, Sutherland realized that roads designed for horse and carriage would not be adequate for automobiles. Because it didn't seem feasible to upgrade all the roads on the planet, Sutherland predicted the advent of a vehicle that rolled forward inside a pair of twenty-foot-high "hoops," one on either side, rather like a child propelling a barrel forward by walking within it:

a rolling railway

> Let the wheel consist of a very small truck-wheel running on the inside of a large, rigid steel hoop. The latter must be supported, to keep it from falling to either side, by means of a steel semi-circular framework rising from the sides of the vehicle and carrying small wheels to prevent friction. We now have a kind of rail which conforms to the condition already mentioned, namely, that of being capable of being laid down in front of the wheel of the truck or vehicle, and of being picked up again when the weight has passed over any particular part. The hoop, in fact, constitutes a rolling railway.

Another innovation predicted by Sutherland was prompted by his concern that in the twentieth century everyone, regardless of their engineering qualifications, would own an automobile. This spelt disaster: an epidemic of fast-moving vehicles navigated by inept amateurs. The solution foreseen by Sutherland was for a safety-rail or guide-line to be constructed along high-speed roads—roads where automobiles would be travelling at thirty miles an hour or more. The automobile would be attached to the guide rail by means of two small wheels "capable of being lifted at any time by means of a lever controlled by the driver."

without the assistance of the guide-rail

Other writers were more accurate in predicting that the twentieth century's profusion of careening automobiles would spawn new laws regulating their operation. Writing in 1901 in *The Grandest Century in the World's History*, the extremely prolific Henry Davenport Northrop noted that France was ahead of other nations in inventing "automobile legislation":

> In France they must be licensed, and the driver must have a certificate of proficiency. Speed must not exceed 18.5 miles an hour in open country, or 12.5 miles in passing a horse, while in narrow thoroughfares it must be reduced to walking pace.

Of course, not everyone believed that the automobile would become prevalent enough to warrant the construction of "safety rails" or the invention of traffic laws. Jesse Quail scoffed at such speculations in an essay called "Forecasts of the Future":

> The anticipation of one writer that before the twentieth century's close every family, however humble, will have its own motor-car, seems over-sanguine; were the prediction realised, it might entail the gradual atrophy of the human organs of locomotion, a result hardly desirable.

Given his concern that motor-cars might lead to the shrivelling of the human leg, Quail would certainly have disapproved of the elaborate "moving sidewalks" that numerous writers forecast for the new century. In his 1900 futurist treatise entitled "Anticipations," H. G. Wells imagined that a series of moving sidewalks, similar to conveyor belts, would be built side by side, each one moving slightly faster than the one to its left. Pedestrians would start on the slowest platform, and then hop successively to the more rapid ones:

the Parisian driver is noted for his carelessness

> If we suppose the space given to six platforms of three feet wide and one (the most rapid) of six feet, and if we suppose that each platform to be going four miles an hour faster than its slower fellow, we should have the upper platform running round the circle at a pace of twenty-eight miles an hour ... To that the man in a hurry would be able to add his own four miles an hour by walking in the direction of motion.

from *En l'an 2000*, a series of illustrated cards by Jean Marc Côté, published by toy manufacturer Armand Gervais, Lyon for the 1900 festivities in France.

By such means, pedestrians could achieve the remarkable velocity of thirty-two miles an hour. The system, thought Wells, would have other enticements as well. One side of the fastest platform would be set with comfortable chairs, and even bookstalls and tobacco shops would be set up to serve the commuters—though it is unclear how Wells would avert disaster when the chairs and tobacco shops reached the end of the moving sidewalk, the point where the rolling platform dipped under the ground and looped back in the opposite direction.

The moving sidewalks would also reduce the number of motor cars speeding dangerously through city streets. This advantage was highlighted when, in the closing days of the nineteenth century, the newly-formed Trottoir Roulant Company announced its intent to build a real moving-sidewalk system in Paris. "One of the chief attractions of the system," reported the *Chicago Tribune* on December 30, 1900, *gas will take us up* "is its life-saving feature, for the Parisian driver is noted for his carelessness and kills and injures a greater percentage of the people of this city each year than the driver of any other city in the world."

On July 2, 1900, Ferdinand Graf von Zeppelin flew the first rigid airship, a covered frame filled with gas. Four years later, on December 17, 1903, Orville Wright flew the first airplane at Kitty Hawk. In between fell January 1, 1901, a moment that inspired countless writers to speculate on whether humans would really fly, as opposed to merely float, in the new century. Many, like Charles Stanley, writing in the *San Francisco Examiner* on the last day of nineteenth century, were certain that the new age would see the invention of a truly navigable aircraft:

> At last the time is come for the perfect fulfilment of the world's dream since the dawn of human invention—the realization of man's ambition to fly. Already the day is here, and within the year just past man has flown. The Von Zeppelin airship was the beginning of practical aerial navigation in actual demonstration ... The advent of aluminum has been a tremendous advance toward producing a ship light and strong enough to be lifted by gas—and gas is, of course, the first essential in aerial flight. Gas will take us up and keep us up ... Such an airship will inevitably open a century of progress never equalled by any previous century, not even the one just closed ... The twentieth century will open with the airship—what it will close with no man can, with any warrant, predict.

Although Stanley seems to be suggesting that the sky's the limit—or rather that there is no limit—for twentieth-century aviation, his buoyant speculations were actually limited to dirigibles and other gas-filled balloon-craft. Of propellor-driven airplanes he wrote nothing. For Stanley, the "most useful and profitable limit to which aerial navigation may be carried" in the new century was nothing more than "an airship capable of carrying the mails and, say, thirty or forty passengers at a speed of seventy miles an hour against natural resistance and a tolerably strong wind, with the ability to descend at the will of the pilot, to answer the call of rudder and elevation planes."

Other *fin-de-siècle* writers, even the most sanguine, seemed to agree that advances in aviation would pertain mostly, if not solely, to dirigibles. In his "Anticipations," H. G. Wells did assert that "before the year 2000 A.D. and very probably before the year 1950, a successful aeroplane will have soared and come home safe and sound"—but the rest of his speculations about human flight, pages and pages of them, were all devoted to balloons of one sort or another.

Of particular interest to Wells was the prospect that dirigibles would become key in twentieth-century warfare. "Great multitudes of balloons," he predicted, "will be the Argus eyes of the entire military organi- *a sort of air shark* zation." The "aeronauts," as Wells called the balloon operators, "will mark down to the gunners below the precise point upon which to direct their fire." More aggressive balloons seemed also to be on the horizon, with Wells anticipating "dirigible aerial devices that can fight." These aircraft, according to Wells, would be fashioned from "a row of contractile balloons"—balloons that could be inflated or deflated at will—attached to a "long car" whose sides "horizontally expanded into wings." From a distance, wrote Wells, such an aircraft would resemble "a soaring, elongated, flat-brimmed hat" and, outfitted with small machine guns, the vessel would become "a sort of air shark."

In contrast, Well's rival, George Sutherland, doubted that aviation would ever amount to anything, either in warfare or in commerce:

from *En l'an 2000*, a series of illustrated cards by Jean Marc Côté, published by toy manufacturer Armand Gervais, Lyon for the 1900 festivities in France.

Military aeronautics, like submarine operations in naval warfare, have been somewhat overrated. Visions of airships hovering over a doomed city and devastating it with missiles dropped from above are mere fairy tales ... The amount of misdirected ingenuity that has been expended on these two problems of submarine and aerial navigation during the nineteenth century will offer one of the most curious and interesting studies to the future historian of technological progress.

misdirected ingenuity

Wells granted Sutherland's point that the submarine had no future; for him it was the vessel's claustrophobic nature that scuttled its prospects:

> I must confess that my imagination, in spite even of spurring, refuses to see any sort of submarine doing anything but suffocate its crew and founder at sea. It must involve physical inconvenience of the most demoralising sort simply to be in one for any length of time.

Poppycock! was John Holland's view of such fears. In 1900, Holland had sold the United States a submarine of his own designing, the first submarine purchased by any navy. It was on the heels of this success that Holland published, in December 1900, an essay entitled "The Submarine Boat and Its Future," chock full of sanguine predictions of twentieth-century travellers employing submarines as casually as trains or carriages. British business men, promised Holland, would soon be commuting to and from the continent on a daily basis, plunged deep in the English Channel:

> For short trips the submarine offers commercial advantages that will render it a dangerous rival of the surface-sailing vessel ... There will be no seasickness, because in a submerged boat there is absolutely no perceptible motion. There will be no smells to create nausea, for the boats will be propelled by electric power taken from storage batteries, which will be charged at either end ... There will

 GLORIOUS year to you all!
    I've paused in the midst of my whirl
    To tell you the reason I'm glad at this season
    I'm a Twentieth Century Girl.

I never could sigh for the days
    When every fun-loving lass,
No matter how winning, must bend to her spinning
    And bleach out the linen on grass;

Where once but a few lucky maids,
    Whose sires were called well-to-do,
Cou'd ravel on pillions. Now our fathers make millions
    And buy us an airship or two,

Just think what our grandmothers missed!
    For surely 'twas frightfully slow
When young blood ran riot, to have to be quiet
    And sit in a corner and sew.

Who'd rather be shut in a tower
    Bound in by a muddy old moat,
Than call in balloon on the man in the moon
    Or sail in a submarine boat?

I care not a caramel's price
    For that era of pastoral joy—
It is good to be here, in this wide-awake year,
    When we handle the world like a toy.

from the *San Francisco Examiner*, December 31, 1900 (and opposite page)

> be no collisions, because the boats coming and the boats going will travel at different depths—say one at twenty, the other at forty feet ... Storms and fogs will have no existence for the traveller, for weather cannot penetrate below the surface of the water.

Such trips would not only be safe, Holland added, they would be downright refreshing:

> The passenger will enter a handsomely fitted cabin at Dover. Electric lights will make it cozy and bright ... Almost without a jar, the boat will put off from her dock on the English side. Practically no vibration will be felt from the smoothly running machinery. Before the traveller fairly realizes that a start has been made, the boat will be fast at her dock at Calais. The three or four hours consumed will be passed in reading, in sleep, or in social intercourse, as pleasantly as though the traveller were at home in his own drawing room. The nervous old lady will have less to worry her than she would find on a drive through the streets of London or Paris. Her husband or son will find perfect comfort in a handsomely appointed smoking room.

"This is no dream," Holland assured his readers. "It is simply a forecast of a trip I myself expect to make some day, and I am fifty-nine years old."

Other forecasters of naval progress confined their speculations to the more familiar surface vessels, though here too their predictions were hit and miss. Writing in the first month of the twentieth century, the renowned historian Sir Walter Besant asserted that

> The ship of the future will be shallow and round in build, like the duck; she will be provided with a row of wing-like propellers; she

A fig for the customs grown stale!
　　A cheer for the freedom that's new!
We'll drink to the deeds that the growing world needs—
　　The wonders that science will do.

Improvement in all things, my friends—
　　In all things but this one: Oh, pray
Kind Heaven above, may men always make love
　　In the same old adorable way!

I own that they're not picturesque,
　　Are absorbed with finance and the "trusts,"
Wear trousers in place of gay knickers and lace,
　　And tourney at football, not jousts;

But because of the work that they do
　　We women can frivol the day;
Can traverse the seas in this go-as-you-please,
　　Delightful, aerial way.

Then here's to the hands and the hearts
　　That sturdily toil and believe;
The brain and the brawn of the century's dawn
　　That struggle and hope and achieve!

Away with the knight of romance!
　　Our knight on a future-made plan
Is the triumph, my dears, of a whole hundred years—
　　The Twentieth Century Man!
　　　　　　　　　　　　　LILLIAN FERGUSON.

will not plough the waters, but will skim them with her electric wings, and her speed will be, not thirty knots, but a hundred and fifty; and it will take not longer to get from Liverpool to New York than it now takes to get from London to Marseilles.

Perhaps because Neil Armstrong rocketed to the moon more than thirty years ago, we are less excited by speculations about speedy travels than Sutherland, Wells, and Besant. We share, though, their excitement in improved communication technologies, probably because the Internet continues to develop on a daily basis, and *electric messages* getting "wired" is genuinely transforming the ways in which we communicate with each other. Similarly, by 1900, convenient long-distance communication was already familiar thanks to the development of the electric telegraph in 1837. What was new, though, was radio telegraphy, invented by Marconi in 1896, and it was this wireless technology that inspired many twentieth-century forecasts.

George Sutherland, for example, predicted that all clocks would become "controlled by wireless telegraphy" with the correct time "being sent from the central station every second or every minute." He added that "the call to awake in the morning will, in cities and towns, be made by wireless telegraphy" and even simple chores such as "lighting the fires on winter mornings, so that rooms may be fairly warmed before they are entered, will be performed by electric messages sent from a central station."

Although many of Sutherland's speculations did not pan out—what family, after all, would want to have a fire lit in their empty house by a stranger sitting half a mile away—many of his other "wireless" predictions did transpire, including a kind of fax machine:

> Drawings will also be despatched by telegraph. For such purposes as the transmission of sketches from the scene of any stirring event, the first really practical application of drawing by telegraph will probably depend upon the use of a large number of code words divided into two groups, each of which, on the principles of coordinate geometry, will indicate a different degree of distance from the base line and from the side line respectively, so that from any sketch a correct message in code may be made up and the drawing reconstructed at the receiving end. Illustrated newspapers will in this way obtain drawings exactly at the same time as their other messages, and distant occurrences will be brought before the public eye much more vividly and correctly than has ever hitherto been practicable.

Telephones, too, aroused much *fin-de-siècle* speculation. It was in 1876 that Alexander Graham Bell transmitted the first voice message—"Mr.

emit spoken words

Watson, come here. I want you"—but not till the closing years of the nineteenth century did the device begin to catch on in homes and offices. Here, too, Sutherland was strangely prescient. In an era when phone connections were made via an operator at a central exchange, Sutherland predicted not just the addition of a numbered dial but even the invention of a "speed dial" and an answering machine. If a "subscriber" were not at home to answer the telephone, Sutherland speculated that the caller would still be able to leave a message. Twentieth-century telephone manufacturers would

> provide the telephone receiver itself with a moving strip of steel, which, in its varying degrees of magnetization, records the spoken words so that they will, at some distance of time, actuate the diaphragm of the receiver and emit spoken words.

In the last month of the nineteenth century, the editor of *Current Literature* speculated that the spread of telephones would mean that in the twentieth century no one would ever leave the house:

> The necessity for taking journeys would practically cease and the passenger business of railroads and steamship lines would be confined to those who travel for pleasure or for the more intimate meeting of their acquaintances and correspondents. The business of the world would be done over wire and not by personal interview or through the mails. Even the five o'clock tea and the social call would become things as far in the remote past as the sedan chair and the hoopskirt.

wired to his church

Already, added E.P. Powell in his essay on twentieth-century farming, "Telephone tea-parties are in vogue—the women of a circuit sit by their 'phones,' drink their own tea, nibble their own cakes, and distribute gossip." The trend, Powell said, would continue in the twentieth century, which would also see the telephone bringing culture to rural areas. "Pho-

Le Théâtre chez soi par le Téléphonoscope.

A "telephonoscope" as depicted by Albert Robida in *Le vingtième siècle*, first published in 1883; reprinted Geneva: Slatkine, 1981.

nographic concerts" would be broadcast over telephone lines because "music is as easily transmitted as conversation." Sermons, too, might be transmitted to a far-flung congregation, as had already happened in Ohio where "a minister has his whole parish wired to his church."

While a telephone concert must have seemed a futuristic marvel to someone living in 1900, it was downright humdrum compared to other, more audacious, speculations. The historian Edward Byrn, for example, wondered whether twentieth-century communication might extend into the realm of the paranormal:

Here at the end of the century comes wireless telegraphy, with untold powers. And by its side appears telepathy, mental telegraphy—the direct action of mind upon mind in a manner analogous to that of telegraphing without wires—of which as yet we know little, yet which may have in it great possibilities of development.

Twentieth-century advances in communications, some predicted, might even extend beyond the earth-bound paranormal to the interplanetary. In the final days of the nineteenth century, astronomers reported seeing luminous activity on the surface of Mars. The reports inspired Nikola Tesla— dubbed by newspapers "the world's greatest electrician"—to predict that the twentieth century would see humans communicate with alien beings. His views were quoted in the *San Francisco Examiner* on January 1, 1901 under the headline "Scientists Look for a Message From Mars":

communication with the Martians

> One idea dominates my mind. I have observed electrical actions, which have appeared inexplicable. Faint and uncertain though they were, they have given me a deep conviction and foreknowledge that ere long all human beings on this globe, as one, will turn their eyes on the firmament above, with feelings of love and reverence, thrilled by the glad news: "Brethren, we have a message from another world, unknown and remote. It reads, 'One—two—three'."

The news item went on to quote Camille Flammarion, founder of the Société Astronomique de France, who explained that Mars "is inhabited by a race more intelligent than ours." Other newspapers, such as the *Chicago Tribune*, reported that Flammarion, like Tesla, believed "it is possible to establish communication with the Martians," and noted that the scientist endorsed a plan to signal the people of Mars, some time in the new century, by lighting seven huge bonfires at strategic points across Europe. The bonfires—in Bordeaux, Marseilles, Strasbourg, Paris, Amsterdam, Copenhagen, and Stockholm—would be recognized by the Martians as representing the Great Bear constellation, thus informing them that earthlings were sufficiently intelligent to devise connect-the-dot puzzles. (When, after ten years, the Martians remained uncommunicative, Flammarion devised a new prediction: that the world would end on May 19, 1910 as the earth passed through the tail of Halley's Comet.)

While many scientists forecast twentieth-century marvels such as human flight and interplanetary communication, others looked forward to advances that would benefit the human body more directly. In the field of medicine, the French scientist Marcellin Berthelot predicted that coming generations would synthesize superior foods "with carbon extracted from carbonic acid, with hydrogen taken from water, with nitrogen and oxygen taken from the atmosphere." Whatever bounty Mother Nature now produced, said Berthelot, "we shall accomplish it better, in a fashion more extensive and

a ball of fatty matter

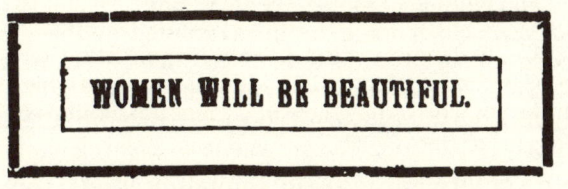

WOMEN WILL BE BEAUTIFUL.

headline from the *Chicago Tribune*, December 31, 1900.

more perfect than by the action of Nature—for such is the power of chemistry." In fact, continued Berthelot,

> In the next century, the day will come when everybody will carry his little gaseous tablet, his ball of fatty matter, his little bit of sugar, his little bottle of aromatic spice, according to his personal taste; all these things produced more economically and in inexhaustible quantities by our chemical manufactories.

Some scientists were sceptical of Berthelot's prediction: Henry Roscoe, former president of the Chemical Society and aficionado of hearty English fare, doubted whether a laboratory could provide "even in the course of a century, a satisfactory substitute for bread, beef, or mutton."

No, we haven't yet succumbed to a breakfast of fatty matter, at least in ball form (though some would say the granola bar is a fair equivalent). And even fewer of us have contracted the services of a phrenologist to diagnose our mental health by palpating the bumps and indentations of our skulls. This *remedial treatment of the insane* would have dismayed the author of *The Wonderful Century*, Alfred Russel Wallace, whose ranking of the greatest inventions of the nineteenth century we saw in an earlier chapter. Wallace predicted that the neglected science of phrenology would revolutionize twentieth-century medicine:

> In the twentieth century phrenology will assuredly attain general acceptance. It will prove itself to be the true science of mind. Its practical uses in education, in self discipline, in the reformatory treatment of criminals, and in the remedial treatment of the insane, will give it one of the highest places in the hierarchy of the sciences; and its persistent neglect and obloquy during the last sixty years of the nineteenth century will be referred to as an example of the almost incredible narrowness and prejudice which prevailed among men of science at the very time they were making such splendid advances in other fields of thought and discovery.

Despite the inaccuracy of Wallace's prediction, it was this anticipation of medical advances that prompted many people living at the end of the nineteenth century to foresee a significant increase in the human lifespan. Soon, predicted the *average of life will soon be raised to fifty years* renowned Russian physician Ilya Mechnikov, most people would be living five decades, and by the time the year 2000 rolled around, even a century might not be an unusual age to achieve:

The men and women of the new century may be in active maturity when 100 years old. A noted savant has pointed out that the general rule among animal creatures is for life to extend over a period of six to seven times longer than the time required to attain complete maturity. And the same biologist concluded that the human animal should easily last 200 or 250 years whenever events allow him to die of old age ... Now that competent physicians are everywhere to be found, instead of ignoramuses licensed to kill; now that the importance of rational feeding and exercising is taught as soon as the alphabet; now that boards of health are in every community enforcing proper sanitation in the school and the home and the shop, that police regulations look to the security of the masses in streets, in the railways, and places of amusement; that the foul hovels where humans used to dwell are forcibly torn down and replaced by healthy dwellings; now that we know how to circumscribe and smother contagion, the claim that the average of life will soon be raised to fifty years certainly seems reasonable.

A prodigious lifespan was not the only thing that medical advances and improved living conditions would bestow upon twentieth-century people. As progress vanquished the social conditions which devoured the beautiful and left the hideous to breed, a cuter humanity would arise. That, at least, was the theory Carolus Duran put forth in the *Chicago Tribune*'s last issue of the nineteenth century:

a far more comely lot

> Will the next century see women more beautiful than exist at the present day? Yes. The next century will have handsomer men and women. Humanity of today is ugly, hideously ugly, yet this is explainable. The imperfect anatomy of the present generation is the result of ages of irrational, haphazard living and reproduction. For centuries the human race has been devastated by war, disease, cares, and passion. And in our breeding the most elementary laws of heredity have been utterly disregarded. Throughout the nineteenth century the conditions which kept up the debasement of our physique have been vigorously attacked and rendered less pernicious. Another hundred years will see their complete elimination. Already the present adult generation is, as a whole, more handsome than the one that preceded it, and again, the children of today are a far more comely lot than were those of thirty years ago. Another hundred years and no imperfect being will be allowed to reproduce itself and inflict upon society a spreading perpetuation of his taints.

Science and improved social conditions would not act alone in changing the appearance of twentieth-century humans. Evolution would also effect needful mutations, or at least that was the belief of many. Writing on the last day of the nineteenth century, Ernst Haeckel predicted that natural selection would have several effects on human physiology:

omit the little pig

> The first stages of the development of mankind will be mostly mental, the evolution of a better and finer brain. When man's brain begins to develop rapidly there is no further need for great changes

Man's Little Toe
Is Disappearing,

A WRITER in the Atlanta Journal-Record of Medicine is convinced that the time will come when mothers who play " This little pig went to market " with their babies will have to omit the little pig that " cried ' Wee! wee! ' " The little toe, he says, is degenerate and must go. After quoting numerous cases where organs once indispensable have disappeared in the march of progress, such as the hairy coat of man's simian ancestors, and

from the *Chicago Tribune*, December 30, 1900.

in his body. And yet some physical changes are still going on. Man will probably lose some of this teeth, there being not the use for them that there was, and there are signs that the little toes will also disappear, leaving man a four-toed animal.

Although four-toed humans are still something of a rarity, Haeckel was not alone in forecasting the demise of the *digiti minimi pedis*. In the December 30, 1900 issue of the *Chicago Tribune*, a reporter devoted a lengthy article to the prospect:

> A writer in the Atlanta Journal-Record of Medicine is convinced that the time will come when mothers who play "This little pig went to market" with their babies will have to omit the little pig that cried "Wee! Wee!" The little toe, he says, is degenerate and must go ... Gnarled with corns, incurved, warped, with rudimentary nail or none at all, can it be doubted that man is losing his little toe? Who in these Procrustean days of shoes can "show up" an extremity that could call forth that burst of admiration, "Thy feet are beautiful upon the hills. O Benjamin! Thy feet are beautiful!" ... The little toe is degenerate and must die.

As the body was working out its evolutionary destiny on its own, the mind called out for attention. Here the future of education was central, as it always is to visions of the future. Some imagined *a five-story building!* that the new medium of photography would revolutionize teaching. Writing on the last Sunday of the nineteenth century, Ernst Haeckel described the power of the photographic image:

> The beautiful and accurate pictures of animals and plants now obtainable, where thirty years ago there were almost none, is an instance of one of the smaller and yet important influences of modern life. Pictures convey ideas swiftly and accurately, therefore they serve as a new and powerful factor in education, scientific education in particular. A man may become comparatively familiar with

the animal forms of the world in a short time through the perfect pictures now obtainable, whereas a few years ago it would have taken a lifetime.

Similarly, George Sutherland anticipated that photography would facilitate the teaching of the humanities. "The production of pictures for the millions," he wrote, "will be practically the highest achievement of the graphic arts in the twentieth century." Reproductions of the works of Raphael, Da Vinci, and Rossetti would become easily available to the "vulgar people" for their enjoyment or edification. For E. P. Powell, education would not be confined to a distant schoolhouse or to mere book learning. "There is no reason," he said, "why every home shall not have laboratories and museums as well as libraries." In a letter to a friend, Anton Chekhov speculated that knowledge and ideas might increase so rapidly in the twentieth century that storing them would become a challenge in itself: "Given the development of cultural life today, who can be certain that twenty-five or forty years from now the library may not require a five-story building!"

Five stories of books! And to think that most of those books in Chekhov's library would be Canadian. That, at least, was the implication of Henry Davenport Northrop's speculations on Canada's literary future. For Northrop, Canadians had been too preoccupied in the nineteenth century to produce much of artistic merit, but at the dawn of the twentieth century they were poised for a literary breakthrough:

as much sought after as Canadian bacon

> The Canadian people is still too young and too busy to have much of a record of intellectual achievement. But be it remembered that there is in them the blood of the most intellectual races in the world. Their ancestry is all right and their climate is such as to enforce mental activity. They are not the people to be satisfied with purely material greatness. Such progress as they have already made in the arts must be taken with all allowances for the circumstances. And when all these allowances are made, it must be admitted that the achievement has been wholly creditable. Having regard for what has been done, it may confidently be predicted that the time will come when Canadian books will be as much sought after as Canadian bacon; when Canadian thought will be as widespread as Canadian ships; and Canadian literature as stately a growth as the Canadian forest.

Besides photography and bigger libraries, twentieth-century teachers would develop pedagogical techniques that would make learning a snap. That was the forecast E. P. Powell made in 1901:

> I will picture what I believe to be the common school of the twentieth century. There will be handsome schoolhouses in abundance, placed in the center of large gardens. The children will study books half a day, and things the other half. The brain will not get any more

training than the hands. Manual culture, which is already a part of the school life of a few towns, will be a part of school life everywhere. The school will have its shops and its gardens—and to use tools will be the chief end of culture ... I believe we shall see the days when boys and girls who are in our common schools together, without damage, can be co-educated in all other grades of school life.

The progressive pedagogy envisioned by Powell would also extend into the university system. According to Daniel Gilman, president of John Hopkins University, the "colleges of the twentieth century" would have teachers ready and able to exploit the latest advances in neurology, physiology, and psychology:

Teachers also are to understand much better the nature of the brain and nervous system and the subtle influences by which the mind affects the body and the body the mind. They will learn to observe the signs of degeneracy and lassitude before the *the glory of* scholar is conscious of them, and will aid the physi- *American education* cal director in his endeavours to apply the appropriate remedies to all who show any physical infirmities. Not only will everybody receive special care, but every mind will be an object of personal attention ... The growth of laboratories, the establishment of gymnasia and fields for sport, the breaking down of the stately formalities which used to be barriers between the faculty and students, the increasing number of assistants and instructors, and the smaller classes which result from the eclectic system are all helps to individual education, the training of each person according to the gifts that God has given him.

For others, progressive pedagogy meant developing better ways to beat, shock, and hurl the truant student. That at least, was the modest proposal set forth by a tongue-in-cheek "Uncle Richard" in the December 30, 1900 issue of the *Chicago Tribune*:

Uncle Richard Tells of the Bad Boys of the New Year 2000

Your Uncle Richard has told you of the bad boys of many lands, from the very gray streaking of history's dawn down to the construction of the Drainage Ditch. He will now peer ahead into the gray mists that veil the future and tell you what is on the cards for the year 2000, and whether or not it will repay you to sit around and wish that you could be a boy at that time.

In the first place it would not be a good idea to wish to be a bad boy in that year, for there will be no bad boys then. Inventions will have been made so wonderful that the bad boy will have to become a nice sweet child or step off the earth. The teachers in the schools will have wonderful instruments on their desks that will record the name of every boy that whispers, and all the teachers will have to do to bring swift punishment to the malefactors will be to press a certain button on the desk, and a current of electricity will shoot through the victim, and make him think he is a human pin-cushion and that he is working overtime.

UNCLE RICHARD TELLS OF THE BAD

from the *Chicago Tribune*, December 30, 1900 (and opposite page).

Fond parents when they wish their offsprings to arise in the morning will not have to shout up the back stairs fifteen or twenty times and finally spring that old gag about coming "right up there now with this apple tree switch, do you hear me?" No, indeed. The parent of the year 2000 will press a small button in the sitting-room, and the bed in which the boy is sleeping will have convulsions, and the boy will be hurled clear across the room. An electric spanker will then do a few stunts, and the boy will be glad to make haste in attiring himself suitably for appearance in polite society.

If the boy sulks when he is downstairs, his mother will punish him by not permitting him to sail with Jimmy Jones in his new airship in the afternoon. No bad boy will runaway from home to kill Indians, for there will be no Indians at that time except the ones who play football on the Carlisle Eleven. Besides nobody is going to run away if they know their fond mamma is going to pursue them with the velocity and ease of the Great or Bald eagle. For individual flying machines will be in great vogue that year, and mammas, as well as papas, will flit about through the air with great ease, and when they spy their offspring they will pounce down on him from some dizzy height, and bat him over the head with an aluminium wing if he gets gay and says he won't promise never to smoke those nasty cigarettes again. Don't you think if your pa or your ma was liable to drop out of clear sky most any old time and land you a good one with an aluminium wing that you would be good? At least it would hold you for a while.

BAD BOYS OF THE NEW YEAR 2000.

ELECTRIC SPANKER FOR
PUNISHING BAD LITTLE BOYS
IN SCHOOL - IN THE YEAR 2000.

Familiarity breeds boredom if not contempt: by the time 1901 was five days old, the new century had become as unremarkable as an old pair of slippers. Suddenly, the week-old forecasts of the marvellous twentieth century seemed naive and embarrassing. Inevitably the sanguine predictions spawned a cynical progeny, including this satire that appeared in London's *Pick-Me-Up* on January 5, 1901:

> The future is one of the best advertised institutions in the world, and just now it is having an unusually vigorous boom. The present condition of the human race has become so painfully third-rate, that people are returning for relief to a surmise of what the world will be like in a few hundred years' time. There is no need to keep it a secret any longer. In a century or so remarkable changes will take place; and the earth is going to be under entire new management.
>
> As everybody knows, the good time that is coming, boys, has been a mighty long time on the road; but all deep thinkers, and people who have to get a living by writing rubbish, are agreed that it will soon be on hand now.
>
> Remarkable changes will take place in the domain of art, the region of science, and price of drink. Everybody will be everybody else's brother or sister; nobody will ever be allowed to be hard up; and there will be a special Act of Parliament passed enabling you to help yourself to your neighbour's chickens when your own fall short. There'll be work for everyone—not too much, of course, but just a comfortable little lot; and if anyone feels he'd rather go fishing,

someone else will cheerfully step up and do his work for him while he's away.

You have only to turn to the scientific papers to learn what changes will take place in the human race during the next few generations. It has been noticed that we are nowadays getting bald very rapidly; and more people than you'd imagine wear wigs instead of the natural thing, to say nothing of the imitation scraps of frizzle that adorn the foreheads of the fair. But this won't be a drawback at all in the future, because the coming race is to be positively hairless, and toothless besides. The poet of the coming time will indite frenzied sonnets to the charms of his loved one, and will sing with metrical magnificence of her shiny pink head as bald as an egg or a pollywog; and instead of chanting a lay (I believe that is the professional term for stringing rhymes) to her pearly teeth, he will yearn to bless her little gums in very blank verse. Then there is going to be perfect equality between the sexes—in the future. Instead of Parliament consisting as it does now of a parcel of vain glorious men, the women will have a fair share in ladling out unsatisfactory laws. An honourable member won't be able to tell his wife then that he's going down to the House, and doesn't expect to be home till after the clubs are closed. Not a bit of it. As likely as not she will be an honourable member for somewhere herself; and she'll go down with him just to make sure that the coachman doesn't mistake a lively music-hall for the Houses of Parliament, as coachmen have been known to do in these degenerate times. It will be just a little awkward at first when the Prime Minister of the future finds his wife is the leader of the opposition; but it will always be open to the House to adjourn the meeting and get the debaters to go home with their seconds and the press people, and finish the argument in the drawing room. Then the present ridiculous fashion which denies to a woman the privilege of proposing matrimony to the object of her choice, will have died out altogether. If the girl of the future has a mind to do it, she will be quite within her rights in leading a bashful youth down a quiet country lane at eventide, and pouring words of love into his delicate, pink ear, till he falls on her neck with a loud splash and stammers out, "Oh, Jezebel, Jemina, this is so sudden!"

And then we shall all be so good—in the future. It is difficult to describe precisely how good we shall be, because there'll be so much of it. There won't be any lying or cheating; and if the sinful practice of betting on the wrong horse survives the ages, a scheme will be arranged so that everybody will back the winner. And there will be no crime anywhere, and such a thing as a burglar won't exist. If you come home late at night and find a strange man hiding under the kitchen stairs, it'll be all right. He will have only come to borrow a little of your family plate; and in the goodness of his heart he is hiding there till you have gone away so that you may not feel hurt at not having offered the use of it before. And if there is any money in the country it'll all be divided equally around once a week, and nobody will have anything to complain of, and—and the moon will be made of green cheese.

and the moon will be made of green cheese

THE FLYING MACHINE OF THE FUTURE WILL PROBABLY BE BASED UPON THE STRUCTURE OF A FLYING BIRD, THE LOUVRES IN THE WINGS CORRESPONDING TO THE ACTION OF THE BIRD'S FEATHERS.

LIFE IN OUR NEW CENTURY.

THE MOST STRIKING OF NEW INVENTIONS.

By W. J. WINTLE.

IN this age of progress no one will dispute that the twentieth century, on which we have now entered, will see marvellous advances and improvements on every hand.

To try to peep into the future is the work of the seer or the prophet, and we make no claim to be either the one or the other. But there are certain tendencies of modern progress and discovery which will become translated into actual facts within a very few years, and it needs no prophet to forecast what these will be.

THE COMING OF THE AIRSHIP WILL NECESSITATE ROOF STATIONS. THIS IS OUR ARTIST'S SUGGESTION FOR ONE AT THE MANSION HOUSE CORNER, LONDON.

In the present article we shall indulge in no imaginative speculation, but shall restrict ourselves to the task of recording various wonders that have already been accomplished in the laboratory, and that only await further development and testing to be introduced to the world.

The man of the twentieth century will

(531)

no longer confine his travels to land and sea—he will navigate the air as well. It is beyond question that the flying-machine will soon become a practical reality.

Already the experiments of Count Zeppelin and others have proved that a balloon can be navigated and can be propelled against the wind. The trial voyages of balloonists from Paris last October marked an epoch in the history of aerial navigation. The aeronaut is no longer at the mercy of every passing gust of wind.

Travelling by a steering-balloon, however, has its limitations. It is obvious that the voyager is dependent upon his supply of gas holding out, and experience has shown that with every precaution a very serious leakage takes place. The flying-machine of the future will need to be to a large extent independent of contained gas.

Experiments in this direction have been made by several inventors, but it was Mr. Hiram S. Maxim, whose name is so well known in connection with the Maxim gun, who first succeeded in making a machine that would actually raise itself from the ground and fly.

Everyone knows that a kite, or, indeed, any light article presenting a large horizontal surface, such as a piece of cardboard, can be supported by the wind if it can only be kept facing it. This is the principle of the aeroplane flying-machine, designed by Mr. Maxim, in which 4,000 square feet of lifting surface were presented to the wind.

A small engine of high power but light weight drove the propellers, and the whole affair, including three passengers, weighed almost 8,000 lbs. Experiments proved that

from *Harmsworth Magazine*, January, 1901 (and following pages).

invented a system of pocket telegraphy, by means of which a man may carry his own apparatus in his pocket and receive messages even from people who do not know where he is.

The inventor takes his small receiver with him when he goes out to lunch, and places it beside him on the restaurant table. If his clerks need him they simply depress a key connected with the transmitter in the office, and the bell of the receiver in the restaurant at once rings.

This can be done in open country over a space of six miles, but in a town, with so much metal and waste electricity about, the range is much more limited.

The illustration below, taken from a photograph, shows Mr. Rosenberg in his private residence, actually receiving a message from his clerks at the office.

This inventor has also made it possible to watch a scene at a distance of hundreds

THE CLERK IN THE OFFICE PRESSES THE BUTTON, AND BY MEANS OF POCKET TELEGRAPHY—

MR. ROSENBERG, THE INVENTOR OF THE SYSTEM, RECEIVES THE MESSAGE IN HIS PRIVATE HOUSE.

why in ten years' time we should not be crossing the Atlantic at a pace of forty miles an hour, or even more.

The new method not only vastly increases the speed but reduces the size and weight of the engines, practically annihilates vibration, and economises fuel.

The last fact is one of vital importance, for the fastest liners of the present day carry 2,500 tons of coal for a trip across the Atlantic. A greater speed would mean more coal, and this would increase the size of the vessel to an impracticable extent.

Probably the twentieth century will see liquid air used in marine engines instead of steam, and then this difficulty will be overcome.

We have already indicated electricity as the great power of the future, and it is from this source that the greatest wonders may be expected. The discovery of the Hertzian waves—which are really a kind of invisible light—and the transmission of telegraphic messages without wires have marked an enormous stride in advance.

Mr. A. Rosenberg, one of the most brilliant electricians of the day, has

---

when this machine was driven along rails at a good speed it rose from the ground and exhibited a lifting power of 10,000 lbs. It was not tested at full speed, or it would doubtless have been seen to possess a still greater lifting power.

There can be little doubt that the successful flying-machine will be constructed on the principle of the flying bird. After all, nature has shown us how to fly, and it only remains for us to copy her methods. Our artist has drawn a machine on these lines, the louvres in the wings being designed to act in much the same way as the large feathers of a bird. We present this idea gratis to the capitalist in search of some pleasant way of getting rid of a little superfluous cash!

On land, also, the twentieth century will see great advances in the way of locomotion. It is now an established fact that a suitably designed electric car can be safely run at a speed of 120 miles an hour on the monorail system, and such a line will shortly be constructed in England. At present it does not appear possible to go any faster than this with safety, but, no doubt, greater things will be achieved in the future.

The motor car is already a familiar sight, and there can be no question that, before the century is far advanced, automobiles will be the usual, rather than the exceptional, vehicles seen in our streets. But there is no reason to suppose that they will altogether supersede the horse, nor is that useful quadruped likely to be relegated to a paddock in the Zoological Gardens.

The ocean greyhound of the present day will be quite eclipsed by the rapid ships of the future. The latest step in advance is seen in the adoption of the turbine propeller for steamship purposes. Quite a sensation has been caused in nautical circles by the performances of H.M.S. *Viper*, which travels at the rate of forty-three miles an hour. This extraordinary speed has been obtained by fitting her with steam turbines (page 538). Up to the present no passenger ship has been fitted on this principle, but such an ocean liner has been designed, and it is contemplated to fit some of the future Channel packets with turbines.

There seems to be no reason

BY MEANS OF THE TELECTROSCOPE WE SHALL NOT ONLY BE ABLE TO LISTEN TO THE DISTANT ORATOR BUT SHALL WATCH HIS ACTIONS AS WELL.

invented which will fire over 3,000 shots per minute with a muzzle velocity approaching 2,000 feet per second. The shots are impelled without the use of gunpowder or other explosive, and consequently there is neither noise nor recoil. Electricity is the motive power, and a small oil motor, mounted on a gun carriage, will work several guns.

Another feature of war in the future will be the firing of mines—or even guns—by means of the Hertzian waves, which require no wires or other contact.

Signals and messages will very probably be sent by the lumiscriptor, an invention which, by means of a pantagraph acting on a blackened glass slide, and a powerful condenser (see next page), re- produces in gigantic lines of fire any message or

HOW THE PAPER OF THE FUTURE MAY BE EDITED.

It will be possible for the Editor to set his own copy—

by means of an Electrical Linotype.

drawing done by the operator on a small board.

In naval actions the submarine boat will doubtless play a leading part, and it is notable that Mr. Rosenberg has now invented a system by which the crew of the submerged boat can see all that is going on above water.

But the most notable and significant fact of all in connection with naval warfare will be the extermina- tion of the torpedo, which will be rendered worthless by the use of a new projectile that is now occupying the attention of the Admiralties of the great powers.

We shall shortly give an account of this new projectile, so we say no more about it now.

Coming lastly to the pen, which is said to be mightier than the sword, we note that journalism will advance by leaps and bounds in the new century. We will not dare to predict what precise forms of " New Jour- nalism" may become fashionable, but there are certain directions, which we may indi- cate, in which the mechanical production of the newspaper will probably advance.

It is within the bounds not of probability but of practical fact that the editor of the future may set up his paper himself. Seated at a typewriter, or dictating to one, the leading article will be composed, and by an

By electricity an entire edition of a paper will be printed at the same moment.

electric connection the depression of the key of the typewriter will depress the corre- sponding key of an improved linotype machine, and thus the editor will actually set up his article in type.

---

of miles. By the use of the electroscope it will be possible for busy men, who cannot attend the races, to simply call at the nearest theatre at the right time and wit- ness the race being run, as here shown.

The same contrivance can be adapted to private use, and the invalid confined to his room will be able not only to enjoy the scenery of the mountains and sea, but also to witness a review at Aldershot, or anything else that may be happen- ing.

Not only can we in London hear our friends talking in Paris by means of the telephone, but the telauto- graph has now made it possible

larly an artist can send his sketch of any event to a newspaper as quickly as the reporter can transmit his "copy". This will be one of the commonplaces of the twentieth century.

Before leaving the subject of electricity we must note that Mr. Rosenberg has devised an entirely new system of electric

THE ELECTROSCOPE WILL BE CON- NECTED WITH THE LONDON THEATRES, WHICH WILL ENABLE US TO WATCH THE RACES WHILE THEY ARE BEING RUN—THE THEATRES BEING SPECIALLY OPENED FOR THAT PURPOSE.

to transmit autograph handwriting or drawings. By a simple but very inge- nious mechanism the writing done on the transmitter in London is simultaneously reproduced in exact facsimile by the re- ceiver—say in Leeds.

Thus a business transaction can be done in writing without the loss of time involved in sending a letter through the post. Simi-

lighting, which will dis- pense with all wires and connections. A series of vacuum tubes arranged on the ceiling or walls of a room give out a diffused, lambent light as long as a small coil, which may be in another part of the house, is in action. The new century will not be very old when this system becomes widely adopted.

Turning now to the sometimes necessary, but always deplorable, art of war, there is little doubt that improvements in the range of guns will more and more tend to make it impossible. A gun has lately been

The commencement of the new century witnesses advance all along the line, and he would be a bold man who should say that we are more than on the threshold of scientific discovery and practical invention.

The British Patent Office records some five hundred new inventions every week, and although many of these prove on trial to be impracticable or unremunerative, yet the presence of so much inventive genius in our midst is in itself a most significant sign of the times.

That life in the new century will experience many and great social changes can hardly be doubted, but here it is more difficult to forecast the course of events.

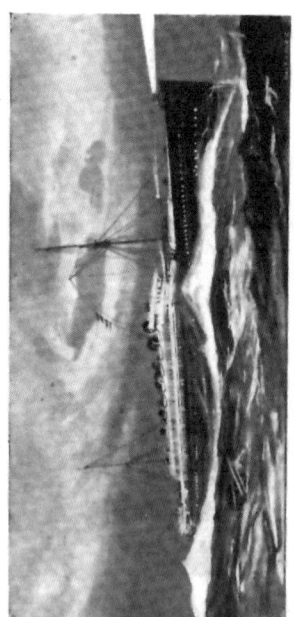

But co-operation and centralisation will more and more tend to control commercial life. The development of "stores" and "universal providers" will probably sweep the small trader out of the field, and then it will be but the next step for the municipality to take over the control.

Whether such a development would be for the ultimate good either of the individual or the community is a very complex question, and one not admitting a general answer. Fortunately we are not called upon to discuss the matter here.

Other times bring with them other manners. New modes of life will necessitate a new code of etiquette. The ways of the eighteenth century seem odd to us to-day.

THE ATLANTIC LINER OF THE FUTURE WILL HAVE TURBINE PROPELLING MOTORS, WILL TRAVEL OVER FORTY MILES AN HOUR, AND WILL PERHAPS BE DRIVEN BY LIQUID AIR.

THE LUMISCRIPTOR WILL REPRODUCE IN GIGANTIC LETTERS OF FIRE WHATEVER IS WRITTEN ON THE TABLET.

Or again, by similar means the type may be set in the form of opaque impressions on a sheet of glass. This in turn can be placed upon a pile of suitably prepared sheets of paper, and by sending the X rays through them, by means of powerful Crookes tubes, the whole of the sheets will be simultaneously printed.

This is no mere visionary dream. It is an accomplished fact, and has been successfully used in printing cards and other small matters.

At the present time another system of printing by electricity, without the use of ink, is in process of development and has already yielded very satisfactory results.

We need hardly point out that the production of newspapers will be much more rapid when these new methods take the place of the present ones.

Here, as everywhere else, it will be seen that electricity is the secret of progress. It is not too much to say that as the last century saw the development of steam as the great motive power both on land and sea, so the new century will see steam supplanted to a very large extent by electricity, which will undoubtedly become the great mechanical power of the future.

At the end of the twentieth century the man in the street will read with amused wonder—perhaps mixed with a little contempt—of the slow modes of locomotion, the imperfect lighting, the inadequate telephone system, and the generally unsatisfactory state of affairs prevailing in 1901, and will wonder how his ancestors could have existed with such a lack of the conveniences to which he himself is accustomed.

Shall we advance in the direction of socialism? Who can say? Yet it is pretty certain that the tendency is for the Imperial Government and the various local and municipal authorities more and more to take charge of the affairs of the individual. The supply of gas, water, and electricity, the provision of dwellings for the artisan classes, the education both of children and adults—these and many other similar matters are no longer left wholly to the enterprise of individuals. To a large extent they are now provided by the State.

It is probable that the new century will see very considerable advance in this direction, though he would be a rash prophet who should predict the complete municipalisation of the domestic and business life of the community.

and probably a hundred years hence our great-grandchildren will smile as they read about us.

Will the world be better and happier in the new century? To us it seems that the answer should be unquestionably in the affirmative. Scientific progress tends to moral advancement.

A moment's reflection will show that aerial navigation, rapid transit, the electroscope, and other inventions that we have named, will all tend to make crime and war more difficult, while improved social conditions will make them less attractive.

The facts we have stated in this article are but a few of the many that might be adduced in evidence of the immense progress in all directions which the new century will witness.

THE TELAUTOGRAPH WILL TRANSMIT MESSAGES IN THE ACTUAL HANDWRITING OF THE SENDER.

Chapter Seven

Zeroing In

THE YEAR 2000 is the only year that has its own "hieroglyph." The acronym Y2K, standing for Year Two Thousand, was devised by computer programmers when they realized that many of the world's computer systems would be unable to distinguish the year 1900 from the year 2000. But the year 2000—along with its neighbours, 1999 and 2001—didn't really need the threat of cyber-catastrophe to get famous: they've fascinated writers and artists for centuries.

Some early Christian scholars, for instance, believed that human history was divided into three periods of two thousand years: 2000 years from Adam to Abraham, 2000 years from Abraham to Jesus, and 2000 more till Jesus returned and conquered Satan. (At that point, a 1000 years of heaven on earth would begin, a period known as the Millennium.) Long after those Christian scholars had vanished, some vestige of their tidy theory may have inspired the sixteenth century seer, Nostradamus, to make his most specific prophecy: "In the year 1999, the seventh month, from the sky will come a great king of terror." Centuries later, in 1925, the poet W. B. Yeats also wrote a book about the two-thousand-year cycles of history, and one year after that, Fritz Lang set his futuristic film *Metropolis* in the year 2000. In 1968, Arthur C. Clarke teamed up with Stanley Kubrik to make *2001: A Space Odyssey*, and in 1996, well before the year 2000 computer glitch hit the media, Prince declared that he wanted to "Party like it's 1999."

But Yeats, Lang, Kubrik, and Prince are only the most famous artists to fetishize Y2K. Other visionaries, most of them as obscure then as they are now, also zeroed-in on the year 2000. Whether they wrote in prose or verse, these visionaries were essentially story-tellers, and for them the year 2000 represented a kind of nether land, a time when the world could seem both intriguingly strange and distressingly familiar. Many of these writers were moralists—their narratives depict either ideal worlds which are intended to rouse the reader into virtuous emulation, or dystopic ones which give us the creeps. But what is strangest of all is that the year that seemed so impossibly remote to them contains the date of our next dental check up.

In 1821, Thomas Hood, poet, humourist and editor of the *London Magazine*, set his macabre poem "The Last Man" in the year 2001. The premise of Hood's poem is simple: in the opening months of the twenty-first century, all humanity has been destroyed by a plague—all, that is, except the poem's spiteful narrator and a poor, wandering rogue:

'Twas in the year two thousand and one,
A pleasant morning of May

The Last Man   I sat on the gallows-tree, all alone,
A chaunting a merry lay,
To think how the pest had spared my life,
To sing, with the larks that day!

When up the heath came a jolly knave,
Like a scarecrow, all in rags:
It made me crow to see his old duds
All abroad in the wind, like flags;
So up he came to the timbers' foot
And pitched down his greasy bags.

After eating some of the kindly wanderer's mouldy food, the dastardly narrator decides that the planet is not big enough for the two of them:

Now a curse (I thought) be on his love,
And a curse upon his mirth,
If it were not for that beggar man
I'd be the King of the earth,
But I promised myself, an hour should come
To make him rue his birth!

For the time being, however, the narrator tolerates the wanderer's company, and the two of them explore mansions that now, in this apocalyptic world of 2001, belong only to the dead:

For the porters all were stiff and cold,
And could not lift their heads;
And when we came where their masters lay,
The rats leapt out of the beds:
The grandest palaces in the land
Were as free as workhouse sheds.

Days pass and the narrator nurses his hatred of the wanderer. Suddenly his fury erupts. He seizes the wanderer, binds him, and brings him to a mock trial:

But God forbid that a thief should die
Without his share of the laws!
So I nimbly whipped my tackle out,
And soon tied up his claws,
I was judge, myself, and jury, and all,
And solemnly tried the cause.

After stringing him up on the gallows, the narrator exults, but only for a moment—the full consequence of his murderous act crashes upon him:

> So there he hung, and there I stood
> The LAST MAN left alive,
> To have my own will of all the earth:
> Quoth I, now I shall thrive!
> But when was ever honey made
> With one bee in a hive!
>
> My conscience began to gnaw my heart
> Before the day was done,
> For other men's lives had all gone out,
> Like candles in the sun!
> But it seemed as if I had broke, at last,
> A thousand necks in one!

The death of the wanderer—a stranger—fills the narrator with more anguish and horror than that of his entire family. Now, he realizes, he is truly and forever alone:

> I've buried my babies one by one,
> And dug the deep hole for Joan,
> And covered the faces of kith and kin,
> And felt the old churchyard stone
> Go cold to my heart, full many a time,
> But I never felt so lone!

The turn of the twenty-first century—the year 2000 to be exact—is also when Sir Herbert Croft set a strange collection of satires that he first published in 1788. The book—entitled *The Wreck of West-minster Abbey, Alias The Year Two Thousand*—purports to **Alias The Year Two Thousand** be a volume of epitaphs that were engraved on the tombstones in London's Westminster Abbey, which collapsed early in the year 2000. Fortunately, says the imaginary editor of the book, the epitaphs were transcribed just before the building collapsed, and thus his degenerate twentieth-century readers can continue to model themselves on the unabashed depravity which the epitaphs celebrate. One such epitaph—inscribed on the tomb of a renowned earl—was supposedly penned by a Dr. Luke, a physician who treated venereal disease by inducing excessive salivation:

> In gratitude I must confess his Lordship
> was one of the best Customers I ever had.
> Ninety-nine times, to my own knowledge, I have salivated him,
> but the hundredth operation proved his mortality.
> I have had him under my care for a clap.
> Two thousand five hundred virgins by their own confession have
> been seduced by the uncommon graces of his person.
> And, to sum up the whole, I would not desire more
> than half a dozen similar Customers.

Still earlier than either Thomas Hood's poem or Herbert Croft's collection of satires is Samuel Madden's *Memoirs of the Twentieth Century*. Written in 1733, Madden's narrative is a series of letters supposedly written by

Madden's great-great-great-great-great-grandson, "who would be chief Minister in the End of the Twentieth Century." Madden received these

28,967 sentences that have meaning in them

letters, he explains, from an angel or "good Genius" who transported them from the future. The same angel also revealed to Madden that the end of the twentieth century will be "the last days of the world" because a "general conflagration" will occur at that time.

Still stranger than his time-travelling angel are the lengths to which Madden goes—or claims to go—to prevent others from altering his letters from the future: he gives a statistical breakdown of his book so that no one can add or delete passages without a numerical change being evident. "There is in this collection," he says, "28,967 sentences that have meaning in them, 1,232,356 words, 2,125,245 syllables, and 6,293,376 letters." Of these letters, he adds, "2,992,644 are vowels (exclusive of 'y' and all diphthongs), as any careful reader may find, who will cast them up with equal diligence."

The imaginary letters that make up Madden's narrative are mostly dry as dust. As he travels by horse and carriage through Europe in the closing months of the twentieth century, Madden's great-great-great-great-great-grandson writes letter after letter to his Lord High Treasurer, dutifully reporting on international events, most of which concern the Pope's continued and wicked attempts to gain control of Protestant nations—one letter, for instance, contains a twenty-six-page list of holy relics that the Pope auctioned off on April 25, 1998 to raise money for his coffers. The bizarre relics—for Madden was clearly an anti-Catholic—include the foreskin of "our Blessed Saviour" and a small amount of cheese made from the milk of the Virgin Mary.

Only one of the letters in *Memoirs of the Twentieth Century* dabbles in a subject that strikes the modern reader as truly "futuristic." While entertaining the Grand Vizier of Turkey with a new and powerful telescope, Madden's great-great-great-great-great-grandson explains why there must be "men in our moon." The telescope reveals the moon to be dotted with pleasant lakes, but Madden's main reason for believing it to be inhabited is that God would not have bothered to create that sphere unless he intended it for some alien race:

> It was absurd to suppose that the wise Maker would have formed such immense, solid, opaque globes, rolling by rules, and in orbits he has prescribed them in the Heavens, as bare useless heaps of matter, and unwieldy lumps of rock or clay, to no end, but to give an imperfect light to our system, and to be looked at by the eye.

Of course not all "futuristic" stories from the eighteenth and nineteenth centuries zeroed in on Y2K. In 1772, Louis Mercier published *L'an deux mille quatre cent quarante*—that is, *The Year 2440*—a story about a man who falls asleep and wakes up seven hundred and thirty two years

MEMOIRS

OF THE

Twentieth Century.

Being Original LETTERS of STATE,
under *GEORGE* the Sixth:

Relating to the moſt Important Events in *Great-*
Britain and *Europe*, as to CHURCH and STATE,
ARTS and SCIENCES, TRADE, TAXES, and TREA-
TIES, PEACE, and WAR:

And Charaƈters of the Greateſt PERSONS of thoſe Times;
From the Middle of the Eighteenth, to the End of the Twentieth
CENTURY, and the WORLD.

Received and Revealed in the Year 1728;

And now Publiſhed, for the Inſtruƈtion of all Eminent
Stateſmen, Churchmen, Patriots, Politicians, Projeƈtors,
Papiſts, and Proteſtants.

In SIX VOLUMES.

VOL. I.

Μάντις ἄϱιστ⊙ ὅστις εἰϰάζει ϰαλῶς.　　Eurip.

Bon Dieu! que n'avons nous point veu reüſſir des conjeƈtures de ce temps
là comme ſi c'euſſent eſté autant de Propheties?
　　　　　　La Mothe Le Vayer Diſcourſe de l'Hiſtoire. Tom. 1. p. 267.

Hoc apud nos quoque nuper ratio ad certum produxit. Veniet tempus,
quo iſta quæ nunc latent, in lucem dies extrahat, & longioris ævi dili-
gentia. Ad inquiſitionem tantorum ætas una non ſufficit, ut tota cœlo
vacet. Itaque per ſucceſſiones iſta longas explicabuntur. Veniet tempus, quo poſteri noſtri tam aperta nos neſciſſe mirentur, non licet ſtare
cœleſtibus, nec averti: Prodeunt omnia; ut ſemel miſſa ſunt, vadunt.
Idem erit illis curſus, qui ſui finis. Opus hoc æternum irrevocabiles
habet motus. *Senecæ Nat. Quæſt.* lib. 7. cap. 25.

---

title page from *Memoirs of the Twentieth Century*
by Samuel Madden, London, 1733.

later. (When translated into English, the title became *Memoirs of the Year
Two Thousand Five Hundred* because, according to the eighteenth-century translator, "there appears no reason for fixing it to any
particular year.") Jules Verne, writing in 1863, set his *Paris au
vingtième siècle* in the year 1952. And Albert Robida, writing in
1883, set his novel *Le vingtième siècle* in 1952. As the end of the nineteenth
century approached, however, a spate of novels and short stories set spe-
cifically in the year 2000 poured forth.

*Le vingtième
siècle*

One of the first was Edward Bellamy's *Looking Backward: 2000–1887*, a
novel in which the hero—Julian West, an inveterate insomniac—pays a

hypnotist to make him fall asleep. That night, a series of unfortunate coincidences unfold: Julian's house burns down, killing the servant who was to wake him; the hypnotist, the only other person who knows of

Looking Backward   Julian's whereabouts, suddenly decides to leave Boston; and it doesn't occur to Julian's betrothed, Edith Bartlett, to look beneath the ashes of the house for a secret room in which Julian lies snoozing. When Julian's secret chamber is finally stumbled upon, he is awakened and learns that "this is the tenth day of September, in the year 2000," and he has "slept exactly one hundred and thirteen years, three months, and eleven days."

Initially disturbed that he has been wrenched from his own time, Julian eventually adjusts to his new world, forgetting about his nineteenth-century sweetheart as he falls in love with her great-granddaughter, Edith Leete. He also comes to realize that the world in the year 2000 is a socialist paradise, a world of "enlightened and care-free men and their ingeniously simple institutions" and that everywhere is a "universal reign of comfort." Boston, like all cities at the end of the twentieth century, has become so beautiful that Julian does not recognize his home town:

> At my feet lay a great city. Miles of broad streets, shaded by trees and lined with fine buildings, for the most part not in continuous blocks but set in larger or smaller inclosures, stretched in every direction. Every quarter contained large open squares filled with trees, among which statues glistened and fountains flashed in the late afternoon sun. Public buildings of a colossal size and an architectural grandeur unparalleled in my day raised their stately piles on every side. Surely I had never seen this city nor one comparable to it before.

In Bellamy's novel, not only have the cities improved by the year 2000, so have the citizens. "Persons of average constitution now live to eighty-five or ninety," Julian learns from his new sweetheart's father, Dr. Leete. This life span—twice what it was in the late nineteenth century—comes as only a small surprise to Julian, who can see with his own eyes that the people of the year 2000 are vigorous and physically fit:

> The magnificent health of the young people in the schools impressed me strongly. My previous observations, not only of the notable personal endowments of the family of my host, but of the people I had seen in my walks abroad, had already suggested the idea that there must have been something like a general improvement in the physical standard of the race since my day, and now, as I compared these stalwart young men and fresh, vigorous maidens with the young people I had seen in the schools of the nineteenth century, I was moved to impart my thought to Dr. Leete. He listened with great interest to what I said.

And how did these improvements come to be? The doctor explains:

> In your day, riches debauched one class with idleness of mind and body, while poverty sapped the vitality of the masses by overwork,

MAISON TOURNANTE AÉRIENNE

A rotating aerial house as depicted by Albert Robida in *Le vingtième siècle,* first published in 1883; reprinted Geneva: Slatkine, 1981.

bad food, and pestilent homes. The labor required of children, and the burdens laid on women, enfeebled the very springs of life. Instead of these maleficent circumstances, all now enjoy the most favorable conditions of physical life; the young are carefully nurtured and studiously cared for; the labor which is required of all is limited to the period of greatest bodily vigor, and is never excessive; care for one's self and one's family, anxiety as to livelihood, the strain of a ceaseless battle for life—all these influences, which once did so much to wreck the minds and bodies of men and women, are known no more ... Insanity, for instance, which in the nineteenth century was so terribly common a product of your insane mode of life, has almost disappeared, with its alternative, suicide.

The people of the year 2000 are happier because of their perfect socialist system. In Julian's new world, where the retirement age is forty-five, workers are paid not according to how much work they do, but according to how hard they try—and in the year 2000 everyone, as Dr. Leete explains to an incredulous Julian, tries equally hard:

> "We require of each that he shall make the same effort; that is, we demand of him the best service it is in his power to give."

"And supposing all do the best they can," I answered, "the amount of the product resulting is twice greater from one man than from another."

"Very true," replied Dr. Leete; "but the amount of the resulting product has nothing whatever to do with the question, which is one of desert. Desert is a moral question, and the amount of the product a material quantity. It would be an extraordinary sort of logic which should try to determine a moral question by a material standard. The amount of the effort alone is pertinent to the question of desert. All men who do their best, do the same."

Julian also learns that all workers—whether bricklayers or surgeons—are paid by the State, but not with money. Instead, credit cards are issued to every citizen at the beginning of the year, and these are used to purchase all domestic goods and services. As well, since all nations, in the year 2000, have achieved socialist governments, a citizen's credit card is accepted even beyond his or her country's borders. "An American credit card," Dr. Leete patiently explains to Julian, "is just as good in Europe as American gold used to be."

Julian is especially surprised to learn that the State, in the year 2000, treats men and women as equals:

"Are credit cards issued to the women just as to the men?"

"Certainly."

"The credits of the women, I suppose, are for smaller sums, owing to the frequent suspension of their labor on account of family responsibilities."

"Smaller!" exclaimed Dr. Leete, "oh, no! The maintenance of all our people is the same. There are no exceptions to that rule, but if any difference were made on account of the interruptions you speak of, it would be by making the woman's credit larger, not smaller. Can you think of any service constituting a stronger claim on the nation's gratitude than bearing and nursing the nation's children? According to our view, none deserve so well of the world as good parents. There is no task so unselfish, so necessarily without return, though the heart is well rewarded, as the nurture of the children who are to make the world for one another when we are gone."

The women of the year 2000 are also the equals of men in affairs of the heart. Their frank approach to love relationships means that unhappy unions have become all but unknown:

"And so the girls of the twentieth century tell their love."

"If they choose," replied Dr. Leete. "There is no more pretense of a concealment of feeling on their part than on the part of their lovers. Coquetry would be as much despised in a girl as in a man. Affected coldness, which in your day rarely deceived a lover, would deceive him wholly now, for no one thinks of practicing it."

"One result which must follow from the independence of women I can see for myself," I said. "There can be no marriages now except those of inclination."

"That is a matter of course," replied Dr. Leete.

from *En l'an 2000*, a series of illustrated cards by Jean Marc Côté, published by toy manufacturer Armand Gervais, Lyon for the 1900 festivities in France.

"Think of a world in which there are nothing but matches of pure love! Ah me, Dr. Leete, how far you are from being able to understand what an astonishing phenomenon such a world seems to a man of the nineteenth century!"

Still searching for the fly in the ointment, Julian asks "Who does your housework?" when he discovers that socialism has done away with the "menial" class of servants:

"There is none to do," said Mrs. Leete, to whom I had addressed this question. "Our washing is all done at public laundries, at excessively cheap rates, and our cooking at public kitchens. The making and repairing of all we wear are done outside in public shops. Electricity, of course, takes the place of all fires and lighting. We choose houses no larger than we need, and furnish them so as to involve the minimum of trouble to keep them in order. We have no use for domestic servants."

Culture, too, flourishes in the last year of the twentieth century, thanks to technology. Rather than cluttering their shelves with vinyl records, eight-track tapes, or compact discs, the clever citizens of Julian's new world indulge their musical tastes through live concerts broadcast over the telephone line:

"Please look at today's music," she said, handing me a card," and tell me what you would prefer. It is now five o'clock, you will remember."

The card bore the date "September 12, 2000," and contained the longest programme of music I had ever seen. It was as various as it was long, including a most extraordinary range of vocal and instrumental solos, duets, quartettes, and various orchestral combinations. I remained bewildered by the prodigious list until Edith's pink fingertip indicated a particular section of it, where sev-

from *En l'an 2000*, a series of illustrated cards by Jean Marc Côté, published by toy manufacturer Armand Gervais, Lyon for the 1900 festivities in France.

eral selections were bracketed, with the words "5 p.m." against them; then I observed that this prodigious programme was an all-day one, divided into twenty-four sections answering to the hours …

"There is nothing in the least mysterious about the music, as you seem to imagine. It is not made by fairies or genii, but by good, honest, and exceedingly clever human hands … There are a number of music rooms in the city, perfectly adapted acoustically to the different sorts of music. These halls are connected by telephone with all the houses of the city whose people care to pay the small fee, and there are none, you may be sure, who do not …"

Near the end of Bellamy's novel, Julian goes happily to bed and wakes to find himself not in the year 2000 but back in the squalor of 1887. It was all a dream! But then—joy!—he wakes again and discovers that it was his return to 1887 that was the dream, and that in reality he is still in the year 2000. Relieved, he thanks heaven that he can "breathe the air of this golden century."

In 1890, two years after Bellamy published *Looking Backward*, Alvarado Fuller published a similar "time travel" novel entitled *A.D. 2000*. This nov-

A.D. 2000   el's middle-aged hero—Junius Cobb—devises a peculiar way to make his fortune: he intends to invest all his wealth and then place himself in suspended animation for a hundred years—when he awakes, the interest accrued on his investments will have made him a rich man.

His plan will necessitate forsaking his sweetheart, the sixteen-year-old Marie Colchis, but—as he consoles himself—she was really too young for him anyway. However, despite her youth, or perhaps because of it, Marie persists in pining for the money-hungry Junius long after he retreats to a secret lair and places himself in a hundred-year sleep. After many years, her sympathetic father decides to place the now-older Marie in her own state of suspended animation, to be awakened in the distant future when Junius regains consciousness and finds her. All this eventually comes to pass, the only snag being that Junius's "century alarm clock" runs a bit slow. Instead of awaking in 1987, he opens his eyes to the last year of the twentieth century:

> "Tell me, what is the year? Are we in 1800 or 1900?
> "Neither, sir," answered Rawolle. "It is A.D. 2000."
> "My God! Have I been asleep since 1887?" and he pressed his hands to his brow, clutching his hair as if endeavouring to tear aside the veil of the past, that a realization of the moment might be made plain to him. "Have I slept a hundred and thirteen years? Am I now alive? Or is this some terrible nightmare? No! No! I heard your voices. I live! I live again! Thank God! I have not failed in my undertaking."

As in Bellamy's *Looking Backward*, Fuller imagines life in the year 2000 to be idyllic, but not because the State has subscribed to socialism or any other innovation in governance. The United States to which Junius awakes is—politically—much the same as it was when he fell asleep, the only major difference being that its territory now extends northward to the Arctic Circle. In 1917, as President Craft explains to Junius in an informal history lesson, "Canada desired annexation to the United States." Hoping for a peaceful resolution, the United States offered England $500,000,000 for Canada. When the offer was refused, says the president, the plight of the Canadian people could not be ignored: "Indignation prevailed throughout the United States, and public opinion demanded that assistance be given to the suffering people in their struggle for freedom." The United States quickly declared war against England, whose forces were defeated at the decisive Battle of Ottawa on August 5, 1917.

If political ideologies in the year 2000 are much the same as they were in the late nineteenth century, the same cannot be said for technology. Life in Junius's new world is faster, better, than the one he remembers. In the year 2000, a strange new invention called "the sympathetic telegraph" allows messages to be communicated through the air: when an operator moves the specially treated needle of one sympathetic telegraph, its "mate" replicates the movement, even though the needles are thousands of miles apart. In the year 2000, a single national paper, its articles distributed by sympathetic telegraph to printing presses in every city, keeps the American nation informed and up-to-date. In the year 2000, the eastern coast of North America is warm and balmy thanks to a huge barrier constructed off the coast of Newfoundland that redirects the Gulf Stream. In the year 2000, a central telegraph station ensures that all clocks keep perfect time (a minor invention but one that delights Junius, still disgruntled by the imprecision of his own "century alarm clock").

It is the advances in transportation, however, that most excite Junius. He relates his first encounter with a vehicle that pervades the city streets:

> At the curb stood an elegant four-seated carriage of very light con-
> struction, with a driver upon the seat. There were no horses attached
> to the vehicle, which was very low in build, and with wheels of fair
> size. The driver sat in the rear, on a sort of raised single seat, with a
> small wheel, like a tiller-wheel in front of him.

"It is an electric drag," Junius's friend, Rawolle, explains to him. "The
batteries, or accumulators, are very small, but with great power ... The
accumulators are charged at the rate of about fifty cents per set, which is
a six-hour run." Stepping into the electric drag, Junius marvels as he takes
his first ride in the year 2000:

> Away, and at a rapid gait, sped the drag, its wheels of rubber giving
> no sound on the elastic pavement of the street, its headlight flashing
> out a brilliant beam, while ever and anon the driver caused a muf-
> fled-toned gong, whose sound was low and musical, to indicate the
> approach of the carriage.

Junius also tries out every other form of transportation the end of the
twentieth century has to offer: a "pneumatic train," propelled by creating
a vacuum in front of the train in its air-tight tunnel; a "submarine boat,"
complete with a "handsomely furnished room, containing all that one
could desire in a thoroughly well-appointed apartment"; and an "aerial
ship," whose precise specifications Junius miraculously divines in a single
glance:

> The vessel was 377 feet long, and was built in a very peculiar man-
> ner. The balloon part of the vessel was in the form of a huge cigar,
> through the center of which extended a rod 380 feet long, with
> trusses to keep it rigid. The cones of the balloon were covered with
> aluminum shields, which extended toward the center to a distance
> of 60 feet ... Depending from the central rod, by stiff hangings, and
> just under the gas envelope, was the car, built of bamboo, canvas,
> and aluminum rods. The car was 100 feet in length, and 15 wide,
> and had an area of 1500 square feet ... The rear point of the cone
> carried a wind propeller of 46 feet in diameter ... The balloon, when
> inflated, was 377 feet from point to point of the cones, and 100 feet
> in diameter. Its displacement of air was 2,000,000 cubic feet, or
> 153,000 pounds, under the pressure of one atmosphere.

Junius brings the same eye for detail to his description of what people
wear in the year 2000. His account of late-twentieth century fashion begins with menswear:

> The main features were: tight-fitting breeches, but coming a little
> lower down than those of the old style; black silk stockings and low-
> cut shoes, the shoes having large gilded buckles upon the instep;
> vest low in front, but closing at the neck; close-fitting cutaway coat
> without tails, unbuttoned in front, but held together by frogs; nei-
> ther collars nor cuffs, but in their place small and neat ruffling.
> There was no shirt-front visible.

STATION CENTRALE DES AÉRONEFS À NOTRE-DAME

An aeroport atop Notre Dame Cathedral as depicted by Albert Robida in *Le vingtième siècle*, first published in 1883; reprinted Geneva: Slatkine, 1981.

"No other style of clothing but this is worn by men," Junius is told. He then turns his eye to the fashionably dressed woman of the year 2000:

> All the women wore short dresses, none reaching lower than within eight inches of the ground. Their feet were covered with low-cut shoes, in some instances; in others, with small, neat patent-leather top-boots, the top of the boot just hidden under the dress. He noticed very few silks were worn, most of the dresses being heavy goods. No bustles were worn, and the dresses were close fitting with jacket basques in most cases. Hats were the prevailing style.

In yet another novel set in the year 2000, *The Day of Prosperity*, written by Paul Devinne in 1901, the men and women of the late twentieth century reveal an even more conservative fashion sense. No ruffles and gilded buckles for the men, and no short dresses for the women—instead, the citizens in *The Day of Prosperity* dress ***The Day of Prosperity*** rather like Ichibod Crane, as the novel's time-travelling hero, Albert Burnham, reports:

> He wore a thin, black summer coat resting comfortably over a pleated, white unstarched shirt, under the broad turnover collar of which was loosely tied a red necktie, resembling a neckcloth. Knick-

erbockers, with belt, stockings, and low shoes, exactly like mine, completed his costume. Puzzled, I looked at the other gentlemen who stood nearest to us. All wore the same costume, except that the colors varied. I saw gray, blue, brown, though the most noticeable color was black ...

I scanned the women. Straw hats like the men's were set tastefully on their well-dressed hair. Under the summer jacket, loose and provided with pockets, a vest could be seen, as well as a portion of the shirt, with broad, turnover collar and a coloured necktie. The costume was completed by a skirt, fastened with a belt, and reaching to the ankles, and by graceful low shoes which the skirt left distinctly visible. I looked for ornaments, but saw none except the plain gold band of wedding rings.

Albert's comment that he is "surprised by the novelty of this costume of the year 2000," amuses his new friends:

"Fashions," replied Mrs. Donnelly, with a smile. "Well, the present style is about fifty years old, and I see no signs of change."

"How could you suspect us of such frivolity, Mr. Burnham?" put in Miss Donnelly, who had shown some symptoms of abstraction during her uncle's remarks. "We outgrew all that ages ago. You know, women give hardly a thought to their external appearance now."

"You leave the men to be attracted wholly by the beauties of the mind?"

"Of course."

Like Julian West in *Looking Backward: 2000–1887*, and like Junius Cobb in *A.D. 2000*, Albert Burnham ends up in the year 2000 thanks to a very long sleep. Unlike Julian and Junius, though, Albert's century-sleep is surreptitiously induced by an obsessed scientist, Dr. Rudini. Upon meeting Albert in 1900, Rudini becomes enamoured of him and devises a secret plan: he will give both himself and Albert a sleeping potion that will keep them in suspended animation until the year 2000. When they finally awake, they will experience the end of the century for a few days, and then Rudini will administer another dose of sleeping potion that will take them to the end of the next century:

"We shall go forward, you and I, from century to century, tasting the present, waiting in restful slumber for the future. A thousand years hence shall see us waking again to a new morning of existence."

To Rudini's chagrin, Albert is not enthusiastic about spending eternity as the time-travelling darling of a mad scientist. In fact, after awaking in the year 2000—the "day of prosperity"—Albert wants nothing more than to stay put, settle down with Miss Donnelly, and enjoy the idyllic society of the late twentieth century.

Many of the novelties that delight Albert are technological. He admires Miss Donnelly's electric fountain, electric piano, electric shoe polisher, and especially her electric coat cleaner:

> At the side I discovered several buttons. I turned one of them at random, and my coat began to move, the rods beat it and the brushes whizzed merrily, while a strong current of air, entering through a tube, drove out the dust ... Connected with this machine was another, the use of which I discovered by similar investigation, for removing stains and grease-spots.

Albert also listens politely as Miss Donnelly shows off her marvellous "electric cooking range":

> "We could stand here and cook, dressed in white and wearing white gloves, without getting soiled in the least. Owing to all the inventions and improvements made since your time, cooking has no longer any terror for us."

Cleanliness, Albert soon learns, is in fact something of a national obsession in the year 2000. "You are certainly much cleaner than were the people of my day," he remarks. "Yes," replies Mr. Donnelly,

> We have entirely put an end to many dirty and disease-spreading habits. You must have noticed the universal cleanliness which prevails everywhere—in the streets, in our houses, on railway, and in street cars. Our authorities for the enforcement of cleanliness are our women, in whom the love of cleanliness is inborn, and every woman has the right to call to task anyone who breaks any rule of health.

Good living has done much for the people of the year 2000. "Your men," Albert tells his new friends, "are stronger, handsomer, and more erect than were my overworked contemporaries." Teeming with such virility, the citizens of the late twentieth century exude a radiant glow:

> They seemed a different race—proud, glorious men and women, conscious of their strength, accustomed to a lavish enjoyment of the good things of this life, knowing nothing of hunger, care, sorrow, or privation except by hearsay.

Still, the quasi-socialist society that Devinne imagines in *The Day of Prosperity* is not without its dark corners. As Miss Donnelly tells Albert, unmarried women such as herself are segregated, willy-nilly, from the married population:

> "I live in a spinster's hotel, you know."
> "A spinster's hotel?"
> "Yes, we unmarried women live by ourselves."
> "Do you enjoy it?"
> "We may sometimes think we don't. In reality, I believe we do."
> "Your hotel must be very attractive."
> "Not very. Just comfortable, like your own quarters. It is only the married people who are entitled to luxury."

Nasty habits, too, have been extirpated by the state in the year 2000, as Albert learns when he expresses a barbarous desire to smoke:

Perchance to Dream.

A ROMANCE OF THE YEAR 2000.

By George B. Lloyd.

[CONTINUED FROM THE SUNDAY TRIBUNE.],
SYNOPSIS OF PRECEDING CHAPTERS.

On a day in the year 2000 Venike and Gwyne Bodeck, members of the Council of One Hundred of the Yukon Kingdom (a state formed out of former British and United States territory in North-west America, and a republic until 1925, when Justus I. was proclaimed King on the overthrow of the too socialistic government), are seated in the Utopian club in Lekyond, the capital, discussing the state of their country. Venike, the reformer, whose dream is a return to the old republican form of government which existed in the United States before that country became the Columbian Em-pire, grows eloquent in his denunciation of the abuses practiced upon the people by Justus II., describing the election of a Council without any power as a fraud upon the electors, and declares for a revolution, which shall be bloodless if possible. He tells Bodeck that he (Bodeck) is looked upon as a coming leader, that he hopes he will not go astray in choosing his position, and that he must not allow himself to become too much entangled with the King's daughter, with whom, he has noticed, Bodeck has of late become a favorite. While they are talking a message calls Bodeck to the palace, where the Princess Lubentia desires to see him.

from the *Chicago Tribune*, December 31, 1900.

"Dear me, Mr. Burnham, how amusing! Why, no one uses tobacco now. It is generations since anyone has smoked."

"I can remember when I was a girl," interposed Mrs. Donnelly, "some elderly people who smoked, and some who took snuff."

"But not many," added Mr. Donnelly. "The practice gradually died out. The women were opposed to it, and by degrees it was forbidden."

As for any atavistic sot who is caught overindulging in spirits, the state has a strict program of "rehabilitation":

If he manages to get liquors elsewhere and to become intoxicated again, then he is brought before the court, which usually deprives him entirely of the right of drinking for a certain length of time. If even this does not cure him, and he is found drunk a third time, he is condemned to a ten hours' day of forced labor for a shorter or longer period.

Even more sinister is that the every citizen in the year 2000 is issued a hundred-page "passport" which details the personal history of its bearer. The passport must be carried about at all times, ready to be scrutinized by any curious official:

On the first page is the owner's photograph. Then follow the names of his parents, his own name, place and date of birth, and dwelling. These particulars are entered by the manager of the hotel in which he is born, or by the head doctor if he is born in any other institution. The pages following contain short notes concerning his school years, his progress and acquirements, and this information is filled in by school officials. Then comes the marriage date, entered by the manager of the hotel. Next the positions he has filled, and the undertakings of importance which he has accomplished. These entries are made by the officials of the factories, farms, schools, or studios.

Here, too, are entered all the journeys made, changes of dwelling, names of children, illnesses, misdemeanours, and penalties paid, if any—in short, everything of importance.

Still, in spite of its spinsters' hotels, its strict temperance laws, and its prying officials, the year 2000 in Devinne's *Day of Prosperity* is much preferable to that envisioned by George Lloyd in his *Romance of the Year 2000*. Published in the *Chicago Tribune* in the first week of the twentieth century, *The Romance of the Year 2000* tosses out the old I-fell-asleep-and-woke-up-a-hundred-years-later convention. Instead, the story begins and ends in the year 2000, tracing the unsuccessful attempt of Venicke to overthrow the Justinian dynasty which has ruled the Yukon, now a world power, since 1925. Written nearly a hundred years ago, *The Romance of the Year 2000* is not entirely accurate as a snapshot of how we now live in the late twentieth century:

> "Heigh-ho, Venicke!" exclaimed Gwynne Bodeck, stretching himself mightily as he allowed the mouthpiece of his hookah to fall to the floor.

After this jolly greeting, Bodeck and Venicke lounge in their togas—the *de rigeur* outfit of the year 2000—and exhaust themselves by explaining to each other how the United States, decades earlier, evolved into the mighty Columbian Empire. Later, as Venicke daydreams about his revolution, Bodeck goes gaga over the attentions of Princess Lubentia, who wants him to read a treatise she has written about the "lower strata of society." So turgid are these three characters that the reader rejoices when they are all undone. The Columbian Empire invades the Yukon and banishes the princess and Bodeck, and Venicke—for plotting against his government—is forced to step onto the "execution disk" where he is reduced to "a handful of ashes."

Execution disks in the year 2000? Absurd. How much more accurate—and pleasant—is the year 2000 in *A Journey in Other Worlds: A Romance of the Future*. Written in 1894 by John Jacob Astor, a great-grandson of the fur-trader who founded the Astor dynasty, this vision of the year 2000 sees its techno-heroes attempting to straighten the axis of the earth so that the planet's seasons will become unchangingly temperate. This project demands, of course, a field trip to Jupiter where the young scientists have a jolly time tracking, hunting, shooting, and eating a bevy of rare prehistoric creatures. Along the way they remind each other—constantly—of the benefits of scientific progress in the year 2000: a huge build-up of aerial bombs by rival nations prevents any one of them from attacking the other; policemen catch speeding motor carriages by photographing them with Kodaks mounted on tripods; and scientist-theologians have discovered "apergy," the natural force by which Jesus was transfigured and carried to heaven. Truly, as one of the novel's heroes affrims,

This period—A.D. 2000—is by far the most wonderful the world has yet seen. The advance in scientific knowledge and attainment within the memory of the present generation has been so stupendous that it completely overshadows all that has preceded.

Twelve years into the twentieth century, John Jacob Astor booked what turned out to be a one-way ticket on one of the scientific marvels of his own era—the *Titanic*.

CLOSING WORDS ABOUT CLOSING WORDS—it's a gloomy prospect. And although we don't reject gloom as a prudent inclination at the end of a century, it's not the only mood available. Still, pessimists will be given the floor first, not because we want to get them out of the way but because it's best to peer into the darkness before we adjust our eyes to the light.

The Pessimist's Narrative

SOME OF US get queasy just thinking about all those zeroes, not to mention that alien numeral 2. There is something abhorrent about the year 2000 and it's not just because it reminds us of so many overwrought constructions of science fiction. Our aversion goes deeper: in the year 2000 we arrive blatantly in the *Alias the year two thousand* future, the date of our birth now made quaint. We stand with nothing in front of us but a ribbon of naughts, time untouched by the human hand, without content. What can we feel but vertigo? It's like stepping out of an airplane into the clouds.

WHAT IS THE NAME of that sensation, when we cross a bridge or stand on top of a high building, that pulls us toward the edge, almost compels us to throw ourselves over the parapet, as if called by ghosts on the other side? The couple who ended their lives in *this monstrously numbered century* Courtney's Hotel on the last night of the nineteenth century obviously felt it and tied their foreboding to this precarious moment in time. How odd that the measurement of time can carry so much psychological weight. Yet we know that when the once-familiar digits become strange to us, we have lost our home in time. We don't just become nostalgic; we are in fact exiled.

MANY OF US will feel estranged in the twenty-first century for the rest of our lives. Anyone born before 1980 may feel forever false when writing "2" as the first numeral of the year. We meas- *still knitting in the old century* ure and tell time by means of systems invented by minds that enjoy that kind of ordering. It's imposed on us from the outside and has very little to do with how our hearts attend to the world. But months, days, years, pick up emotion like lint. Canada adopted the metric system in 1971 but many who spent their childhood with teaspoons, inches and acres still hold those measurements as the true ones. Nearly thirty years after the conversion, the cake still takes three cups of flour and, eating it, we gain by the pound.

OF COURSE IT'S difficult to adapt to any change but especially so when we move toward something so empty of content, so dark, so unknowable. In

the big black avenue that gapes in front of us

truth, this is the nature of all future time. It's a wasteland as far as we know. Thomas Carlyle is reputed to have said that he would rather be in hell than in the next century—he was a man who lived in the same house for more than fifty years. A fear of change and a fear of time's unfathomable doings are the same thing—what do we glimpse in that dark road ahead? Freud knew.

CROSSING FROM THE nineteenth century into the twentieth, where he would seem so completely at home, Freud had not a lot to say. But he did

the dates of our deaths

penetrate the core of our aversion to going forward—the next century will see our death. Even if technology and science promise to expand our lifetimes considerably, we cannot imagine, or desire, much beyond a hundred years.

BETWEEN the pessimist for whom the future is a variety of hell and the optimist who sees a shining paradise, there is a neutral space, a limbo.

same old mitten

Here in a kind of suspension we find the wry and the wan, for whom each day, each century, each millennium, is the same as the next. Everything is "the same as it ever was" and all we discover is that "same old mitten" over and over again. "Put Back Those Whiskers, I Know You," said Ogden Nash to the New Year who was just the Old Year, clean-shaven and diapered.

IT IS POSSIBLE, if you have sufficient funds, to experience the millennial eve by not experiencing it at all. The Four Seasons Hotel in London is

stuff their ears with cotton wool

offering a special package to those who love simple peace and quiet—a suite on the ninth floor with full blackout draperies and soundproofing, an absolute absence of clocks and calendars and a special pre-1950s menu. Only black and white movies will be shown. The going price for the suite is about US$1,500 but the hotel hopes to get substantially more at auction. Profits will go to the British Red Cross.

AFTER CHIDING HIS friend for seriousness, Hilaire Belloc took him to lunch

great whacking things like centuries

at the Villa-Vita, not to celebrate the new century, which he shrugged off, but just to enjoy a warming hour. Across the centuries food sustains, even exhilarates. On the first day of the nineteenth century, the Reverend James Woodforde noted with satisfaction—"Giblet-Soup & rost Rabbit"—and made no mention of crossing the temporal divide.

HENRY JAMES DID attend an end-of-the-century party but insisted that he just wanted to sleep through the festivities. Whether or not he left early we don't know. As little feeling as we may profess for the millennial threshold, few of us will get *convey my poor old bones to bed* away with ignoring it. It seeps into all the days beforehand, do what we will.

The Optimist's Narrative

OPTIMISTS ARE CREATIVE—they may be marketers of junk souvenirs, devisers of new calendar systems, or ecological activists. While ethical intents differ wildly among them, they all see the millennium as a chance to do something. For them it's a beginning not an end and they give us heart, even when our natural inclinations are less joyfully visionary. Maybe the twenty-first century needn't be "the same old mitten" after all.

IN 1700 NO ONE saw the new century as a promotional opportunity. Mostly it was a chance for a good sermon or perhaps a public declamation of weighty verse. Politicians in 1801 saw the new century as a symbolic moment to unite Great Britain and *making the darkness radiant* Ireland, much as a hundred years later, Australia became a commonwealth. And whereas the pyrotechnical displays at the beginning of the nineteenth century were natural ones (a meteor at Camborne, for example), the twentieth century opened by demonstrating every imaginable festive use of gunpowder and electricity.

WHEN PEOPLE GATHERED to celebrate the new century, they generally did so for free. Tin pipes and hats may have been hawked but no one cornered the market on trademarks and patents for end-of-the-century souvenirs and mementos. Some of our present cynicism *a pocket full of boodle* about the millennial passion comes from our aversion to hype and commercialism. The millennium as a marketing man's dream brings sorrow to those who hope for some social transformation in the next century.

AND YET, ENVIRONMENTALISTS, pacifists, social activists, and more have been at work bending the public imagination toward the possibility of good works. End-of-the-world scenarios have always been yoked to the millennium; now these *and then we shall all be good—in the future* undercurrents of doom bring a sense of urgency to the task of sustaining the planet. The Millennium Institute and its Millennium Alliance, for example, are supporting many events that will be used to generate some excitement about the possibilities of changing the future. The concept of Millennial Gifts is being promoted as a way to encourage governments, corporations and individuals to work together to create a better world by offering something material to the future, actions as well as funds.

THE BEGINNING OF the twentieth century was mad for speed. Everything accelerated. Now we dream of peace and quiet. The popular movements of our time emphasize simplifying and slowing down (except of course for access to the Internet—it's never fast enough).

I really want to live differently somehow—brighter, faster

Interestingly, many important millennial celebrations are taking place over the period of a year or more, from the autumn of 1999 to January 1901 at least. Does this reveal a new thoughtfulness? Are we deliberating?

NO MATTER HOW uninterested we are in the millennium, nor how gloomy about the future, we can't escape it. Time, unlike space, is out of our hands; we can't really manipulate it. In space we are here and there; in time we are all in it together. In celebrating a new century we include an entire community of people whose days and years are ordered and named by the same calendar.

rise to greet the author of time

We ought to remember that while 2 billion will celebrate the advent of the year 2000, another 3.8 billion will not, having their own systems of time. Still, for most of the Western world, midnight December 31, 1999/January 1, 2000 will see us "teetering on the fulcrum of destiny" as the Millennial Project (a group hoping to colonize the galaxy) has it. If that's too dizzying a prospect, we might just give destiny a kick in the right direction, drink a bumper (standing), and hope for the best.

A BRIGHT NEW YEAR TO EVERYONE.

BROOKE'S SOAP,
MONKEY BRAND
WON'T WASH CLOTHES.

advertisement from *Punch,* January 2, 1901

Sources

Astor, John Jacob. *A Journey in Other Worlds: A Romance of the Future.* New York: D. Appleton and Company, 1894.

Backus, Charles. A Sermon Delivered on Jan. 1, 1801, containing a brief review of some of the distinguishing events of the eighteenth century. Hartford: Hudson and Goodson, 1801.

Balfour, Arthur. *The Letters of Arthur Balfour and Lady Elcho (1885-1917).* London: Hamish Hamilton, 1992.

Bellamy, Edward. *Looking Backward: 2000-1887.* New York: Dover Publications, 1996.

Belloc, Hilaire. *Letters from Hilaire Belloc.* London: Hollis and Carter, 1958.

Bennett, Arnold. *Letters.* Edited by James Hepburn. London: Oxford University Press, 1966.

Bennett, Arnold. *The Journals of Arnold Bennett.* Edited by Newman Flower. London: Cassell, 1932.

Berkeley, Maud. *The Diaries of Maud Berkeley.* Adapted by Flora Fraser. London: Secker and Warburg, 1985.

Besant, Walter. "The Burden of the Twentieth Century." *North American Review,* January 1901.

Bowles, John, *Reflections on the Political and Moral State of Society at the Close of the Eighteenth Century.* London: F. and C. Rivington, 1800.

Bridges, Robert. *The Selected Letters of Robert Bridges.* Edited by Donald E. Stanford. Newark: University of Delaware Press, 1983.

Burja, Abel. *Ein Gespräch über die Frage: ob das Neue Jahrhundert mid dem Jahre 1800 oder mid 1801 Anfängt?* Berlin: Bei C. F. Schone, 1799.

Burroughs, John. *The Life and Letters of John Burroughs.* Edited by Clara Barrus. Boston: Houghton Mifflin, 1925.

Byrn, Edward. *Progress of Invention in the Nineteenth Century.* New York: Munn and Co., 1900.

Cantzlaar, Jan. *Voorstelling dat het Jaar 1800, en niet het Jaar 1801, het Begin der Negentiende eeuw is of moet Zijn.* Rotterdam: N. Cornel, 1799.

Chekhov, Anton. *Letters of Anton Chekhov.* Translated by Michael Henry Heim in collaboration with Simon Karlinsky. London: Bodley Head, 1973.

Chekhov, Anton. *The Three Sisters.* Translated by Rose Cullen. London: Faber and Faber, 1990.

Coleridge, Samuel Taylor. *Collected Letters of Samuel Taylor Coleridge.* Edited by Earl Leslie Griggs. Oxford: Clarendon Press, 1956.

Coleridge, Samuel Taylor. *The Notebooks of Samuel Taylor Coleridge.* Edited by Kathleen Coburn. London: Routledge and Kegan Paul, 1957.

Croft, Herbert. *The Wreck of Westminster Abbey, Alias The Year Two Thousand. Being a selection from the monumental records of the most conspicuous personages, who flourished towards the latter end of the eighteenth century.* London, C. Stalker, 2001 [i.e. 1788].

Croly, Jane Cunningham. *Memories of Jane Cunningham Croly, "Jenny June."* Women's Press Club of New York City. New York: G. P. Putnam's Sons, 1904.

Dana, James. Two discourses: I. On the commencement of a New Year II. On the completion of the eighteenth century; delivered January 11th 1801. Library of Congress Pamphlet.

De Blowitz, Henri. "Past Events and Coming Problems." *North American Review,* December 1900.

Devinne, Paul. *The Day of Prosperity.* New York: Arno Press, 1971

Dobbs, Francis. *A Concise View From History and Prophecy of the Great Predictions in the Sacred Writings that have been Fulfilled; Also of Those That are Now Fulfilling, and That Remain to be Accomplished.* London: S. Sael and Co., 1800

Dolman, Frederick. "Science in the New Century." *Strand Magazine,* January 1901.

Eberhardt, Isabelle. *Departures.* Translated and edited by Karim Hamdy and Laura Rice. San Francisco: City Lights Books, 1994.

Farington, Joseph. *The Diary of Joseph Farington.* Edited by Kenneth Garlick and Angus MacIntyre. New Haven: Yale University Press, 1979.

Forel, August. "Human Perfectibility in the Light of the Facts of Evolution." *International Monthly,* August 1901.

Freeman, James M. "An Old Magazine." *Ladies Repository,* April 1867.

Freud, Sigmund. *The Complete Letters of Sigmund Freud to Wilhelm Fliess.* Translated and edited by Jeffrey Moussaieff Masson. Cambridge: Harvard University Press, 1985.

Fuller, Alvarado. *A.D. 2000.* Chicago: Laird & Lee, 1890.

Gates, Charles Marvin. *Five Fur Traders of the Northwest.* St. Paul Minnesota Historical Society, 1965.

George, Prince of Wales. *The Correspondence of George, Prince of Wales.* Edited by A. Aspinall. London: Cassell, 1967.

Gilbert, W. S. *His Life and Letters.* Edited by Sidney Dark and Rowland Grey. London: Methuen, 1923.

Gildersleeve, Charles. A Century Sermon, Delivered at Midway, January 1st, 1797. Savannah: Seymour and Woolhopter, 1797.

Gilman, Charlotte Perkins. *The Diaries of Charlotte Perkins Gilman.* Edited by Denise D. Knight. Charlottesville: University Press of Virginia, 1994.

Gilman, Daniel C. "Colleges of the Twentieth Century." *Chicago Tribune,* December 31, 1900.

Gissing, George. *The Letters of George Gissing to Eduard Bertz, 1887-1903.* Edited by Arthur C. Young. New Brunswick, N.J.: Rutgers University Press, 1961.

Goethe, Johann Wolfgang von. *Letters from Goethe.* Translated by M. von Herzfeld and C. Melvil Sym. Edinburgh University Press, 1957.

Goethe, Johann Wolfgang von. *Selected Letters (1770-86).* Oxford: B. Blackwell, 1949.

Gorky, Maxim. *Selected Letters.* Edited by Andrew Barrett and Barry P. Scherr. Oxford: Clarendon Press, 1997.

Gregory, Lady. *Lady Gregory's Diaries, 1892-1902.* Edited by James Pethica. Gerrards Cross: Colin Smith, 1996.

Harper, Ida Husted. "Women Ought to Work." *The Independent,* January 1901.

Harrison, Frederic. "The Eighteenth Century." *Choice of Books.* London: Macmillan and Co., 1886.

Harrison, Frederic. "Christianity at the Grave of the Nineteenth Century." *North American Review,* December 1900.

Harrison, Frederic. "The Day of All the Dead." *Positivist Review,* March 1900.

Henry, Alexander. *The Manuscript Journals of Alexander Henry and David Thompson.* Edited by Elliott Coues. Minneapolis: Ross and Haines, Inc., 1897.

Hickey, William. *Memoirs of William Hickey.* Edited by Alfred Spencer. London: Hurst and Blackett, 1925.

Hobhouse, "The Battle of the Centuries." *Contemporary Review,* March 1900.

Holcroft, Thomas. *Memoirs of the Late Thomas Holcroft, Written by Himself and Continued to the Time of His Death.* London: Longman 1816.

Holland, John. "The Submarine Boat and Its Future." *North American Review,* December 1900.

Holland, William. *Paupers and Pig Killers: The Diary of William Holland, A Somerset Parson.* Edited by Jack Ayres. Gloucester: A. Sutton, 1984.

Hood, Thomas. "The Last Man." *Selected Poems of Thomas Hood.* Edited by John Clubb. Cambridge: Harvard University Press, 1970.

Horner, Francis. *Memoirs and Correspondence of Francis Horner.* Edited by Leonard Horner. London: John Murray, 1853.

James, Henry. *Letters.* Edited by Leon Edel. Cambridge: Harvard University Press, 1984.

James, Henry. *Selected Letters of Henry James to Edmund Gosse, 1882-1915.* Edited by Rayburn S. Moore. Baton Rouge: Louisiana State University Press, 1988.

Jenkins, James. *The Records and Recollections of James Jenkins.* Edited by J. William Frost. New York: Edwin Mellen Press, 1984.

Kartini. *Letters from Kartini.* Translated by Joost Coté. Clayton, Australia: Monash Asia Institute, 1992.

King, Edward. *Remarks on the Signs of the Times.* London, 1798.

Kipling, Rudyard. *The Letters of Rudyard Kipling.* Edited by Thomas Pinney. Basingstoke: Macmillan, 1990.

Lamb, Charles. *The Complete Works and Letters.* New York: Modern Library, 1935.

Lang, Andrew. "The Decline of Intellect." *The Critic,* December 1900.

Lawrence, J. *Remarkable and Recent Predictions! Of Many Great and Astonishing Events that are to Happen Before and at the Close of the Present Century.* Bristol, 1794.

Mackay, John. *The Commencement of the Nineteenth Century Determined upon Unerring Principles.* Aberdeen, 1800.

Mackenzie, Compton. *My Life and Times.* London: Chatto and Windus, 1964.

Madden, Samuel. *Memoirs of the Twentieth Century.* New York: Garland Publishing, 1972.

Mechnikoff, Elie. "Will be Young at 100." *Chicago Tribune,* December 31, 1900.

Mercier, Louis. *Memoirs of the Year Two Thousand Five Hundred.* New York: Garland Publishing, 1974.

Merry, Andrew. *The Last Dying Words of the Eighteenth Century.* London: J. Lee, 1800.

Modersohn-Becker, Paula. *1876-1907. The Letters and Journals of Paula Modersohn-Becker.* Metuchen, N.J.: Scarecrow Press, 1980.

Nordau, Max. *Degeneration.* London: William Heinemann, 1898.

Northrop, Henry Davenport. *Grandest Century in the World's History, containing a full and graphic account of the marvelous achievements of one hundred years.* Philadelphia: National Publishing Co., 1900.

Piozzi, Hester. *The Intimate Letters of Hester Piozzi and Penelope Pennington.* Edited by Oswald G. Knapp. London: John Lane, 1914.

Piozzi, Hester. *The Piozzi Letters.* Edited by Edward A. Bloom and Lillian D. Bloom. London: Associated University Presses, 1989.

Plaatje, Sol T. *The Boer War Diary of Sol T. Plaatje.* Edited by John L. Comaroff. Johannesburg: Macmillan, 1973.

Powell, E. P. "Farming in the Twentieth Century." *The Arena,* April 1901.

Quail, Jesse. "Forecasts of the Future." *Macmillan's Magazine,* December 1901.

Resol, A. "Quand a Fini le XVIII siècle? Quand a Commencé le XIX?" *L'Intermediaire des chercheurs et curieux,* January 25, 1870.

Robida, Albert. *Le vingtième siècle.* Geneva: Slatkine, 1981.

[Roget, Peter Mark.] Emblen, D. L. *Peter Mark Roget: The Word and the Man.* New York: Thomas Y. Crowell Company, 1970.

Rose, John. *The Grand Chronological Dispute, or The Question in What Century is the Present Year 1800?* Bristol, 1800.

Sassoon, Siegfried. *The Old Century and Seven More Years.* London: Faber and Faber, 1938.

Schiller, Friedrich. "Correspondence Between Goethe and Schiller 1794-1805." (*Studies in Modern German Literature,* Vol 60). Translated by Liselotte Dieckmann. New York: Peter Lang, 1994.

Schleiermacher, Friedrich. *The Life of Schleiermacher.* Translated by Frederica Rowan. London: Smith, Elder and Co., 1860.

Sewall, Samuel. *The Diary and Life of Samuel Sewall.* Edited by Mel Yazawa. Boston: Bedford Books, 1998.

Sichel, Edith. *The Life and Letters of Alfred Ainger.* London: Archibald Constable and Company, 1906.

Slate, Ruth. *Dear Girl: The Diaries and Letters of Two Working Women.* Edited by Thompson Tierl. London: Women's Press, 1987.

Sloan, Margaret. *The Shattered Dream: A Southern Belle at the Turn of the Century.* Edited by Harold Woodell. Columbia, S.C.: University of South Carolina Press, 1991.

Strindberg, August. *Strindberg's Letters.* Edited and translated by Michael Robinson. Chicago: University of Chicago Press, 1992.

Sutherland, George. *Twentieth Century Inventions: A Forecast.* London: Longmans, Green, and Co., 1901.

Taylor, Ann. *Autobiography, and other memorials of Mrs. Gilbert (formerly Ann Taylor).* Edited by Josiah Gilbert. London: Kegan Paul, 1878.

Thompson, David. *The Manuscript Journals of Alexander Henry and David Thompson.* Edited by Elliott Coues. Minneapolis: Ross and Haines, Inc., 1897.

Tolstoy, Leo. *Tolstoy's Diaries.* Edited and translated by R. F. Christian. London: Athlone Press, 1985.

Trench, Melesina. *The Remains of the late Mrs. Richard Trench.* Ed. by her son, the Dean of Westminster. London: Parker, Son, and Bourn, 1862.

Verne, Jules. *Paris in the Twentieth Century.* New York: Ballantine Books, 1996

Victoria, Queen of Great Britain. *The Letters of Queen Victoria (1896-1901).* Edited by George Earle Buckle. London: J. Murray, 1932.

Victoria, Queen of Great Britain. *Queen Victoria in her Letters and Journals.* Selected by Christopher Hibbert. London: John Murray, 1984.

Wallace, Alfred Russel. *The Wonderful Century.* London: G. Allen & Unwin, Ltd., 1925.

Wells, H. G. "Anticipations: An Experiment in Prophecy." Serialized in *North American Review,* June 1901 to December 1901.

Windham, William. *The Diary of the Right Hon. William Windham.* Edited by Mrs. Henry Baring. London: Longmans, Green, 1866.

Wyndham, George. *Life and Letters of George Wyndham.* Edited by J. W. Mackail and Guy Wyndham. London: Hutchinson, 1925.

Woodforde, James. *Diary of a Country Parson.* London: Oxford University Press, 1931.

Woods, Margaret. *Extracts from the Journal of the late Margaret Woods.* London: John and Arthur Arch, 1829.

***

Unless indicated otherwise in the text, items from the following newspapers and periodicals are all taken from either the first or last issue of the century under discussion. For example, December 1800 or January 2, 1901: *Atlantic Monthly, Aurora General Advertiser, Bell's Weekly Messenger, Boston Herald, Chatauquay, Chicago Tribune, Connecticut Courrant, Contemporary Review, Cosmopolitan, Current Literature, Dial, Gentleman's Magazine, Harmsworth Magazine, Humane Review, International Monthly, Kansas City Star, Literature, London Times, London Post, Manitoba Free Press, New York Times, New York Tribune, New York World, Nineteenth Century And After, North American Review, Oracle, Outlook, Overland Monthly, Pick-Me-Up, Poor Robin's Almanac, Popular Science Monthly, Porcupine's Gazette, Puck, Punch, Review of Reviews, Saint John Globe, San Francisco Examiner, Spectator, Temperance Caterer, Toronto Star, Washington Evening Star, Worcester Telegraph, World's Work.*

Recommended Web Sites

Talk 2000: http://humnet.humberc.on.ca/talk2000.htm
Everything 2000: http://www.everything2000.com/
The Year 2000 Information Center: http://www.year2000.com
Center for Millennial Studies: http://www.mille.org
The Millennium Institute: http://www.igc.org/millennium/index.html
World Wide Observatory of the Year 2000: http://www.tour-eiffel.fr/an2000_uk/
Mission pour la célébration de l'an 2000: http://www.celebration2000.gouv.fr/uk/index.htm
Greenwich 2000: http://www.greenwich2000.com
The Billennium: http://www.billennium.com
World Peace 2000: http://www.worldpeace2000.com
Club 2000: http://www.club2000.com
Countdown 2000: http://www.countdown2000.com
The Millennium Report: http://www.2000cdn.com
Countdown to the Millennium: http://familyeducation.com/topic/front/0,1156,1-4421,00.html
Canada and the Millennium: http://www.millennium.gc.ca
World Future Society: http://www.lucifer.com/~sasha/refs/wfsgbc.html
Earth Link: http://home.earthlink.net/~hipbone/mille.html

About the Authors

Growing up on the Prairies, MARK MORTON endured endless chicken-feeding and combine repairs by holding fast to a mighty dream. "Someday," he whispered as he filled the pig trough, "I will complete a Ph.D. in Renaissance literature, teach English on the French Riviera, and return to become a professor at the University of Winnipeg, broadcast word-origin columns for CBC Radio, and write books." Mark Morton did all this. He is the author of *Cupboard Love: A Dictionary of Culinary Curiosities.*

GAIL NOBLE was born in Halifax in the third quarter of the century, and since then has completed her Ph.D. in Renaissance drama and published a collection of poems, *Truant.* She bides her time waiting for the millennium while walking her dogs and working as a freelance editor. She lives in Toronto.